I am an ANGLICAN

I am an ANGLICAN

Margaret Killingray
and
Joanna Killingray

Photography: Chris Fairclough

Consultant: The Bishop of Tonbridge

FRANKLIN WATTS

LONDON/NEW YORK/SYDNEY/TORONTO

Joanna Killingray is ten years old. She and her family live in Kent. Her father, David, teaches at London University. Her mother, Margaret, looks after the home and does some writing and office work. Joanna has two grown-up sisters, Kate and Fiona, who work in London. She goes to the local county primary school.

Contents

The Anglican belief	6
Going to church	8
The Family Service	10
Baptism	14
Getting married	15
Junior Worship	16
Helping other people	18
Advent and Christmas	20
Lent and Easter	22
The church family	24
Learning more	26
The Anglican Year	28
Facts and figures	30
Glossary	31
Index	32

© 1986 Franklin Watts   12a Golden Square   London W1

ISBN 0 86313 428 9

Design: Edward Kinsey
Photographs: page 7;
The Press Association
Illustrations: Tony Payne
Cover Design: Steve Wilson

Printed in Italy

The Publishers would like to thank the Killingray Family and the Congregation of St Nicholas's Parish Church, Sevenoaks, Kent for their help in the preparation of this book.

Special thanks are due to Canon Kenneth Prior, The Reverend Jeremy Thomson, David and Wendy Crosland, Mike and Margaret Talbot.

The Anglican belief

My family are Christians. We are members of the Anglican Church.

Anglicans, like all Christians, believe in one God who sent his Son, Jesus Christ, to live on earth. They believe God sends His Holy Spirit to help them live lives that please Him. The Christian faith is divided into different Churches. The Anglican or Church of England, separated from the Roman Catholic Church over four hundred years ago.

We have two Archbishops. They are the leaders of the Church of England.

The Archbishop of Canterbury (above left) is senior in rank to the Archbishop of York (above right). Under them are Bishops who look after an area called a diocese. Joanna's church is in the diocese of Rochester. The diocese has many parishes each with its own Church and ministers. The Anglican Church is the official Church for England. The Queen must be a member of the Church.

Going to Church

Our church is called St Nicholas. Around it are graves of people who died many years ago.

The parish church, named after a Christian Saint, is usually the most ancient building in any English community. In earlier times it would have been the only church. St Nicholas was built in the 12th Century. Today there are many types of Christian Church in most communities.

Once a month I go to a church service with my family. We are given song and service books at the door. Bibles are always left on the seats.

A Family Service is held on the first Sunday of each month at 10.30 in the morning. On other Sundays young people go to a church school called Junior Worship. There are services at the church every Sunday in the morning and evening. All services last about one hour. Once people have found a seat they usually say a short prayer before the service begins.

The Family Service

The service begins with a prayer asking God to forgive us for our sins over the last week. Then there is a Bible reading.

The Ministers lead the service but other people, especially young people, do many things during the service. The Family Service is meant to bring young and old together in the worship of God. It is a joyful occasion for everyone. Here two sisters are reading a story from the Bible.

I am in the recorder group which sometimes plays at the Family Service. The Church Choir sings special hymns.

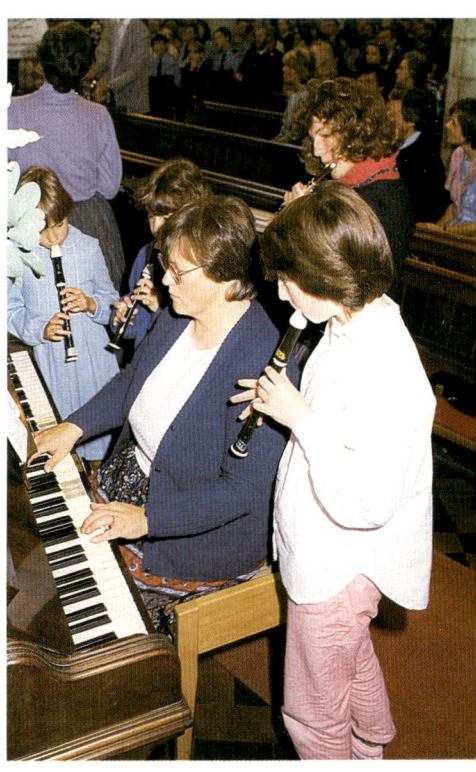

Music to accompany hymns is usually played on the organ. There is also a small orchestra of guitars, flutes and recorders. The choir is made up of people with very good voices. They have to rehearse at least once a week. The choir leads the whole Church in singing God's praises. Some hymns and songs come from the Anglican Hymn Book. In the Family Service many different songs are sung.

Everyone with a birthday during the next month is given a card. A Junior Worship choir then sings and there are more prayers.

The minister prays for those people with birthdays. He asks God to look after them all in the coming year. Anglicans use the Prayer Book for their services. In it are orders of service, including prayers that are used for confessing sins, the Creed in which all Christians state their belief and The Lord's Prayer. All these are said out loud by the congregation.

A minister always gives a talk called a sermon. He sometimes asks children to help him.

Sermons are meant to make people think about their lives and actions in relation to the teachings of Jesus. The speaker here is explaining the parable or story told by Jesus about a farmer seeding his field. Seed falls on different kinds of ground and grows well or badly. The same is true of how people respond to the Christian gospel. The service ends with a hymn and prayer. Many people then stay to talk and have a cup of coffee.

Baptism

Many babies are baptised at the Family Service. The Minister pours water on the head of the baby.

Baptism or Christening is the ceremony at which people first become members of the Church. The Minister makes the sign of the Cross on the baby's forehead. The parents and godparents promise to help the baby grow up as a Christian.

Getting Married

I like weddings very much. Everyone dresses up in their best clothes and the church is full of flowers.

The bride and groom promise to love and look after each other for all their lives. These promises are made in front of their family and friends, in the sight of God. The couple then sign the church Marriage Register which is a record of all weddings in the church. Photographs are then taken outside the church and everybody goes to a party called a reception.

Junior Worship

I go to Junior Worship on most Sunday mornings while my parents go to church. I play in the recorder group.

The church year begins a month or so before Christmas with a time called Advent. During this time Christians look forward to celebrating Jesus' birth and remember that He promised to come again one day as Judge and King of all the earth. Christmas is a festival for which special food is prepared: mince pies, puddings and a Christmas cake.

We write plays and act in them for the other children. We always end with songs and prayers.

All the children then come together in the big hall. The leaders of Junior Worship think of many interesting and enjoyable ways for the children to worship. The children write their own prayers and choose which songs to sing. There are prayers for anyone who is ill. When they reach eleven years, children move on to another Sunday School called Centrepoint at which they stay until fifteen.

Helping other people

At Junior Worship we also pack up parcels of clothes to send to poor children in Africa.

Junior Worship has for many years kept in touch with Jacaranda Cottage, a home in Kenya for about thirty boys of up to sixteen years old. The home is looked after by a married couple who provide a caring Christian family life for the boys. Some of the boys are orphans or from poor families. St Nicholas church takes much interest in such work.

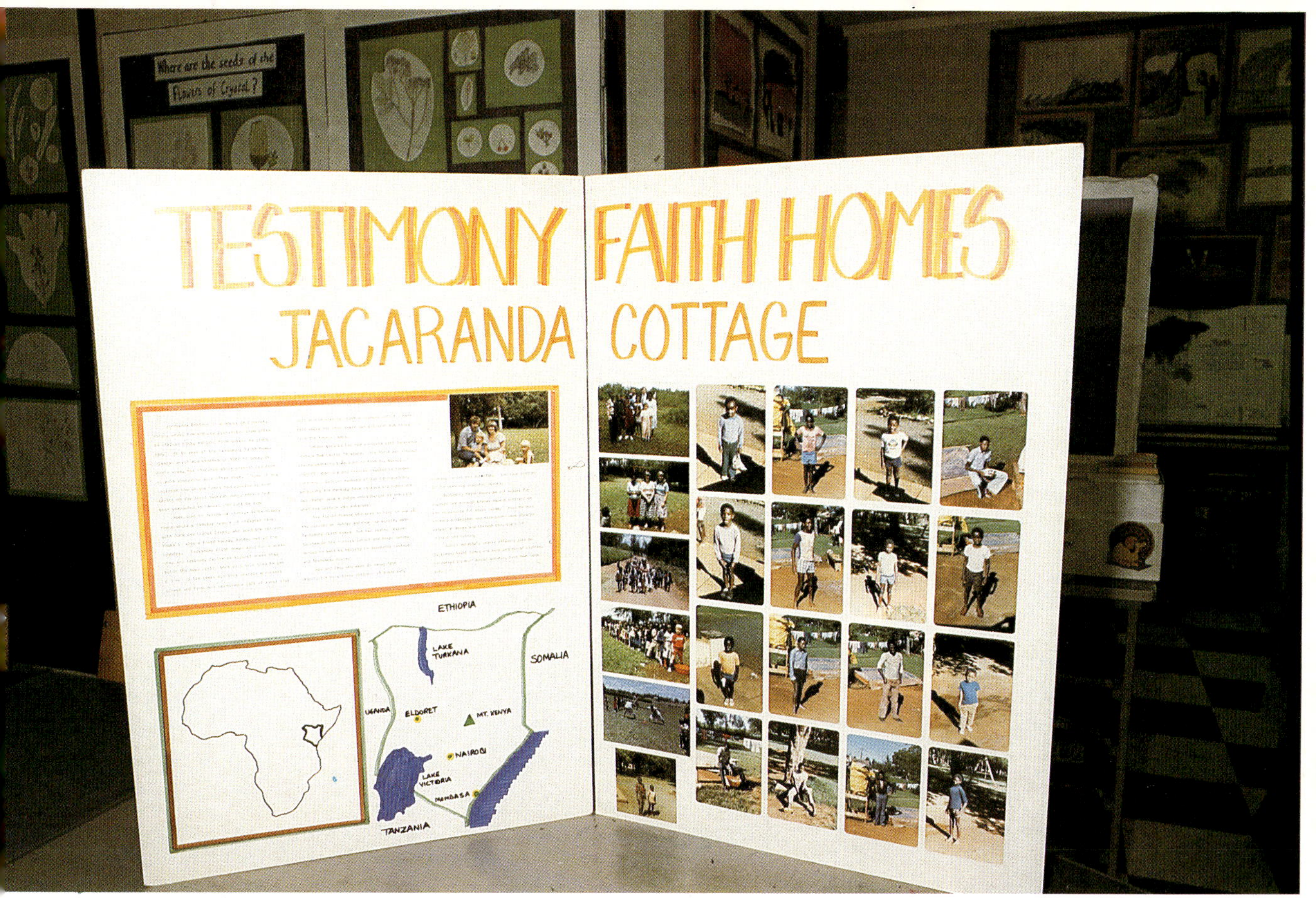

We have seen many photographs of Jacaranda Cottage and the boys. We collect money at Junior Worship to send to them.

The house parents at the Cottage send back photographs and regular letters giving news of the boys. Prayers are said at Junior Worship for special needs at the Cottage. Two members of St Nicholas have recently been to Kenya and visited Jacaranda Cottage. They gave a talk to Junior Worship about the daily life of the Cottage.

Advent and Christmas

Christmas is a very exciting time. I count the days to Christmas by opening a window a day on my advent calendar.

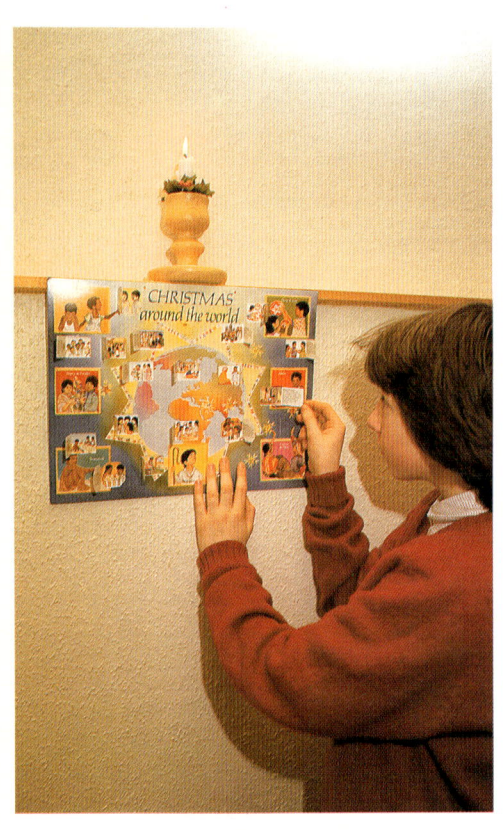

The church year begins a month or so before Christmas with a time called Advent. During this time Christians look forward to celebrating Jesus' birth and remember that He promised to come again one day as Judge and King of all the earth. Christmas is a festival for which special food is prepared, mince pies, puddings and a Christmas cake.

I was a shepherd in my school nativity play. We have a huge Christmas tree at our church.

Christmas is a time of celebration and great joy for all Christians. The church is brightly decorated and most churches have a tree. At midnight on Christmas Eve there is a candlelit service at many churches to welcome the birthday of Christ. On Christmas morning a special service is held before the traditional Christmas meal.

Lent and Easter

The Cross reminds us of the death of Jesus at Easter.

Lent is the forty days of preparation before Easter when many Christians pray more and give up some luxuries. At Easter Christians remember the last week of the life of Jesus on earth. He was put to death on the Cross, on what is now known as Good Friday. The Cross is seen as a symbol of God's love for man.

Easter Sunday is a happy day as Jesus came to life again. Pictures on the windows of our church show Him and His disciples.

On Easter Day Christians celebrate the resurrection of Christ from the dead. Christ gathered His disciples together and told them to preach the gospel throughout the world. The disciples started the Christian Church by telling everyone about Jesus and baptising those who believed in Him. The Anglican Prayer Book gives special prayers and readings for Easter as well as other festivals throughout the year.

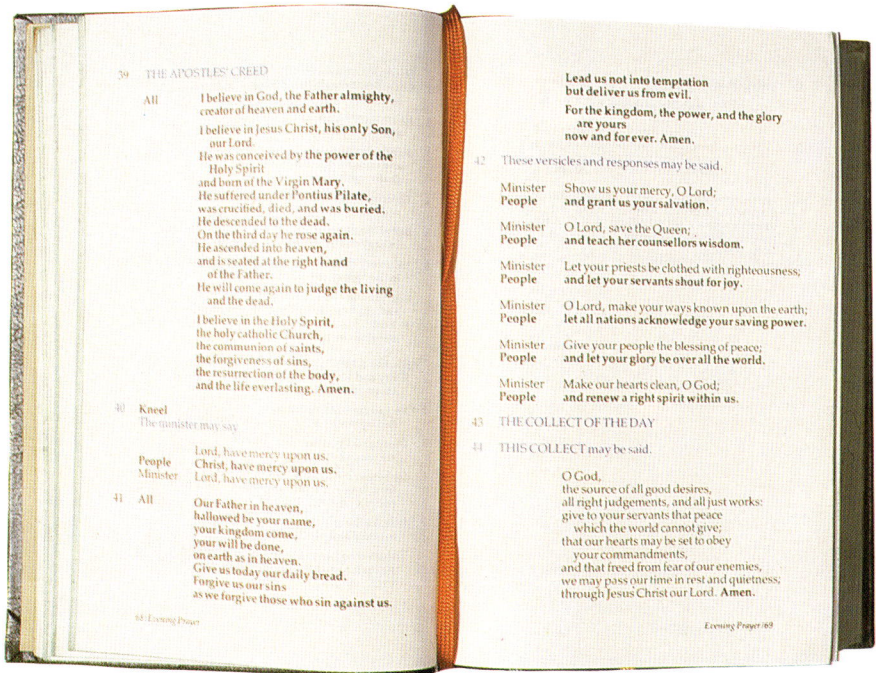

The church family

Sometimes we go away for a summer holiday together. We stay in a school and I sleep in a dormitory with my friends.

Members of the church see themselves as part of a large family. It is thought essential for everyone to get to know each other well. It is not enough just to attend a service on a Sunday. On each day of the holiday there is a talk on a Christian subject and a time for worship. There are also walks, sports and other outings.

We also get together on a day. summer. There are many things to do. We have picnic lunches.

In the morning people can take part in different hobbies, including knitting, drama, playing music, doing jigsaw puzzles and lots of other things. After lunch there are football matches and races. Days like this draw the members closer together, and those who are lonely can feel part of a family. After Family Service on summer Sundays everyone has a picnic lunch together.

Learning More

At the back of our church there is a bookshop. Sometimes my friends and I look at the books.

The bookstall sells Bibles and a wide range of other books and magazines on Christian subjects. Bible study is seen as a very important means of understanding God. During the week small groups of church members meet to discuss the Bible and pray together.

Before I go to sleep I read the Bible and pray to God.

Joanna's family prays together, thanking God for his gifts and asking Him to look after them. Joanna will need to decide when she is older whether she wants to become a full adult member of the church. Once a year the Bishop comes to the church and gives a confirmation service when all those who wish to join the church make the promises that their parents and god-parents made at their baptism, for themselves. After being confirmed a person can take part in the Holy Communion service which recalls the last meal of Christ with his disciples. It is the most important service for all Christians.

The Anglican Year

The church year is based on the normal calendar year but starts with the season of Advent at the end of November/beginning of December. Apart from the major festivals some churches remember days named after saints.

CHRISTMAS DAY
25th December
The celebration of the birth of Jesus Christ.

ADVENT
November/December
The season of preparation for Christmas which begins four Sundays before Christmas.

EPIPHANY
6th January
Remembers the visit of the Magi (kings or wise men) to the baby Jesus.

LENT
40 days
Begins on Ash Wednesday and ends at Easter. It is a time of prayer and fasting in preparation for Easter.

HOLY WEEK
March/April
This begins with Passion or Palm Sunday which remembers Jesus' entry into Jerusalem. Maundy Thursday commemorates the Last Supper at which Jesus washed the feet of his disciples. Good Friday was the day when Jesus was crucified.

EASTER SUNDAY
March/April
The day on which Jesus rose from the dead. It is the beginning of the season of Easter which lasts for 50 days.

ASCENSION DAY
May
This is the Thursday 40 days after Easter Sunday when Jesus finally left earth and no longer appeared to human view.

PENTECOST
(Whit Sunday)
May/June
The last day of the Easter season when the Holy Spirit came upon the followers of Jesus Christ and they went out to present the gospel to the whole world.

The dates of Lent and Easter change each year according to the date of Good Friday which is the Friday following the first full moon after the spring equinox. Good Friday is usually in April.

Facts and Figures

Christianity is the largest religion in the world, with about 1,000 million members throughout the world. About 700 million are Roman Catholics. The Anglican Communion, a worldwide fellowship of Churches derived from the Church of England, has about 47 million members. The Church of England has about 2 million of the 7 million members of Christian Churches in Britain. The Church in Wales, The Episcopal Church in Scotland and Church of Ireland all have links with the Church of England.

The Church of England is divided into two Provinces: Canterbury, having 30 dioceses (including the Diocese of Europe) and York with 14 dioceses.

The Archbishop of Canterbury is called the "Primate of all England" and the Archbishop of York is Known as the "Primate of England." A bishop is in charge of each diocese. The Parishes have a vicar or rector with assistants called curates. There were 13,400 Anglican ministers in the United Kingdom in 1985.

The Church of England's roots go back to the first Christians who came to Britain during Roman times. During the 16th century Christians all over Europe were challenging the authority and ideas of the Roman Catholic Church under the Pope. Queen Elizabeth I made the final break with Rome and established the Church of England as the State Church. The Sovereign must now be a member of the Church and uphold it.

The governing body of the Church of England is the General Synod in which the Archbishops, Bishops, Clergy and lay members are represented.

The Anglican Church bases its beliefs on the Bible which is divided into the Old and New Testaments. The Old Testament tells of God's creation of the world and the history of the Jews. The New Testament tells the story of Jesus Christ's life on earth and how the Christian Church began. The Anglican Prayer Book was written originally in the 16th century but has recently been revised into more modern English.

The Anglican Church is a leading member of the World Council of Churches which brings together some 300 different churches in over 100 countries.

Glossary

Baptism The sacrament in which a person becomes a member of the Church. Water is used to symbolize the gift of new life in Christ.

Bible The holy writings of Christianity said to be the word of God. They are divided into the Old and New Testaments.

Bishop A leading minister who is in charge of an area called a diocese which has many individual churches with their own ministers.

Communion The sacrament which recalls the last meal of Christ. Bread and wine are used to symbolize the body and blood of Christ.

Confirmation The service where a bishop places his hands on the head of a Christian who has decided to "confirm" the promises made on his or her behalf at baptism by parents and godparents.

Creed A statement of belief which is used by almost all Christian Churches

Gospel The word comes from an old word meaning "Good News." It is the name given to the essential message of Christianity. It is also used for the four versions of Christ's life in the New Testament.

Minister A person who has had training in theology and has been ordained by a bishop to lead the Church and to lead church services. At present only men can be ordained in the Church of England.

Parish Every part of England is divided into parishes each served by a church.

Prayer Book This sets down all the Church of England services and form of prayers for the year.

Resurrection The event when Jesus was raised from the dead.

Sacrament A ceremony with a visible sign of a gift to to a person from God. There are two, Baptism and Communion, which Jesus instructed Christians to do.

Sermon A talk given by a minister during a church service.

Sin The Christian word for wrong-doing and disobedience to God.

Index

Advent 20, 28, 29
Archibishop of Canterbury 7, 30
Archibishop of York 7, 30
Ascension day 29

Baptism 14, 23, 27, 31
Bible 9, 10, 16, 26, 27, 30, 31
Bishop 7, 27, 30, 31

Cathedral 7
Centrepoint 17
Choir 11, 12
Christening 14
Christian 6, 8, 12, 13, 14, 18, 21, 22, 23, 24, 26, 30, 31
Christmas 20, 21, 29
Church family 24
Confirmation 27, 31
Creed 12, 31
Cross 14, 22
Curate 30

Diocese 7, 30, 31
Disciple 23, 27

Easter 22, 23, 28, 29
Epiphany 29

Family Service 9, 10, 11, 14, 25

God 6, 10, 11, 12, 15, 22, 26, 27, 30
Godparents 14, 27, 31
Good Friday 22, 28
Gospel 13, 23, 29, 31

Holy Communion Service 27, 31
Holy Spirit 6, 29
Hymn Book 11

Jesus Christ 6, 13, 20, 21, 22, 23, 29, 30, 31
Junior Worship 9, 12, 16, 17, 18, 19

Last Supper 29
Lent 22, 28, 29
Lord's Prayer 12

Marriage Register 15
Minister 7, 10, 12, 13, 14, 30, 31

Palm Sunday 29
Parish 30, 31
Prayer 9, 10, 12, 13, 17, 22, 23, 26, 27, 39, 30, 31
Prayer Book 12, 31

Resurrection 23, 31
Roman Catholic Church 6, 30

Sacrament 31
Saint 8, 28
Sunday School 16, 17
Sermon 13, 31
Service Book 9
Sin, 12, 31

Vicar 30

Wedding 15

THE
Someone is dead. Someone needs to pay.
MEANNESS
What would you do for revenge?
OF THINGS

SJ SIBISI

First published by SJ Sibisi, 2024
Copyright © 2024 SJ Sibisi 2024

ISBN: 979-8-322-20411-4

Imprint: Independently published

Cover design and typesetting by Gregg Davies Media
www.greggdavies.com

All rights reserved.

SJ Sibisi has asserted her right under the Copyright Act 1978 to be identified as the author of this work. This novel is a work of fiction. Names and characters are a product of the author's imagination and any resemblance to actual persons, living or dead, is coincidental.

This book is sold subject to the condition that it shall not, by way of trade or otherwise, be lent, resold, hired out or otherwise circulated without the author's and publisher's prior consent in any form of binding or cover other than in which it is published and without a similar condition including this condition being imposed on the subsequent purchaser.

Additional copies of this book can be purchased
from all leading book retailers worldwide.

To my dear mother, Harriet Ngubane.
You will always be the light guiding my path.

And to Michael Komape.
You will always be remembered.

1. Charlie

Tooting Bec
London, UK

Charlie jerked up from the mattress, sweat running down her back, her breaths coming in short, sharp gulps. For a few seconds, she could still feel the flames of the burning car scorching her flesh, the curdling screams of her parents ringing in her ears. Then her bedroom came into focus and fear dissolved into the dull weight of living.

Groaning, she leaned back against the headboard and closed her eyes, counting backwards from ten, centring herself. When she reached one and the nightmare was safely tucked away, she took a deep breath and opened her eyes again, ready to face the world. Her mouth was dry as the desert, her sandpaper tongue rasping against its roof, the taste of alcohol clinging to her lips. The culprits responsible sat sheepishly on the nightstand: A stash of sleeping pills, a half-empty bottle of wine and a cup of hot chocolate, now cold and stale after she had passed out before she could drink it. Her potential saviour, standing as her sole defence against such evidence of reprobation, was a tall glass of water, so tantalising she could almost smell it. However, she couldn't touch it yet. Routine was key. The golden path to letting go of harmful habits and embedding new ones. At least according to one of her many, many past psychologists. Hence, with a sigh, Charlie ignored the water and began her daily mantra.

"I live in the present to heal my past. I live in the present to heal my past. I live in the present to heal my past...."

As the words echoed in her head, she concentrated on her breathing, deep and long, pushing the air down with her diaphragm to her stomach, just like she'd been taught. With each breath, she tried to relax her limbs one by one, starting with her neck, then her shoulders, arms and fingers, down through her torso, hips, legs, and eventually her toes. Focusing just on her breath, slowly lifting the tension until…

Fuck.

Damn thing never worked.

Giving up, Charlie chugged down the water and checked her phone. Nearly 6 a.m. Seven hours of sleep and she was still exhausted. One hour to go before her alarm went off. She cast a wanton eye at the soft pillow beside her, longing to burrow back under the duvet. Then she dismissed the idea. One nightmare was quite enough for one day.

Forcing her legs to move, she got up and dragged herself to the bathroom. As she sat on the bog, she caught up on the news and checked her messages, mentally ticking off the things she would need to follow up on later. With nature temporarily satiated, she dropped the phone on the laundry basket and absently opened the bathroom cabinet, catching her reflection in the mirror. The woman who looked back at her seemed older than her thirty-one years, her pointy caramel face blotchy, her big, brown eyes dull and red, the fade of her mohawk desperately in need of a trim. So much for beauty sleep.

Turning on the shower to heat the water, Charlie reached for her toothpaste and brush, her hand skimming past a dusty pill bottle on the middle shelf. She paused, staring at the vail, its contents long expired, remembering the days when she'd needed four pills just to summon the will to get out of bed. Now the dreams forced her out. Guess that's what you called progress.

After brushing her teeth, she stepped into the shower, smiling as tiny pinpricks of blazing hot rain cascaded over her face, clearing the fog in her head, and kneading out the stubborn knots in her shoulders. She washed with her mother's favourite, vanilla and coconut soap, the lather a longed-for caress against her skin. Cosseted in thoughts of better days gone by, when her mobile chimed for attention, she let it go to voicemail. After a few moments, it rang again, MJ this time, her emergency number.

Cursing, she stepped out of the shower and grabbed her phone.

"Arthur," she said brusquely. "Do you know what time it is?"

Silence. She waited a few beats then said, "Whatever this is, it better be good."

Still nothing.

Wait - was that faint, strained breathing?

"Arthur? …Arthur, are you there?"

His voice was a hollow whisper.

"She's dead."

2. Missing

Regent's Canal
London, UK

It was quiet down by the canal. There, the shrieks, bangs, and bustle of the morning London rush hour four metres above seemed like a distant world. Apart from the faint hum of traffic, the dominant sounds were tweeting birds, the swoosh of willow trees in the gentle breeze and rippling water shimmering in the pale autumn morning light. It would have been almost idyllic, Charlie thought, if it wasn't for the dead body under a tree.

She stood taking photos a metre from the crime scene on the narrow canal walkway, her five-foot, three-inch frame clad in a black bomber jacket with matching jeans and suede boots, a felt cap shielding her head from the cold.

Further up the path, about eight metres behind her, Arthur, her informant, hovered nervously near the battered tent he called home, warily looking up and down the path for any casual passers-by. Face covered in white stubble, his long, grey hair tied in a ponytail, he stood hunched over, tightly clutching around him an oversized duffle coat as if protecting himself against all the evils of the world. They had met five years ago when she had been covering a story about a spate of murders among London's homeless or, as some would say, 'rough sleepers'. She hated it when people called them that as if the only problem the likes of Arthur had was thrashing around in bed and hogging the duvet. She knew why they did it, of course. To shift the blame and avoid calling it what it was. A failure of family, government, and society. Arthur had never told her the details of his story, just that - like so many other people - he had spent his life living pay cheque to pay cheque, getting knocked down and getting up until, one day, he just couldn't. They had never found the Rough Sleeper Killer but eventually the murders had abruptly and mysteriously ceased. Yet, brought together by chance, she and Arthur had stayed in touch, bound together by a strange form of kinship. Two souls looking for different kinds of home.

As Charlie circled the body capturing the scene from different angles, she ran through different headlines in her head, trying not to think about the cloying aroma of decaying flesh, the bitter taste of copper on her tongue or the horror before her eyes. In front of her was a small bump, almost imperceptible in the tall green foliage that grew from the back of the tree and up the high retaining wall that bordered the canal and the street above. The bump was a little girl, maybe five years old, her head almost severed from her neck, her pink dress raised to her chest. The girl's stomach had been sliced open, her guts hanging over her legs, her once-white stockings torn and covered in blood. The worst, however, was the wide smile that had been carved into the little girl's face. A crimson grimace, wailing from beyond the grave.

"You, ok?"

Charlie stopped shooting and turned to the voice at her side. Arthur had crept up behind her, his face still a ghostly pallor.

"Yes. I'm fine. Why?"

"You look like you're about to puke."

"I said I'm fine." She swallowed, warding off threats by her chilli tomato, egg, and bacon breakfast sandwich to make a reappearance.

Arthur gave her a searching look, his eyes sceptical. "Anyway, you told me to call. If I heard or found anything. So, I did. Just in case it was them."

She forced a smile, "Thank you, Arthur – I appreciate it."

"So, do you think it's them?"

"Could be." Charlie looked up, scanning the windows of the blocks of flats on the other side of the canal, wondering if anyone had seen anything and making a note to find out.

"What does that mean?" Arthur said gruffly.

She looked back at him. "Have to wait for the post-mortem. See if the pattern fits." She paused then added. "If it is, what they're putting these little kids through is getting worse."

Her companion nodded gravely, like an expert on the subject agreeing with a renowned colleague's prognosis. "I read your articles, you know. About - what you call it? – that paedophile ring?"

"Oh?" Charlie stepped away from him, partly to take a few more photos from further up the path and partly to hide her irritation. She preferred to be left alone when she was working, otherwise, she might miss something. However, Arthur clearly wanted to talk. Needed to talk.

"Yeah," he said eagerly, dogging her footsteps, "wanted to be informed, see? Just in case. What they do to these children is horrible. Entrapping them. Using them. Keeping them for months so they can push them around to multiple sites. Then discarding them like they were nothing better than garbage." He spat as if something nasty had slid into his mouth. "Terrible. Absolutely terrible."

"Yeah, I know."

"I read about you too. Said you'd been nominated for a Pulitzer. For the lengths you've gone to. To uncover the story, like."

Charlie shrugged dismissively. It wasn't about prizes. It was about justice. Giving voice to the voiceless. The problem was, after all this time, all this death, she was still no closer to finding the ringleaders behind it.

"What time did you find her again?" she asked.

"Just before I called you. When I got up for my morning dump."

"And she definitely wasn't here last night?"

"Nope. Not by midnight when I went to bed. Didn't hear anything in the night either but, then again, I sleep like the dead." Arthur guiltily peeked at the girl then away again, suddenly realising the inappropriateness of his analogy.

"Ok. Well, I think I'm done here," Charlie pocketed her phone. "I'm sure someone in those flats will have already called it in, so the police should be here soon."

Arthur's face turned sour, his experience with cops less than pleasant.

"Do you want me to help you move?" Charlie asked. "Find a new place until the police are done and you can come back home?"

He shook his head, "No thank you, dear. I'll be fine. Used to it, after all these years."

"Well, as long as you're sure," she tapped his shoulder, "I'll see you around, yeah?"

He nodded goodbye, "Yeah."

Charlie turned and started to walk back up the canal towards the stairs that would take her to her car. As she went, she opened an app on her phone, tapped and swiped then put the phone back in her jacket pocket.

Five seconds later, Arthur called her name. She turned to see him holding his phone to his chest, his rheumy eyes shimmering. "300 bucks? You didn't have to do that!"

"It's the least I can do," Charlie yelled, walking backwards. "Once you're resettled, go get yourself a nice breakfast."

"But this is enough for ten breakfasts! Lunches and dinner too. I can't-."

"Yes, you can!" Chuckling, she turned as she reached the stairs, shouting over her shoulder, "Cheers Arthur. Thanks again for all your help!"

Ignoring his ongoing protestations, she bounded up the stairs and onto the street above. She'd just unlocked the driver's door of her prized Mini Cooper when her phone rang. An unknown number.

"Hello?"

"Hi C, it's me."

"Vusi?" Charlie said, surprised. She hadn't expected it to be her cousin. "Where are you calling from?"

"The station."

"Oh? Are Constables allowed to make international calls now?"

"They aren't," he replied, sounding annoyed. Vusi hated being teased, which was exactly why Charlie loved doing it. "Look," he continued, "I don't have much time. Is this a good time to talk?"

"Sure," she said, silently laughing at his huffy tone, "What's up?" Putting her phone on speaker, she started the engine and eased into traffic.

"Remember that girl I told you about? The one who promised to sell me her laptop so that I can study online?"

"Yeah. What about her?"

"She finally got back to me with a price."

Charlie knew what was coming but she said it anyway, "And you're phoning me because…?"

"Eish! Don't be like that, C. You know I'm good for it."

"Didn't you say that the last time? *And* the time before that?"

"Black tax, Couz. Once I get my law degree, I'll pay it all back, I promise. Just help me out, one more time. Ppppleeaaassse."

Despite herself, Charlie softened. Vusi always found a way of making her go against her better judgement. Probably because he was one of the few family members she had left. "Fine. Send me the details and I'll see what I can do."

"Awesome. You're the best cousin ever!"

She heard a door bang in the background. "What's that?" Charlie asked.

"Looks like Serg just arrived. I better go."

"That's strange. Usually, your boss is still having breakfast at this time."

"I forgot to tell you. A new case just came in related to your part of the woods."

"Oh?" she heard papers shuffling.

"A missing person. Some high-flying banker."

"Define 'high-flying'?"

"Umm…let me check," more shuffling papers. "Here it is – a CEO at Yeats Bank, London."

"Really? How long?"

"Over twenty-four hours."
That long and not a peep?
Interesting.
"Circumstances?" she asked.
"Last seen going through security into departures at Heathrow airport. Then he didn't pitch at any of his meetings in Sandton yesterday. Also hasn't checked into his hotel and no one can get hold of him."
"And the guy's name?"
"Murdoch," Vusi said, "Derrick Franklin Murdoch."

3. A Scoop

Islington
London, UK

Charlie took the scenic route from Regent's Canal to the Torch offices in Islington, listening to her favourite aria to remind herself there was still some beauty left in the world. Luckily, when she arrived, the newsroom floor was still deserted apart from a few blurry-eyed souls emerging from an all-nighter. That meant that most of the hot desks were free including her favourite place near the coffee machine. Dumping her stuff on the desk, she went in search of the News Editor.

Famous for being an early bird, Kathy was already ensconced in her glass-fronted office engaged in her usual first task of the day, picking through the stories vying for the afternoon headlines. With a recessed chin and forehead, both of which paled in comparison to her long, pointy nose, she had a habit of sniffing and wriggling her snout as she read as if trying to detect the winner headline by smell alone. A habit which had earned her the loving sobriquet, The Ferret. Each story was either met with an excited gleam in her eye or a sour sneer as she placed it on the relegation pile and, as far as Charlie could tell, this morning the rejects were winning by a mile.

Charlie knocked and then walked right in, not wanting to give the News Editor the chance to turn her away. "Five-year-old girl found dead, mutilated. Possible Vic of the paedophile ring I've been tracking. Any chance of a spot above the fold?"

The Ferret didn't pause or look up. "Local?"

The question seemed innocent enough. After all, Londoners were bound to take more notice if it was one of their own. However, Charlie also knew that 'local' was also code for so much more. "Does it matter?" she said defiantly.

The editor didn't say it, but her face spoke volumes: I wish it wasn't so, but we both know brown and black toddlers are always a harder sell. Nevertheless, she gave Charlie a lifeline. "Name and angelic photo taken when she was alive?"

"Not yet," Charlie replied. "I'm hoping MISPERS will cough something up." Sadly, the Met's missing persons database was full of young minors, with dozens being added every day.

The Ferret looked at her with impatience. "Anonymous dead girls are just a statistic – you know that." She returned to her task. "Get me a name, a smiling photo and a quote from the grieving parents and you've got a shot for the evening slot."

"Cool. You'll have it in your inbox ASAP." No way was she going to have all that info by then, Charlie thought to herself, but a slot was a slot and hopefully, she would be able to gather just enough for people to care.

As she backed out of The Ferret's office, she heard a yelp behind her as she nearly bumped into someone. "Hey! Watch yourself!"

"Sorry," she pivoted to find the Business Editor scowling at her. Quickly shifting her face into what she hoped was a beguiling smile, Charlie followed her new quarry down the corridor. "Though, this *is* a happy coincidence."

"Is it?" Wearing a pristine business suit, her blonde hair slicked back into a bun, Bulldog Barbara neither smiled nor broke her stride as she headed for the lifts. "I don't have much time. I'm already late for a breakfast meeting at Canary Wharf."

Unflustered by the cool reception, Charlie hurried behind her and pressed on. "I was wondering if you've heard of a guy called Derrick Murdoch. Works for Yeats Bank?"

"Yeats? The CEO of the Africa division?"

"I believe so."

"Well, I don't know of another Derrick Murdoch who fits that description."

"Then I guess that's the guy. What can you tell me about him?"

"Quite a lot. We've run several pieces about him, in fact."

"Oh? On what?" Charlie kept on Bulldog's heels as she stepped into an empty lift.

"Some of them were the usual fluff pieces. Changes in the bank's portfolio or leadership, the bank's expansion into various African countries, that sort of thing. But more recently, Derrick started making headlines because of the changes he was making in the division. As you know, many international banks have received a lot of bad press lately relating to allegations of money laundering involving corrupt politicians and foreign moneymen. Well, unlike leaders in many of the other international banks, Derrick seemed to be getting ahead of the curve, introducing initiatives to tighten corporate governance, and letting go of several senior executives who had allegedly been involved in wrongdoing."

"So, he's one of the good guys?"

"I wouldn't go so far as to say that!" Bulldog demurred. "You know these City types. All wandering eyes and insatiable appetites. But professionally, he seems to be on the up and up. Even, some would say, an anti-corruption hero."

"No scandals? Enemies?" They stepped out of the lift into the underground carpark.

"Not that I know of. Rumour has it that some of the guys he fired weren't too happy. The bank, of course, tried to cover the firings up. Resignations and early retirements, that sort of thing. Wouldn't do to have any hint of scandal, after all. Anyway, why all these questions about Murdoch?"

"Because he's gone missing."

Barbara shot her a look of bemusement. "Missing? When?"

"As far as I know, more than 24 hours ago."

"How'd you know?"

"A source."

"Local?"

"No – SA. Where Murdoch disappeared."

"South Africa?" Bulldog's eyes twinkled with mirth. "One of your local connections, was it?"

Charlie smiled to herself. Was Vusi a connection or more like a stone around her neck? "Something like that."

"Why there?"

"Not sure yet. Probably a business trip. Anyway, I'm pretty sure it's going to be a while before anyone else picks up the story."

Bulldog turned as she got to her car, finally giving Charlie her full attention, her eyes shining with anticipation. "So, you're hoping this is going to be a scoop?"

Charlie briefly pondered her reply. Overplaying her hand might backfire but, at the same time, she needed enough bait to get the fish on the hook. "I think so," she said evenly.

"Good," she got into her car and rolled down the window. "Send me the copy for review as soon as you can. If we go ahead, I'll give you a good rate."

"Perfect."

"By the way," Bulldog said as she was about to drive off. "What do you think happened to him?"

"I've no idea," Charlie replied. "But whatever it is, I've no doubt it's going to be interesting."

4. The Marked Man

Alexandra Township
Johannesburg, South Africa

Thabo was on the prowl, his eyes sweeping back and forth, searching. He stood in the torrential rain on a small hill overlooking the river that stole his parents, barefoot, dressed in torn jeans and a raggedy t-shirt, trying to ignore the gnawing ache in his belly.

He had spent much of the morning at his usual spot, a traffic light intersection in a rich, white, Joburg suburb. Traffic lights were the best hunting ground, each switch to red a brief opportunity to grab a driver's attention and spur some kindness or inspire a little pity.

His patch was on a tree-lined street with huge mansions on either side, each fronted by green lawns and scented flower beds. Each mansion had prison-high walls and electric fences, the street patrolled twenty-four-seven by armed, private security guards.

Thabo had never understood why the settlers locked themselves in. Maybe it was the remnants of *swart gevaar* when, decade after decade, the ruling white apartheid elite were fed horror stories about what "the blacks" would do to them if they ever got a chance. Or perhaps it was due to guilt-inspired fear, each step inside their gilded cages accompanied by the crunch of bones cracking under their feet, each lash of rain against their windowpanes the drumbeat of the African dead demanding recompense. Whatever the reason, all that mattered was that it evoked just enough feeling to open up the purse strings. Especially for a fourteen-year-old black boy with a face like an angel.

The Meanness of Things

Yet today he had come up empty. The car windows had remained stubbornly shut, drivers pretending to be blinder than usual to his pleadings. It could have been the pouring rain that did it. Or they might have sensed the deep resentment in his heart. No matter which, after three hours without even a cent, he had been forced to turn back and look for better pickings closer to home.

As he had walked from the suburbs, past the industrial area, through Alexandra township to a shack settlement on the banks of the Jukskei river, green lawns had been replaced by dry, brown brush, the scent of flowers by the reek of open sewers, the mansions by tightly packed corrugated-iron shacks and the trees by tall, wooden electrical poles, their black wires covering the sky like a spider's web.

Now, standing on the hill above the settlement, Thabo watched as the sewers became streams and the streams flowed into the rising river. Dozens of his neighbours desperately tried to bail out their shacks with plastic buckets, while those with homes too close to the riverbank, frantically tried to save their prized possessions from the river's grasp. Back and forth, they waded into the churning waters, grabbing all they could before running up the hill to place their belongings next to him on the grass. A place where they thought they would be safe.

He just had to find the right moment. When all eyes were on the river and not on what was happening on the hill. Two, three seconds tops, to reach down, make the lift and be out of there with his prize. That was the theory anyway. Yet, how long had he been standing there? Almost an hour? Thabo cursed under his breath. There were too many people on the hill. Too many relaying back and forth to the riverbank.

Hold on – what was that?

Thabo squinted, trying to focus. Halfway between the riverbank and the top of the hill, a shape that looked like a black bag lay near a row of crumbling, concrete pit toilets. The toilets were just another example of a failed Alexandra Renewal Programme, sucked dry by corruption. Or at least that's what his neighbour said. The would-be bag was closest to the last pit latrine in the row. This one had lost all its walls, leaving just the latrine's broken seat sticking up, chair-high, from the ground. Yet, unlike the rest, this seat had a concrete slab on top of it. He cast his mind back.

Had that slab been there yesterday?
No, it hadn't. He was sure of it.

Curious, Thabo walked down the hill to take a closer look. Standing next to the decaying toilet, he discovered the bag was, in fact, a backpack. He quickly did a three-sixty to make sure he wasn't being watched. The way he saw it, whoever had put down the slab had been trying to hide something in a place they thought no one would look. Which meant they wouldn't appreciate it being found, by him or anybody else. Now, the backpack could be linked to that something, and the hiders had left it behind by mistake, or it could be unrelated. Whether it was or it wasn't, he believed in one rule: You could never be too careful.

Once he was sure it was safe, Thabo eagerly opened the backpack. Empty apart from a couple of sticks of chewing gum. That was ok. The bag would still fetch a Bob or two. He gobbled down the gum, relishing the burst of flavour in his mouth and how the sugar briefly eased the pain in his belly, then put the backpack aside.

So far, so good.

Now, Thabo turned to the slab. Placing his shoulder against the concrete block, he pushed with all his might, straining at the effort. After a couple of shoves, he finally managed to shift the slab just far enough to be able to see inside. He jumped back, heart thudding in his chest, his mind whirring.

Was that…?
Couldn't be.
But it looked just like…
Really…are you sure?
What else could it be?!

He took deep breaths, trying to calm himself as he nervously scanned his surroundings again, making sure he was still unobserved.

Come on, Thabo, get a grip. Take one more look. Just to be sure. Then get the hell out of here.

Once his heart had returned to a steady beat, he inched forward and pushed the slab until there was room to put his whole head through the opening. With a hand clasped over his mouth and nose to ward off the stench, he leaned further in. At the bottom of the dark, concrete pit, a white man half-lay, half-sat against one wall, his hands bound behind his back, legs twisted at impossible angles. Part of his body was submerged in water and excrement as flies buzzed all around him, some chomping on the blood that trickled from the top of his head to his chin, whilst others focused on the drool oozing out of his mouth. His expensive suit hung dirty and torn around him, his white shirt ripped open to reveal the man's battered torso and the rivulets of dark liquid that ran across his chest, the skin ripped and ragged as if a serrated knife had carved up his flesh.

The foul stink of blood, faeces and decay started to make Thabo feel sick, but he resisted the urge to look away. There was something about the man's chest he couldn't figure out. Something about the knife strokes. At first, they had seemed random but now…Thabo squinted some more.

Was it some sort of pattern? No – not a pattern. More like…

When it finally clicked, his breath locked in his throat. The man had been marked with a message, each gash a letter stroke, most so deep they had shredded muscle. And for a split second, it seemed like the message had been left just for him. A warning and accusation wrapped in one word.

TRAITOR

5. EXCO

The Strand
London, UK

On a normal day, as he stepped out of the lift onto the penultimate floor of Yeats Bank, John Hilary would have paused to take in the breath-taking beauty of the Strand skyline, his briefcase held firmly by his side, his back ramrod straight and his Roman nose raised precisely twenty degrees to the heavens. However, today was not a normal day.

As he walked briskly down the brightly lit corridor, he passed a few of his fellow Executive Committee members making their way to the boardroom to await the urgent meeting he had called. Greeting each as he passed, he informed them he would be along shortly and hurried to his office.

"Morning, Gertrude. We all set?"

"Morning," his personal assistant rose from the desk in front of his office and followed him inside. "Everyone has confirmed for the Exco except Margaret. She has a client meeting she can't get out of."

Hilary went to sit behind his desk. "Fine. I'll give her a call later to get her up to speed. I've already told the boys I'll be along shortly. Just want to get my thoughts together."

"Of course. Shall I take your cappuccino through to the boardroom in the meantime?"

"Yes, please."

Hilary opened his briefcase and took out his notebook. Just shy of six feet with a runner's build, he had long crafted a quiet and unassuming demeanour that led to his often being underestimated by friends and enemies alike. Hence, though his rise in the bank had been slower than some, it had been steady, eventually securing him the role of Africa division Chief Operating Officer. A post he had safely held onto for the last ten years.

As the COO and Acting Divisional CEO in his boss's absence, it had fallen on Hilary to manage the matter of Derrick's disappearance. And what a matter it was. Of course, it could turn out that the disappearance was merely temporary, with Derrick suddenly emerging after a misguided dalliance or waking up as John Doe in a hospital bed. On the other hand, his boss could be gone for good. Which meant this might be the moment he had been waiting for.

A chance to finally make his mark.

So far, things had gone well. At their meeting that morning, the Group CEO and the Africa Board Chair had taken the news stoically, nodding sagely and mumbling their agreement with the steps Hilary had taken, including reporting the matter to the South African Police Services as well as notifying the British Embassy in Pretoria. The real question had been what they were going to do next - treat it as a crisis or adopt a more cautious approach. In the end, they'd agreed that the best strategy was to try and buy time until they knew exactly what was going on. That meant keeping the matter under wraps and coming up with a convincing tale to explain the divisional CEO's absence to those likely to notice.

Fortunately, when Hilary had spoken to Derrick's Chief of Staff and PA, he'd been glad to find that they readily understood the importance of discretion. Even his wife, Lucy, had put up surprisingly little resistance, sounding lost and confused as if she was still struggling to come to terms with it all. Now, the only thing left was the Africa Division Exco. Derrick's PA had already received urgent enquiries from some of them, demanding to know why the Africa CEO was not answering his phone. However, The Group CEO had insisted that divisional Exco members should still be kept in the dark, arguing that the higher the number of people who knew a secret, the more likely it was going to leak. Whilst Hilary did not disagree with this logic, it meant that he would have to put on his best poker face to get his colleagues to buy into the bluff. The challenge was he had never been much good at poker. To date, he had succeeded at playing the political game through keen observation, patience, and deft strategy, knowing which card to play and when. Bald-faced lies were not his forte, especially under pressure.

So, what was to be done?

Sighing, Hilary closed his notebook and sat back in his chair, allowing his mind to wander. Sometimes, the best way to solve a problem was to not think about it. To let go and let the subconscious have its way. He thought about his drive into work that morning, reading the morning papers in the back seat as

Mark had battled through the rush hour crush. From this vantage point, he had noticed how much his driver had aged recently, like his body's natural deterioration had held back all these years then pounced on him all at once. An unwelcome thought, given that they were the same age. He could scarcely believe it. Inside, he still felt like the twenty-five-year-old intern who had joined Yeats all those years ago, bounding up and down bank corridors, keen to impress. How his Da had radiated with pride when he had told him that he had been accepted into the internship programme! Hilary glanced at the photo of his father on his desk. Ten years since he had passed yet he still felt him standing beside him, gently urging him on.

He jerked upright. That was it. So obvious, he kicked himself for having not thought about it before. Like his Da had always said, the best lies are the ones that are closest to the truth. And that's what he'd do, tell Exco the truth - with just a few omissions, of course. He rehearsed the story in his head: Derrick had gone on a business trip to Johannesburg – which they all knew to be true. Up to this point, he – Hilary - had not known the sensitivity of this trip until he had been informed this morning by the Group CEO. Also true… ish. So sensitive, that Derrick and the Group CEO had agreed that the matter must remain confidential and Derrick incommunicado until his mission was complete. Untrue but - plausible. Thus, the Group CEO had asked all members of Exco to keep this hush-hush until told otherwise and had instructed that he, as Acting CEO of the division, should continue to deal with all matters relating to Derrick's office until he returned. Which was 100% true.

Hilary nodded, feeling pleased with himself.

Yes, that would do nicely.

His preparations complete, Hilary stood up and made his way to the boardroom, wondering how his story and the disruption in leadership would be received. Trudy, the Head of Strategy, and a long-term ally would quickly fall into step, that he was sure of. And even if she had a few private reservations about his tale, she could be depended upon to keep them to herself. She was also very close to Maggie, so he expected no trouble from that quarter either. The same, however, could not be said for Derrick's allies.

The weakest but loudest of these was Jonathan Murphy, the Head of Private Clients. A short, portly man whose personal presence could best be described as underwhelming, Jonathan sought to make up for these defects with a nastiness of temper, sucking up to power and always seeking to elevate himself at other people's expense like a schoolyard bully sidekick. God knew why Derrick had promoted him, but without their boss, Jonathan would never have ascended so high. No wonder, then, that his sponsor's sudden absence had made him such a worried man, with Derrick's PA reporting that Jonathan had kicked up the most fuss about their boss' sudden silence. That meant he was in for a grilling, Hilary thought as he walked down the corridor, with Jonathan on the alert for the slightest hint that something might be wrong. However, the longer Derrick was absent, the more likely it was that Jonathan would start to drown, frantically looking around for the next life raft, which, for his part, Hilary had no intention of providing. Hence, despite his bark, Jonathan was likely to be an irritating but negligible threat.

Then came the Chief Risk Officer. Although Reuben Stott had always tried to project a suave and calm demeanour, aimed at collecting friends rather than enemies, Hilary had always sensed a deep restlessness within him. As if his soul was constantly twisting and turning, sensing danger everywhere. He reminded him of dry kindling, otherwise harmless but quick to ignite when faced with a spark. Would Derrick's disappearance be the match to ignite the flame? Probably not. While Reuben was the other Exco member who had raised concerns about Derrick's whereabouts, indications were that he had seemed more curious than perturbed when doing so. Furthermore, unlike Jonathan, Reuben had a strong track record within the bank and the sector as a whole, which made him more sure of himself. So, most likely, he would take the news in his stride, keeping things close to his chest as he waited to see how it all played out. This meant that, if Derrick didn't return, Reuben could potentially be turned.

Lastly, Hilary's mind turned to Steven Vivekenandan, the Chief Finance Officer. Now there was a sophisticated player, constantly weighing the odds and determining the most profitable path before making his move. Had they lived in a different world, Steven might have indeed been a formidable rival. However, given that Yeats was about as woke as a dead dinosaur, the best people like Steven could hope for was to be cast as a supporting character. He would never get the lead, no matter how good he was. The question was, did Steven know that, or did he still dream of getting to the top? So far, Hilary had nothing to go on. Unlike his colleagues, Steven had made no enquiries about Derrick since he vanished, seeming totally untouched by the matter. Moreover, the CFO had given nothing away as they had passed each other in the corridor, appearing neither anxious nor calm, just his usual unreadable self. Which, of course, was no bloody use to anybody. He would have to watch him closely. If Steven was ever going to make his move, now would be the time to do it.

Rounding the corner leading to the boardroom, Hilary straightened his spine, readying himself to go into battle. Then a nasty thought occurred to him.

What if wily Steven knew something he didn't.

6. Tongue-Tied

Chelsea
London, UK

Lucy Murdoch sat on a window seat in the kitchen of their Chelsea home, wrapped in a blanket and staring blindly into space. Her thick auburn hair was dishevelled and greasy, her large green eyes puffy from crying, her head feeling dull and heavy like it was encased in a thick fog. Despite the combined efforts of the central heating and the blanket, she couldn't stop shivering, the number thirty-nine going round and round in her mind.

Thirty-nine hours since she had kissed her husband goodbye.

Thirty-nine hours in which her life had changed forever.

Thank God her mother had agreed to take the kids until this all blew over. She just hadn't been able to cope with them right now. Did that make her a bad parent? Passing on her kids to their grandparents like unwanted baggage? Yet, what else was she supposed to do?

A bell pealed in the far distance. She burrowed her head into her shoulders and pulled the blanket tighter around her, warding off all intrusions.

Must be from across the street.

The bell rang again. Closer and longer this time. Insistent.

Mrs Dawson's next door. Had to be. Why didn't the deaf bat answer it?

The bell chimed a third time, screeching around the kitchen like a caged bird. When it was promptly followed by three, sharp raps on wood, echoing down the hall and bursting into the room, Lucy finally realised the noise came from her own front door.

Who the hell was that? And couldn't they see she just wanted to be left alone?

She groaned, pondering what to do. Screaming at them to go away might not work. On the contrary, it would just confirm that she was at home, perhaps making them even more determined. Yet, if she continued to ignore them, they would probably keep pressing the bell until they drove her crazy. In other words, she was caught in a double whammy.

The profanities coming thick and fast in her head, Lucy forced herself to stand, her bones creaking with the effort. Feeling a hundred years old, she shuffled across the kitchen and down the hall, then squinted through the front door peephole.

No one there.

That was odd. Maybe it was just a silly prank. Probably one of those snotty, little kids from number thirty-five.

Lucy was about to turn back when something else occurred to her. She bent down to look through the letterbox. She'd been right. Something was lying on the doorstep. Opening the door just a crack, she scanned the front yard to make sure it was empty, then stepped out to inspect the object more closely. A box, about the size of a smartphone, wrapped with brown paper and encased in a clear plastic bag. No address, stamps, or postmarks. Just her name, hand-written on the front.

Her gut told her to leave it alone, to get Maggie to deal with it when she arrived the next day to clean the house. Then again...

A strange package turning up a few days after Derrick's disappearance? What were the odds?

Heart racing, she scurried back to the kitchen, ditched the blanket on the box seat, grabbed a knife and a pair of washing gloves and returned to the porch. Carefully, she picked up the box with gloved hands, keeping her arms extended away from her body to minimise contact. Shoving the front door shut behind her with her foot, she placed the box on the tiled entrance hall floor. Then she stood, hands on her hips, looking at it.

Reckless, that's what this was. Planning to casually open an unknown package that someone had anonymously dropped on your doorstep? Someone who had gone to such lengths not to be seen! Dumber than dumb. At the same time, she couldn't just leave it here, could she?

Taking a deep breath, Lucy knelt on the floor and reached for the package with shaking fingers. She gently shook it and heard nothing but rustling plastic. Sniffing the edges, she picked up faint odours of candle wax, cardboard, and dust. Not exactly harmful biochemical compounds. Yet again anthrax didn't announce itself either. Maybe the best thing was to take things step by step.

First, she sliced open the plastic bag, making sure the opening faced away from her, and smelt the air again. No new aromas. No sudden bout of dizziness or nausea. So, if anyone was trying to kill her, they weren't trying to gas her to death.

Good. On to the next step.

She pulled out the box and examined the wrapping paper. Nothing exceptional. Something that you would find in any stationery store or supermarket. Slowly peeling off the sticky tape holding the brown wrapping in place, she put the paper to one side. What lay underneath the wrapping paper also seemed innocent enough. A plain, rectangular cardboard box with a thick flap on the long edge. She picked the box up and sniffed it again.

What was that smell? Lavender mixed with something she couldn't quite place. Could the package be a gift? Perhaps some kind of homemade deodoriser left by a thoughtful but shy and miserly neighbour? After all, who doused a bomb in lavender? Unless it was those kids, part of their sick little joke? Well, there was only one way to know for sure.

Putting the box back on the floor, Lucy pried open the flap a millimetre at a time with the tip of her knife, haunches tight, ready to jump back in the event of any sudden flashes. When the flap was loose enough to open by hand, she put the knife away, sat back and took another deep breath.

Ok, Luce. It's now or never.

Steeling herself, Lucy quickly opened the flap. Suddenly, she couldn't breathe, her surroundings warping and spinning. Her last thought as she slumped sideways, slipping into unconsciousness, was that she should have fucking listened to her gut. When she hit the floor, her knee kicked the box on its side, tipping its contents onto the shiny hall tiles. A cream satin cushion covered in dark, red stains rolled out first, followed by a man's severed finger, gore glistening on its puckered skin. The last item was a white, blood-smeared card with three words typed on it in black, capital letters.

HOLD YOUR TONGUE.

7. No Trace

Tooting Bec
London, UK

She sat at her favourite spot in her Tooting Bec flat, the breakfast table in her small, cosy kitchen, next to a tall, sash window that looked out onto the back garden. There was something about nature, the foliage changing with the seasons, birds chirping in the trees and squirrels darting through the underbrush that lifted her spirits no matter what was going on in the world. However, after having spent the previous day tracking info on the dead girl without success forcing her to put the story temporarily to bed, the only thing on Charlie's mind that morning was trawling the net for Derrick Murdoch.

It had been more than forty-eight hours since Murdoch had gone missing, but so far no one had publicly raised the alarm. Neither the bank, his wife, nor the police. Perhaps the South African police were just being slow off the mark but for an employer and spouse to be mum in moments like this was very unusual, if not downright suspicious. Which had, naturally, made her even more determined to find out what was going on.

So far, her dive into Murdoch's background had confirmed what Bulldog had said, with a few additional titbits. Murdoch was a man who liked being in front of the camera, either boasting about his successes, most recently his anti-corruption campaign, or schmoozing with London socialites at ridiculously expensive nightclubs and restaurants. Whilst some of the clubs he frequented were notorious cocaine dens or invitation-only gambling joints, Murdoch had been very careful to avoid any hint of scandal as far as that was concerned. However, he seemed to have been less careful about his love life, with rumours of several ex-marital liaisons, many of which had ended badly.

Hence, if something bad had indeed happened to Murdoch, the people who might have had a motive to do the deed – whatever it was - not only included the bank employees he had pushed out, but also his wife and disgruntled ex-mistresses. However, all these potential enemies were in the UK. If they had a grudge against Murdoch, why not act closer to home? Why wait until he travelled to South Africa to do the deed? So, maybe Murdoch also had enemies abroad?

Turning away from her laptop, Charlie picked up her phone and sent a text – 'can you talk?'. Two minutes later she got a reply. 'Give me twenty'. Whilst she was waiting, Charlie made herself a cup of coffee and started to put together an initial framework for her story. As soon as the twenty minutes were up, she eagerly dialled. Vusi picked up on the first ring.

"Sorry about that," he said. "Just had to find a place where it's safe to talk. You checking I got the money? Cos I haven't."

"No," she took the edge off her annoyance with a sip of coffee. "Only transferred it this morning, so it will only show tomorrow. I'm calling you about something else. Heard anything more about that banker?"

"Banker?" Now she wasn't talking about money, Vusi sounded like he couldn't be less interested.

Charlie reminded herself to be patient. For now, he was the only source she had. "Remember – that MISPER you guys got in yesterday?"

"Oh yeah – him. You chasing my tip then?"

"Might be. Depends on where it goes. Got any more intel?"

"Nah. It's been passed on to Priority Investigations."

"The Hawks?" Charlie put down her coffee, grabbed her pad and started making notes. "So, they're taking it *that* seriously?"

"Serg said the politicians think a missing Brit banker is bad for international investment. I hear the team's been told they better find him fast or else."

"Then Murdoch wasn't just hijacked?" Charlie knew it was a stupid question. Murdoch would probably have been traveling in a rental and, generally, hijackers didn't steal rental cars. Too much mileage on the clock. However, there was no harm in making sure.

"Had that been the case, he probably would've turned up by now. Dead or alive." Vusi replied. "But he seems to have disappeared without a trace."

"You sure? Or is it just too early to tell?"

She heard the shrug in his voice, "Seems that way. Heard some of our traffic guys who are supporting the investigative team talking about it in the canteen."

Charlie waited for him to expand but he fell silent. "And they didn't say anything else?" she prompted.

"Nope."

She tried another angle. "But 'without a trace' must mean it was planned, right?"

"Could be," Vusi said, his tone flat.

"I guess, you're not that close to it, are you? Given that the Hawks are running the case."

"Not really," he replied, clearly relieved. "The only other thing I know is that the Hawks bosses are keeping the investigation on lockdown, trying to ensure that there are no leaks."

"What about public calls for information? There haven't been any this side, what about there?"

"Na-huh."

"Why?" Charlie asked. "Surely those who reported him missing would have insisted on it. Do you know who that was?"

"Bank office in Sandton."

"Do you think it was them who gave the instruction? On no public calls, I mean."

"I guess so."

"So, the bank wants him found, but on the down-low?"

"Perhaps. I -"

"But even if that was the case," she said thinking out loud. "Why would Murdoch's wife go along with it?"

"Look," Vusi said emphatically. "I better get back or someone's going to come looking for me."

Charlie finally relented, recognising she had probably gotten all she was going to get. "Sure. Keep me in the loop if you hear anything else."

Excitement coursed through Charlie's veins as she put down the phone and woke up her laptop. She'd been right. There was something more to Murdoch's disappearance after all. Though, first she had to confirm what Vusi had told her.

She quickly searched for Mrs Murdoch's contact details but found that they weren't listed. Then she contacted the bank's Media Relations Officer, who referred her to the Group CEO, who, in turn, referred her back to Media Relations. Lastly, she phoned the Hawks spokesperson who refused to confirm or deny the investigation, simply stating that they would be doing a media briefing on all ongoing investigations in due course. And this told her all she needed to know.

Her reach-outs done, Charlie quickly wrote up the first draft of the story, confirming that she had given all parties their requisite right-of-reply and ending with just enough questions to keep readers wanting more.

What really happened to Derrick Murdoch?

And why are some of those closest to him trying to keep it quiet?

8. Out of the Bag

The Strand
London, UK

Hilary paused on the threshold, soaking it in. Walking into the Group CEO's office was like entering power personified. It wasn't just the expanse of the room, further enlarged by the 180-degree view of London provided by the wall-to-wall, floor-to-ceiling windows. Nor was it the view itself, the sight of dusk falling over the city enough to take your breath away. And it also wasn't the expensive fittings consisting of deep-pile carpets and Persian rugs, a huge, gleaming mahogany desk and conference table, plush, velvet couches before a tall, marble fireplace and a bedroom suite for those all-night stints, discretely tucked behind a hidden panel. Rather, it was the bold masculinity etched into every inch, from the décor to the shiny professional trophies and gilded photos of Spencer smiling next to world leaders. The abode of the ultimate Alpha. A lair that matched the magnetism of the man himself. The charming smile, the rugged good looks, the walk of an apex predator. There was something intimidating yet seductive about being so close to raw, unbridled power. To be amongst those who knew that rules were only for the lowly masses. Would such power ever be his? Possibly, but only if he stayed ahead of the game.

The Group CEO had his back to him, standing at the window taking a call. Sensing he was no longer alone, Spencer turned and waved him in, raising one slim, tanned finger to signify one more minute.

"Have you seen the Torch?" Hilary asked when the call came to an end.

"Yes, this morning, why?" Spencer ambled to one of the two couches in front of the fireplace, indicating that Hilary should join him.

"Then you haven't seen the latest," Hilary replied sitting on the couch opposite.

"No, I haven't." Spencer leaned back, taking up space, spreading his arms across the back of the sofa and crossing his legs. "Merry did say some journo rang yesterday. Never could stand the press. Referred them back to PR."

"Well, I don't know what our team said but the Torch's just added a story to their business pages headlined 'Top Banker Missing in South Africa'."

"Don't tell me Derrick's thing has leaked already?"

"Looks like it." Hilary handed Spencer his phone, the story already open on the screen.

He read quickly, scrolling as he went, his face inscrutable. "Who's Charlie Tate? Not one of ours, is she?" Spencer asked when he got to the end.

"Don't know. Must be a freelancer."

"Well, whoever she is, she's certainly well-informed," he handed Hilary the phone and sat forward, elbows on his knees, his eyes locked onto Hilary's own. "Where's the leak, do you think?"

Spencer's stare was so intense, it made Hilary feel guilty even when he knew he was innocent. "I'm not sure," he said, making a show of pocketing his phone so he could look away. "I'll get bank security to investigate but I would be surprised if it's one of us."

His boss didn't reply, shifting his eyes to a spot just over Hilary's left ear, squinting like he was trying to identify something in the far distance that he couldn't quite make out. Hilary stared silently at the carpet, knowing better than to interrupt him when his cogs were turning. Eventually, Spencer focused on him again, his regard cool. "Will he be found, d'you think?"

"Let's hope so," Hilary said with what he hoped sounded like genuine enthusiasm.

Spencer made a face, pulling some lintel off his trouser leg as if he'd just found a dead insect soiling his sacred person. "All of this would have been so much easier if we had a ransom note. Or, better yet, a body."

Hilary blinked but kept his face impassive. "Yes. Certainty is always best."

"Far neater, don't you think?" Once again, Spencer's eyes bored into his own.

Was this a test?

This time, Hilary held his gaze. "Of course."

A brief, mirthless smile flickered across his boss' face then was gone.

Did that mean he had passed or failed?

"But now the cat's out of the bag," Hilary continued with more confidence than he felt, "we need to discuss what to do next."

Now Spencer was all business. "I need to phone the Board Chairs. Let them know we have this under control."

"And the press? I think we now have no choice but to go public."

"Agreed. We need to get ahead of the story before every tom and dick starts running with it. I also didn't like Tate's insinuation, making it look like we've got something to hide."

"We'll sort that at the presser. I'll also organise a staff briefing to put an end to all the gossip that must be going around by now."

"And please take care of Lucy." Spencer rolled his eyes. "Don't think I could take her particular brand of whining at the moment."

"Will do," Hilary felt a tinge of pity for Derrick's wife but promptly squashed it. One had to keep one's eye on the prize. "Now that the story has broken, I'll need to warn her before her kids get wind of it."

Spencer gave him a "don't bore me with the details" look, checked his watch, and stood. "Was there anything else? Promised my wife to take her somewhere special for dinner this evening."

"Sorry – I won't keep you much longer." As Spencer went to his desk to pack up for the day, Hilary followed. "What shall we do about the divisional Exco?"

Spencer raised a sharp, manicured brow. "What about them?"

"Now they'll realise they were lied to."

"And?" The eye roll was almost imperceptible this time but there all the same. "What do I always say…?"

Hilary flushed, feeling foolish at the reminder. "Need to know means need to know. Yes, …um…I'll be sure to make that clear."

Spencer weighed a file in each hand as if deciding which one he should take then put them both in his bag. "And in the meantime? You've done what I asked?"

"Oh yes," Hilary said. "I've begun with Derrick's major clients. If he was up to anything we didn't know about, that's where we'll find it."

"Excellent. And remember – report whatever you unearth to me and only to me. Got it?"

"Naturally."

"You know," Spencer said softly, zipping up his bag. "You and I might just make a good team. If everything goes to plan."

Warm satisfaction spread across Hilary's chest. Finally, his boss had spoken the words he'd been waiting for.

"Yes, I.." he fumbled for the right phrase, something appreciative without being too gushy. "I promise I won't let you down."

"Good man." Spencer picked up his bag, preparing to head out the door. "And find out what you can about this Charlie Tate, would you? Let's make sure he or she doesn't become a problem for us."

9. Thangs

Tooting Bec
London, UK

Charlie looked at the evidence board in her study and frowned, trying to decide what to do next. After coming back from the Yeats press conference, she had immediately set to work, more convinced than ever that the full Murdoch story had yet to be told. It hadn't been so much what Yeats had said. She had expected a PR job with lots of 'we acted as soon as we could' and 'our thoughts are with the family' type of bullshit. What had struck her more was what they didn't say. The subtle but very real attempt to put daylight between the bank and Murdoch. Either the bank knew more about Murdoch's disappearance than it was saying, or they suspected whatever happened to Murdoch would taint them in some way. Whichever it was, Charlie knew a juicy tale in the making when she saw it.

At the top of the board, Charlie had written the word 'victim?' and placed Murdoch's picture underneath it. In the row below Murdoch, she had created five categories: Current bank employees, ex-bank employees, the wife, mistresses, and others. Under the first category, she had listed the names of Murdoch's current and past colleagues in the Africa division. In the second category, she had included the names of the two ex-employees who had resigned, AKA been sacked, under Murdoch's tenure. In the wife category, she had pasted Lucy Murdoch's photo and noted the names of a couple of Lucy's friends. Under mistresses, she had focused on those who seemed keen to get themselves in the media hoping that it would make them more willing to talk. Lastly, in the 'others' category, she had drawn a couple of upside-down smiley faces, representative of those that might be lurking in the shadows, their contribution to the story as yet unknown.

Now the skeleton of her evidence board was in place, she had to work out how she was going to fill it. There were two obvious places to start but they were also likely to prove the trickiest. The bank and –

Charlie heard the front door open and feet stomping down the passage before a firestorm of red, gold and green flashed past her study door.

"Hey!" Charlie followed the supernova into the kitchen. "Don't you ever knock?"

"Damn girl!' Quicha said, holding her hand to her heart. "Why you got to be so loud? I swear, you're just like my Mama."

Knowing Quicha's mother, Charlie wasn't sure she liked the comparison. Especially coming from someone who epitomized the word 'loud'. Apparently, under the impression that primary colours were a God-given instruction, LaQuicha Johnson Carter's curvaceous 22-year-old frame always blazed from head to toe in a rainbow pick-n-mix, from her beaded braids, popping nail art to her designer footwear, announcing her presence as irrevocably as her Atlanta Georgia drawl.

"No, I'm not," Charlie replied with a mock pout. "Anyway, the key I gave you was for emergencies, not for you to barge in whenever you like!"

Despite the rebuke, Charlie wasn't really mad. In fact, she was glad to see her. Quicha was the kind of neighbour who dropped in to borrow a cup of sugar, ended up staying for hours and made you love every minute of it, emitting a warm glow like a fire on a cold winter's day.

"I'm sorry. My bad," Quicha made a puppy dog face. "But it is. Kinda."

"What?"

"An emergency. I need coffee."

"Again?"

"These exams be killing me. Mama said I better not fail or they ain't taking me to Malibu this Christmas." She began opening and closing the kitchen cupboards. "Remind me – where your coffee at?"

"Where it always is – right cupboard above the kettle." Leaving her guest to it, Charlie went back to her study thinking that, for a rich girl, Quicha's street wasn't bad. She'd asked her once why she spoke that way, given her private school education, and Quicha had just shrugged and said it made her feel cool. The look in her eyes, however, had been all too familiar. Charlie knew exactly what it was like to be rejected by two groups, one because you were Black and another because you weren't Black enough. Maybe that's why they had become friends.

Standing in front of the whiteboard, Charlie heard an "oh snap" followed by more footsteps before Quicha strode into the study carrying a bag of Peruvian coffee beans.

"Wow!" she said, coming to stand beside her. "Is this what they call a murder board?"

"Well – I don't know if it's murder yet. Let's just call it an evidence board for now. I'm trying to put everything up in one place so I can keep track."

Quicha pointed at a photo. "*She* looks an uppity B."

Charlie chuckled. "That's the victim's wife - Lucy Murdoch. Been trying to get hold of her but she hasn't been returning my calls. Even went round to her place. Neighbours said she hasn't come out of her house since her husband vanished."

"Man! I take that back. She must be shook."

"Maybe," Charlie replied, pulling a face.

"Girl, that's cold!"

She burst out laughing. "No, it's not! It's being objective – statistically speaking."

"Awright, I get your point. Always start with the spouse." Quicha shifted her focus, pointing at another category. "You also goin' after those bad boys at the bank?"

"Someone there must know something. Though at the press conference today they pretty much shut down all my questions."

Quicha's eyes lit up. "You went to a presser? Meet anyone special?"

Charlie rolled her eyes, remembering that Quicha had recently appointed herself as custodian of her love life like she was on some kind of rescue mission. "Of course, I didn't. It was a press conference for God's sake." Despite herself, an image floated into her head. "Well, at least not like that."

"I knew it!" Quicha did her happy dance. "What's his name and what does he look like?"

"Jake – Jake Toplin. Works for Business Today. As for looks…" Charlie thought of his face. Curly, dirty blond hair, square jaw, laughing mouth and green eyes speckled with sapphire blue – just like her brother's. At the memory, something welled up inside her, wretched and bruised. She forced it back down, pushing thoughts of her dead brother aside. "Don't know," she said. "Didn't notice."

Quicha grinned. "Yeah, you did. And you like him too. I can tell!"

"I wouldn't say that," she said primly. "Though he seemed nice enough. Even offered to help if I ever needed it. Me being new to the finance beat and all that."

Quicha gasped. "Hold on, girl! Good-looking *and* kind?"

Charlie wasn't sure how to respond. Jake had not needed to make such an offer, there was no doubt about that. Yet, not one to jump to conclusions, it was probably too early to judge what the gesture said about his character.

Moreover, at this rate, if she allowed Q to carry on, she would have her trussed up and married before dinner. Time to pour some water on the flames.

"Or he's got an ulterior motive. People can surprise you, Q. That's why I like being single."

"Mm-mmm," Quicha replied, serving her a huge slice of side-eye with extra-large fries.

"Let's get back to Murdoch, shall we?" Charlie said brightly, tapping the photo at the top of the board. "Murdoch didn't just disappear, Q. Sooner or later, someone has to talk, I'm sure of it."

Quicha huffed in frustration then reluctantly went along with the change of subject. "He loaded?" she asked, gazing at Murdoch's face.

"I presume so. Why?"

"You remember my cousin, Shonda?" Her eyes sparkled like she'd just discovered gold. "You know! The one who recently moved back to LA?"

Unlike her, Quicha came from a massive family, from tens of great-great-grandparents and great-aunts to dozens of cousins, nephews, and nieces, all of whom were always either getting up to something or feuding and fighting with somebody. And while Charlie tried to remember it all, the truth was she just couldn't keep up. However, loath to hurt her friend's feelings, she nodded and smiled, saying, "Oh yes. *That* Shonda."

"Well," her visitor said in the tone of a church gossip about to reveal a pious rival's greatest secret. "She and her man had been hooking up for 'bout 2 years. Talking 'bout getting married and everythang. Then her man gets these new sneakers. Reeeal fancy. Came swaggering in, acting like he was Michael Jordan an' shit. Said he'd been saving up, working extra hours. But I knew the fool was lying."

Though a part of Charlie felt impatient, wondering what the hell this story had to do with Murdoch, another part couldn't help but be drawn in by the vivacity of her friend's portrayal, replete with mimicry. So, before she could stop herself, she found herself saying, "How did you know?"

"Damn fool couldn't afford those things!" Quicha burst forth as if the answer was the most obvious thing in the world. "Extra hours or no extra hours." She leaned in conspiratorially, tapping her nose with a long, bedazzled nail. "Turns out I was right too. You know that show Cheaters? Shonda began to suspect something weren't right, so she rang them up and they started following his ass. Sure enough, they caught him in the middle of the night, sneaking out of his sugar mama's crib!"

Charlie waited for the punchline, but none came. Quicha just crossed her arms and nodded like a sage having just shared their biggest pearl of wisdom. "And your point is?" she eventually asked.

"Thangs, girl. The thangs peeps will do for thangs!"

Before Charlie could reply, Quicha's sports watch beeped.

"Damn! Got to dip. James Jr's baby's due this afternoon and I promised Ma I'd Facetime them to find out how they're doin'." Without waiting for an answer, Quicha turned and headed for the door, yelling over her shoulder, "Thanks for the coffee. I'll see myself out. Don't be a stranger, awright?"

The front door banged shut, leaving Charlie in a depth of silence she hadn't noticed before. Quicha was so larger than life, filling every inch of all the spaces she inhabited, the flat always seemed empty after she'd gone. To counter the void, she went to the kitchen and switched on the radio, dancing along to an R&B song as she made herself a strong cup of coffee to help her get her head back in the game. Then she returned to the study and went through her notes. Over and above getting people to talk, one thing was paramount: Getting an inside track on the Hawks investigation. Vusi couldn't help her with that but, thankfully, she had a backup plan. As Charlie opened her laptop and started to type, she thought about what Quicha had said.

Had she been right? In the end, would it all come down to money?
Or something far more important than that?

10. VIPER

Lower East Side
New York, USA

When her mobile rang, Maria Rodriguez was doubled-up in laughter in the sunny living room of her modest Lower East Side apartment, trying not to piss herself. As she howled at her favourite comedian, tears ran down her dimpled cheeks, her whole body shaking like a baby sumo wrestler.

The chair she sat on was part of a slightly tattered, cream pleather suite, bought from the previous owners of the apartment along with the worn, fake Persian rug that now lay at her feet and the French Impressionist reproductions on the cream walls. A room that spoke of an occupant down on her luck, stretching every dollar, scraping by as best as she could. And that's just the way Maria liked it.

Her apartment sat in a brownstone tenement in the heart of the East Village, three floors up from the doughnut shop on the ground floor which, she wasn't afraid to say, had been part of the attraction when she'd moved in fifteen years ago. That and a neighbourhood made up of a rainbow of art shops, quirky clothing stores and restaurant fare from all around the world. A thousand heady scents had filled the bustling streets in strange synchronicity, promising a new start and a safe harbour. A perfect place for a suddenly single mother thrust into a life she had never imagined.

She had started her career as a chartered accountant working for an international auditing firm, before a car accident in her early thirties had claimed the life of her drunken, English husband and nearly her own. During a long period of recovery, she had not only regained her ability to walk but also the strength to go it alone. She had moved to America, using her auditing skills to get piecemeal jobs, whilst teaching herself to code. After that, she had started consulting, first as a forensic investigator, then eventually building a reputation as one of the best grey hackers in the business.

So, when her phone interrupted her viewing halfway through the fourth episode of her favourite show, Maria didn't do what she normally did with such interruptions, which was to ignore them. That was because this particular notification had a singular tone, chosen by Maria herself, to signify only one thing.

Urgency.

Clicking off the TV, she pushed herself out of the chair and made her way across the living room into the cream-tiled passage. Two doors down on the left, she turned into what looked like a small storage room, lined with grey shelves from floor to ceiling, packed with household items. The middle shelf held white toilet rolls, standing two rows high and eight columns wide. Maria pushed the fourth toilet roll on the bottom row until she heard a click, then pulled it open to reveal a black keypad. Keying in a six-digit code, she waited for the familiar whirr and smiled as the whole back wall of the room slid to the right.

Some things never got old.

Behind the false wall, lay a light-grey room, tastefully furnished in black, white, and chrome. As the downlights automatically came on, their beams bounced off six large, LED screens lining the back wall of the room. Arranged in two rows of three, the screens sat above a black glass and chrome desk, on top of which was an ergonomic keyboard, lying at the ready in front of a black leather chair. This tableau was flanked to the right by a black bar fridge with a gleaming coffee maker on top of it, next to a white leather couch that sat on a deep-pile, Picasso-style rug. Above the couch hung an original Warhol painting. Opposite the couch, taking up the whole of the left wall of the room, stood a bank of head-high, black and chrome filing cabinets, each drawer carefully marked with a different letter of the alphabet.

Maria sat at her desk and tapped the keyboard. The middle screen in the bottom row immediately sprang to life. After biometric authentication, a notification popped up on the monitor.

An email.

From Charlie.

A memory popped into Maria's head of a time before the accident. Her first day at the battered woman's shelter after her third attempt at leaving her abusive husband, hugging her son as they sat shivering with fear in the reception area, convinced he would find them. A young woman in her late teens had come bounding in, her smile infectious, her heartfelt warmth unmistakable. Bit by bit, the woman had helped her find herself again, including summoning the will to leave her husband for good. Even on that fateful night, when her husband, reeking of whisky, had finally tracked them down and forced them into his car before crashing into an oncoming truck, the young woman had been the first beside her hospital bed, giving comfort. That woman had been Charlie and they'd shared a special bond ever since.

The last time they'd spoken, however, was a year ago, when Charlie had started looking into the paedophile ring. Wondering what her friend was up to now, she opened the mail and read her missive slowly and carefully. Then Maria, AKA Viper, closed the message, cracked her fingers, and opened her web browser.

Showtime.

11. The Caller

Alexandra Township
Johannesburg, South Africa

It was the scratching that woke him, coming from something heavy on his chest. As Thabo opened his eyes, the burden lifted, bounding, and thumping across the room in the darkness. Moonlight spilt through the clear plastic window to the left of the door, illuminating the creature's escaping back as it exited through a crack in the corrugated iron walls. A bloody rat the size of a cat.

God, he hated those things!

Thabo sat up on the grass floor mat and brushed his bare chest with his hands, feeling like a thousand fleas were crawling over his skin. Getting up, he tiptoed to the corner, poured some water from the water bottle into the washing bowl and wiped himself down with a cloth. Once he felt clean again, he put the cloth aside, making a note to remind himself to throw out the water before the others got up in the morning so they wouldn't use it by mistake.

Lying back down, Thabo rested his head on the rolled-up t-shirt he had fashioned into a pillow and tried to go back to sleep. The back of his hip bones dug into the mat, his slim buttocks unable to cushion the hard ground. He changed position, hoping lying on his side would be better, but now his shoulder hurt. It was difficult to get used to a cold, hard floor again once you'd tasted a soft mattress. Giving up on sleep, he opened his eyes and rolled back onto his back.

He caught sight of Lucky's sleeping form on the bed across the room. His

The Meanness of Things

asthma had been bad that day so they'd all agreed that he should have the bed to himself. Lucky's breathing was still ragged, his knees pulled up to his bony chest like he was still in the womb. Thinking of childhood reminded him of when they had first met, barefoot in the playground of the orphanage, both having just turned four years old. Gripped in his friend's hand had been a baby blanket, one Thabo soon discovered Lucky carried with him wherever he went, no matter how dirty it became. It had belonged to his grandmother and brought him luck he had said and soon everyone had taken to calling him Lucky, even long after the blanket had frayed and then fallen apart. Best friends ever since, Lucky was the only one who truly knew him, who had his back no matter what. So, when Lucky had one of his spells, Thabo couldn't help but worry. Couldn't help but long to have the old Lucky back with his high-pitched laughter and his crazy, stupid pranks.

On the floor next to the bed, Innocent snorted, once, then fell silent again. He lay sprawled on his back, his muscular tattooed arms folded above his head. If Lucky was the comedian, Innocent was the brawler of the group. Always up for a fight but also ready to smack down anybody who took up against his own. One year older than him and Lucky, Innocent was always jockeying for leadership of the gang, as if age and muscle were all that it took. Even so, he'd been more testy than usual lately. Thabo thought back to the row they'd had earlier. He still didn't understand why Innocent had become so angry over a little thing like who was growing the fastest. Perhaps he needed to spend some time alone with him, find out what was up.

Boy's elbow poked him in the side as he changed position. A fitful sleeper, he was wedged between Thabo and Innocent, flat on his stomach with his thumb in his mouth. At eight years old, he was the smallest of them all. Thabo often wondered what Boy's real name was. He'd turned up last summer dressed in rags, refusing to talk, his eyes full of horror. When he'd started following them around, they'd begun to call him Boy and, before they knew it, the name had stuck. It had taken three months before he had trusted them enough to speak, four before he'd been brave enough to share his toothy smile. Now, whenever he heard Boy laugh, Thabo thought it was the best sound in the world. Yet, he still hadn't told them his real name. Perhaps, for Boy, some things were best left in the past.

The sheets rustled on the bed as Lucky rolled over. Thabo smiled to himself, thinking of the day he'd managed to get enough money to buy it. His first and only hijacking, nearly bungled, bullets whizzing past as they had made their panic-stricken getaway. After that day, he had vowed to stick to petty thieving and begging. Smaller pay-outs sure but a far greater chance of staying alive. It had been worth it, though. With that money, they'd been able to buy this shack and the bed with it. No more sleeping under bridges or shop doorways. He still couldn't believe what a difference a bed had made. He loved the way it hugged his whole body, the warmth as they all huddled together under the blanket. Like…what were the words he was looking for? Yes – that was it. Like a real family. He'd never tell the others that, of course. Wouldn't want anyone to think he was getting soft.

Outside, a group of people hurried past, their drunken voices loud, the light from their torches bouncing off the shack walls and illuminating the bright thread of his brand-new hoody hanging on the wall, gleaming. The hoody he'd bought with the money he got from selling the backpack.

An image of the white man's broken body at the bottom of the pit flashed before him. Thabo felt nauseous just thinking about it. The flies, those twisted limbs, the flaps of skin on his bloody chest, imagining the agony the man must have gone through in the last moments of his life.

He'd never told anyone what he'd found, even the boys. Just pushed the slab back into place, grabbed the backpack and ran out of there. Still, he'd expected the police to show up sooner or later. Called by someone who had found the body just like he did, or after being alerted by a neighbour when the smell had gotten too bad. However, no one had complained, and the police hadn't come.

Strange.

Feeling a buzzing beneath his head, Thabo reached under the pillow and pulled out a phone. It was black, small, and simple. The kind tenderpreneurs used to avoid their calls being eavesdropped. He'd found it in a hidden pocket at the bottom of the backpack, along with a scrap of paper with a number written on it.

The good thing about the phone was that it didn't need a pin and it seemed to have lots of airtime. The bad thing was that someone kept calling. They never left a message. Just kept calling again, and again, and again. From the same number written on the piece of paper. One of the last numbers the phone's previous owner had dialled. The same number now flashing on the phone's screen.

Thabo quickly ended the call and put the phone back under the pillow. He didn't know if the backpack and the phone had belonged to the man in the pit or someone else. He also didn't know if the person who kept calling had been the dead man's friend or foe. However, one thing was for certain.

Some calls were best left unanswered.

12. Patience

The Strand
London, UK

Steven Vivekanandan sat at his desk in his office furiously taping the keyboard, his black, oily hair gleaming, his arms pumping up and down like pistons as his tiny crow eyes tracked the contents on the screen. Today, as always, he was dressed in a tailored black suit over a crisp white shirt with a bright red tie. A uniform of strength and power, telegraphing to the world that he was now a million miles away from the snivelling eight-year-old Hackney boy, crying all the way home every day after being pummelled by racist bullies in the schoolyard.

Another signifier of how far he had come was his office. Whilst it was considerably smaller than Derrick's or Hilary's, as the CFO of the division, his was the third largest, big enough to hold a desk with two chairs in front of it, a four-seater board table, a large bookshelf and two floor-to-ceiling windows that gave him a goodish view. In the prestige stakes, it was all about the real estate. The larger the office, the greater the power. Power Steven wasn't planning on losing.

"Mind if I have a word?"

He looked up to find a sweaty, round head poking into his domain. Steven pinched his lips.

Mind? Of course, he minded.

Yet, not wanting to appear rude, he struck upon a compromise. "My next meeting is in five minutes," he replied, tilting his head in the direction of a chair in front of his desk, inviting Jonathan to sit.

As his colleague took a seat, Steven minimized the window on this laptop just in case his guest caught a glimpse of his screen.

"So, Jon, what's up?" Steven said with practised cheer.

Jonathan's anxious eyes searched his face, perhaps hoping to see beyond the mask. "Reuben and I were talking. You know, about the staff briefing on Derrick the other day?"

"Oh?" Steven rested his elbows on the arms of his chair and steepled his fingers in front of his chest, his face mildly curious.

"Did you believe it? The explanation Hilary gave, I mean."

"Why?" He gave Jonathan a steely look. "Didn't you?"

Jonathan looked flummoxed but quickly recovered. "Anyway, that's not the main reason I'm here. Reuben and I - we wondered...well we thought...since you were also close to Derrick, and you've been on the Exco longer than us..."

God! The man blathered on.

"Wondered what exactly?" Steven interjected, making his impatience plain.

"Well – if we needed to be worried." Jonathan licked his upper lip. "You know - now, that Derrick's gone."

"Why would you be worried?"

Jonathan blinked in surprise. "For what we -"

"Honestly, I don't know what you mean." Steven sneaked a look at the security camera in the ceiling.

Didn't the fool know where they were?

Jonathan followed his gaze, his face reddening with embarrassment. "Sorry. It's the shock."

"Yes, yes. It's been a surprise for us all," Steven pushed his chair back, signalling their time was up. "But Derrick's only been missing a few days. I'm sure he'll soon turn up, safe and sound."

"That's not what I wanted -"

"I'm so sorry, Jon," Steven got to his feet. "I really have to kick you out now so I can head out to my meeting. If you still need to talk, let's schedule a proper meeting, shall we? Perhaps go for a drink outside the office?"

"Sure. I'll...um... ok, I'll do that." Jonathan grudgingly stood up and trudged to the door, saying as he left, "Thanks for...the, uh...chat."

Steven shook his head in disbelief as the door softly closed behind his hapless visitor.

What did he think? Coming in here as if they were all in this together! There was no 'we'. There never had been a 'we' but, clearly, the man was an imbecile. Too dumb to know that Derrick had only seen him as a useful sap!

The Meanness of Things

Sitting back down, he maximised the window he'd been working on, thankful that, from the get-go, he'd remembered to place his desk in such a way that all the security camera saw was the back of his screen. He also took the added precaution of always anonymising his special files by giving them a number rather than a name. Looking at the column of numerical files that filled the screen, Steven went to the file at the top and pressed delete. Whilst he had already wiped all the relevant files on his laptop, he still had plenty of documents to go on the server. This was why, as soon as he had read Tate's piece yesterday evening, he had texted his PA to cancel all his scheduled meetings for the day.

The only thing was, he couldn't remember where exactly on the server he had hidden them all. Too clever by half, that was his problem. Finding them again required trolling through years of data and lots of patience. He didn't mind, though. When it came to saving his own skin, Steven had all the patience in the world.

13. A Race

The Strand
London, UK

Hilary stood up and yawned, having spent the whole day sitting at the conference table in his office. He'd already reviewed all of Derrick's major deals in the last three years and had found nothing out of the ordinary. So, he had switched focus to the money laundering investigation Derrick had been so proud of. Now, he stood surrounded by thirty thick, lever-arch folders, ten of which were stacked on the conference table whilst the rest sat on the floor. He'd only managed to go through nine so far, despite having spent the whole day on the task. Through the window, the night beckoned, the London Eye unmistakable in the distance. Cursing his luck, he picked up his mobile and dialled.

"Hello, darling," he said, putting the phone on speaker as he stretched. "Just checking in to see what you're doing."

"I've just finished dinner and now I'm planning to watch a movie," his wife replied languidly.

He imagined her tucking her shapely legs underneath her on the sofa and the curve of her sweet nape as she reached for the remote control. "I wish I was there with you."

"Oh, Lord! You *do* sound tired."

"Been a long day, Grace. And it's going to be a long night too."

"I'll be thinking about you, darling," she cooed with just the right amount of pity to suggest she felt his pain. "Shall I leave dinner out for you?"

"Don't worry," he said, grateful for the offer all the same. "I asked Gertrude to order something for me before she left."

"All right then, dear. I'll see you later. By the way, if you do get peckish, please remember the microwave's still out."

Hilary groaned. "I thought Jasper had fixed it?"

"You know Jay-Jay!"

"But I paid him to do it!" he spluttered, feeling his temper rising, a common occurrence when it came to his brother-in-law. "Is he going to give me my money back?"

"He says he's still going to fix it, darling."

"Wasn't he supposed to be doing that the first time?"

"Fix it again, I mean."

"But -" Hilary stopped himself and counted to ten.

"Anyway," Grace continued, her tone nonchalant. "I told Jay not to worry. I'll have Mark look at it in the morning."

Finding counting didn't work, Hilary took two deep breaths before saying as calmly as he could, "Mark is a driver, dear. It's not his job to clean up after Jay's messes!"

"That's true, darling. But needs must..." She trailed off, leaving the sentence to finish itself.

"At some point, Grace, we're going to have to talk about your brother."

"Yes, dear. But not tonight," she blew him a kiss. "Don't work too late, darling."

He sighed inwardly and gave up the fight. "I'll try. Goodnight, dear." As he ended the call, Hilary sincerely wished marriage wasn't a package deal where, if you wanted the spouse, you had to have the relatives too. Thinking of deals prompted him to cast a resentful eye at the folders around him. Resisting the urge to pack up and go home, he walked over to the coffee machine to pour himself a fresh mug, needing a shot of energy.

As he sat back at the conference table, coffee in hand, someone rapped on the door, the faint whiff of musk signifying that there was only one person it could be.

"Come in Samuel!" Hilary cried, glad of the respite.

"Have you got a minute?" the bank's Head of Security said as he opened the door.

"Sure," Hilary held up his mug. "Would you like a cup of coffee?"

"No thank you, Sir. I'm good."

Samuel Ferguson was a tall, broad-shouldered man whose smile seemed to be permanently on vacation. An ex-military man, he sported the standard crew cut and rigid walk of a body long conditioned to marching, his eyes constantly scanning his surroundings like a Terminator cyborg. He also perpetually reeked of Old Spice, presumably because someone at some point had told him it would help attract the ladies. Hilary didn't have the heart to tell him it had the opposite effect.

His visitor pulled out a chair and sat. "I thought I would give you an update on Charlie Tate."

"Oh?" Hilary was immediately alert. "What have you found?"

Samuel pulled out a tiny notebook and started reading. "Charlie, Nandi Tate is a freelance journalist known for her work on international criminal syndicates. She was born in London, Hammersmith in 1985, the second child of a British father and a South African mother. Both parents were active in the anti-apartheid movement as well as the Labour Party. Both of them also spent a few hours in jail during the poll tax riots."

Hilary frowned. "Why are you talking about them in the past tense?"

"They died in a car crash in South Africa in 2010. Along with Charlie's older brother, Ben, and his girlfriend. The family had returned there shortly after Mandela was released in 1990 with both parents taking up roles in the new government."

"But Charlie survived the crash?"

"She wasn't there. She was working in London as a trainee at the BBC. After her family died, she returned to South Africa for the funeral and thereafter stayed for two more years, working as a local journalist while also trying to find the culprits."

"So, it wasn't an accident?"

"Yes and no. The crash was precipitated by a blown tire, which in turn was assisted by a bullet from a high-calibre rifle. However, the perpetrator was never found, aided no doubt by the fact that the police docket went missing."

How convenient.

"But that didn't stop Tate," Samuel continued. "And even though she's made no headway, she's still determined to find the truth, by all accounts."

"Wilful and resolute."

"Very. That's also borne out by her track record after she came back to London in 2012. She has a reputation for gnawing at a story. Never letting go until she's gotten down to the marrow."

"So, it was her," Hilary said under his breath, remembering the ferocity he'd seen in the woman's eyes.

"Sorry – what?"

"At the press conference. Some journo bombarded me with questions, but I didn't quite catch her name."

Samuel looked at him blankly.

"All right," Hilary quickly went on, taking a sip of coffee. "We now know the kind of character we're up against. How the hell does she get her info? From our office, the South African Police Services or somewhere else?"

"It must be SAPS," the Head of Security replied, pocketing his notebook. "We've been tracking all communications and movements relating to Joburg employees as well as anyone who might be close to the investigation here. No internal leaks so far."

"Any chance of shutting the SAPS source down?"

"We'd have to find them first. It's not impossible but I think it might be a bit premature to go down that route. Based on the reports we've received so far, after having traced him to his hotel, the SAPS investigation has made little progress. They say that if you don't find a missing person within the first 48 hours, the chances of finding them after that are slim. Derrick's been missing for four days now. Given this, I think that, if no new facts emerge, the SA police will soon put this case on the back burner and turn their attention to more pressing matters. Which means we won't have to worry about leaks from that quarter for much longer."

From your lips to God's ears, Hilary thought. "And Tate? What are the chances of her losing interest once her SA source dries up?"

"That depends," Samuel looked down, suddenly finding a detail on the conference table particularly interesting.

What was that about? Sam wasn't usually this oblique.

Hilary studied him for a moment then gave him a nudge. "On what, exactly."

The Head of Security cleared his throat, a habit that signalled he was about to introduce a delicate subject. "On what led to Murdoch's disappearance. If I may suggest, Sir, we should find out if there is any dirt there. If there is, we should clean it up before Tate can get her hands on it."

Hilary inadvertently glanced at the files on the table. Following his gaze, comprehension dawned in Samuel's eyes.

"My thoughts exactly," Hilary said. "I'll handle things this end while you keep an eye on Tate. We're in a race Sam, we can't afford to lose. So, I want to know everything she gets up to."

As Samuel made his exit, Hilary wearily reached for another folder and began going through its contents. He wasn't looking for anything specific. Just something that seemed odd. An anomaly like bows too neatly tied or coincidences that didn't coincide.

The investigation had been kept hush-hush with Derrick insisting on using an external team of investigators. Not the usual crowd either. A little-known firm that Derrick had argued wouldn't be tainted by "old school ties". Whilst he hadn't questioned it at the time, his boss' sudden interest in money laundering had seemed a little too goody-two-shoes given their type of work. He'd also always wondered about the outcome. If Michael, the former Head of Private Clients, and Patrick, the former CRO, had really done the things they'd been accused of, surely others would also need to have had a hand in it? And what if Michael had been telling the truth and the investigation had just been a cover-up?

If so, a cover-up of what?

14. The Garage

Islington
London, UK

Charlie trudged through the entrance doors of The Torch, feeling the onset of a bad mood. The day had started well enough. She had woken up to three interview confirmations from persons of interest in the Murdoch case. An unusually speedy response from such a motley crew. Thus, it was with a sense of buoyant optimism that she had returned to the block of flats overlooking Regent's Canal, confident that today at least some of the residents would be willing to talk about what they had seen that dreadful morning. However, when each doorbell ring had been met with silence or a gruff "no comment", Charlie's high hopes of gathering witness info on her dead Jane Doe had been dashed. Too depressed to go home, she had decided to swing by the office and have another crack at the Met database.

As usual, the media house's lobby was abuzz with activity, bike messengers dropping and receiving, journos rushing to or from a hot story, and endless rounds of takeout deliveries. The lobby had recently been redecorated, the high-brow chic of wood, brick and black trim replaced by Pollock rip-offs and neon furnishings in multiple colours and shapes. The Ferret had said the redesigned lobby was supposed to be uplifting. To Charlie, it just looked like yesterday's vomit.

Managing to find an empty hot desk despite the mid-morning crush, she'd just put down her stuff and powered up her laptop, when a mail from a familiar address popped into her inbox. Thinking of her friend brought a smile to her face. Viper was nothing if not speedy *and* efficient. Praying that the attachment to her mail contained something to lift her spirits, Charlie opened it and started reading.

Viper began her report by outlining how she had hacked into the Hawk's server and left a back door so she could return anytime. From the length of the description, Charlie concluded that the server must have been locked down tight. However, Viper was too modest to boast about it, merely going on to immediately outline what she had found.

The Hawks had begun their investigation by trying to trace Murdoch's phone based on the view that finding the phone would also lead to finding the man himself. Unfortunately, it turned out that the phone and the man were no longer one, with the latter having been discovered under his plane seat by a member of the cleaning staff. Moreover, upon examination, the phone's contents failed to provide any clues regarding its owner's whereabouts or what had happened to him.

The police had then gone on to examine video footage, beginning with the CCTV cameras in the airport, then traffic cameras along the highway, and ending with the cameras at the hotel where Murdoch was supposed to have stayed. Here, the Hawks had made more progress. The CCTV cameras at OR Tambo showed Murdoch going through passport control, baggage claim and arrivals before being met by a driver who led him to a silver sedan. Using traffic cams, they had managed to track the sedan from the airport to his hotel, whereupon the hotel CCTV showed the sedan driving into the hotel parking garage.

The problem was that was when Murdoch had vanished. There was no record of him having entered the hotel lobby and, so far, the police had not been able to find any witnesses who recalled seeing him anywhere else in the vicinity. Furthermore, neither the car, the driver nor Murdoch had come out of the garage, even though there was only one entrance and exit. At the same time, the sedan was now also missing. It was no longer in the garage and when the police had tried to trace it, they had found that the number plates had been fake. They had also tried to identify the driver but, given that he had been wearing a cap and dark glasses, they hadn't been able to get a good enough look at his face to develop an identikit. In other words, it was as if Murdoch and dissolved into thin air, leaving no trace evidence. No body, no car, no driver, and no witnesses.

The police had also interviewed some Yeats employees in London who had arranged Murdoch's trip and those in Johannesburg who would have had contact with Murdoch during his visit. All those interviewed recorded that there had been nothing unusual about Murdoch's arrangements regarding the trip and that they had not observed any changes in Murdoch's behaviour before it.

The Hawks had then turned their attention to Murdoch's bank accounts to see if they might contribute to solving the riddle. A virtual interview with his wife had revealed that the Murdochs had a joint account which had not recently seen any large, unexpected withdrawals. Mrs Murdoch had also said that, to her knowledge, her husband had not had any other accounts, including ones offshore. Furthermore, when they had asked her if her husband might have had any reason to flee, she had provided such tearful denials they had had to break for a brief recess. Concluding that, if what Mrs Murdoch had said was true, there was reason to believe that her husband had not gone missing of his own free will, when the interview had resumed the investigating officer had asked if she had received any contact regarding her husband, either in the form of a ransom note or any other missive. It was at this point that Mrs Murdoch had refused to answer any more questions, claiming that she was too upset to continue. Given that she hadn't been classified as a potential suspect and they thus had no reason to detain her, the police had terminated the interview, warning her that they could decide to compel her to cooperate should they have reason to do so in future. However, it appeared that the Hawks had not been entirely convinced by the wife's account. Not only had the investigators sought a warrant for Murdoch's bank records, they had also asked Interpol for help in tracing possible additional Murdoch accounts in the UK and offshore.

Lastly, Viper had ended her report with four one-word questions.

1. Burner?
2. Professionals?
3. Kidnapping?
4. Wife?

Charlie sat back and thought about what she had just read. Firstly, she agreed with Viper about the burner phone. Given how much everyone depended on their phone these days, it was inconceivable that Murdoch wouldn't have noticed his phone was missing between the time he got off the plane to when he exited the airport. Of course, there was the possibility that Murdoch, realising his phone was gone, had bought another one at the airport but hadn't had time to activate it before he disappeared. However, this purchase would have been picked up by the CCTV cameras and there was no evidence of this. Hence, it seemed more likely that Murdoch's original phone had been left rather than lost, and he had replaced it with another one that he already had on his person.

Charlie also agreed with Viper on the second question. Going totally off the grid in the modern age is extremely hard. Making someone disappear against their will, especially without leaving any evidence, is even harder. Usually, there's always something. One tiny thing that the perp overlooks. This suggested that professionals had been involved. People who had been well-prepared and meticulous, taking care of every angle and anticipating every possibility. What was as yet unknown was whether they had been of the criminal or clandestine kind.

This in turn meant that the answer to the third question was probably affirmative. In other words, the possible involvement of professionals strengthened the possibility that some sort of kidnapping had occurred, whether it was for financial gain, to exert some sort of pressure or as a prelude to murder. The fact that Lucy had refused to confirm whether she had received a ransom note did not necessarily suggest that Murdoch hadn't been kidnapped nor that a note had not been delivered. The kidnappers could have warned her not to speak to the police. Then again, if he'd been taken in order to kill him there would be no ransom note which would mean Mrs Murdoch was telling the truth. The problem was it was difficult to tell which one might be true.

Which brought her to Viper's last question. As the Hawks had already concluded, there was something off about Lucy's testimony. Her reactions seemed exaggerated and contrived, like those of a ham actor in a burlesque. Viper, however, had hinted at something deeper than just a lack of credibility. At best, Lucy knew more than she was telling, and at worst, the South African investigators might have been premature in disregarding her as a suspect. Both of which moved her higher up the persons of interest list.

After sending Viper a thank you note, Charlie opened her notebook and jotted down three questions. Why had Murdoch switched to a burner? Why had professionals abducted him? And why was Lucy behaving so strangely?

Then she pondered the angle of her story. For now, she would need to play it safe. Focus the next instalment of the Murdoch purely on the facts rather than speculation. She quickly wrote it up, starting with him landing at Joburg airport and ending with the Houdini act in the garage. After having received a 'no comment' from the bank and another brush-off from the Hawks media desk, Charlie pressed send, wondering how long it would take for her story to find its way to Bulldog's anticipatory inbox. Ten minutes later, the Business Editor called her to her office.

"You've got to be kidding me," she said as Charlie walked in. Bulldog stood at a raised desk, pink reading glasses on her head, the story open on her desktop screen. "So, Murdoch was snatched?"

"It looks that way based on the evidence so far. Though, as you can see, I've left it to the reader to come to their own conclusions."

"Yes, yes - I saw." Bulldog shook her head in amazement. "And you think the bank knows this? As does his wife?"

"The police would have told them what they've found, so they must do. Which makes the whole thing stink to high heaven."

"Can't argue with you there." Bulldog drummed her short nails against her cheek, thinking. "Any ideas as to why he was taken?"

"Nope. But the longer he stays gone the worst possibility is going to become increasingly likely."

"That he's been murdered?"

Charlie nodded.

The Business Editor searched her face. "And you're sure about the facts? Your sources are impeccable on this?"

She thought of Viper. "Hundred percent. I have absolute faith in them."

"What about the reach-out to the SA police? You've got that on record?"

"Yep. I recorded the call."

"All right. Then we'll run it ASAP." Bulldog peaked through the smoky glass wall into the office next door, but The Ferret was in a meeting. "I'm going to hook Kathy in on this as well. The way this story is going, it would be a better fit for the news section than the business pages."

"Makes sense," Charlie said coolly, hiding the burst of satisfaction she felt. Now the story was sure to get a lot more traction.

"What's your next step?"

"Interviews with persons of interest. Shake the tree and see what falls out."

"Good." Bulldog turned her back on her, a sign that she was dismissed.

With a new spring in her step, Charlie went to pack up her things. Then, reasoning it was after five pm somewhere in the world, she took herself off for a celebratory drink.

The day hadn't turned out too bad after all.

15. Three

Kensington
London, UK

He had arrived home early for once, just past six o'clock in the evening, but still feeling spent after a busy day. Even the sight of one of his greatest achievements, their four-storey Edwardian home on one of the most exclusive streets in Kensington, hadn't been enough to re-energise him. After briefly greeting his wife with a customary peck on the cheek, Hilary had gone straight to his study, dumped his homework on his desk, and poured himself a stiff drink. He was cradling the drink in his hand, observing how light bent through the amber liquid, when a familiar ring emitted from his phone.

"I take it you're phoning about Tate's latest salvo?" he said, phone pressed to his ear.

"How did you guess?" Spencer said drily. "I see our team has been refusing to comment and referring everything to the SAPS?"

"Well, kidnapping is hardly in our line of business, is it? Better to let the experts handle it and put as much distance as possible between us and the investigation." Hilary delicately sniffed his glass as he crossed the room, soaking in the complex aromas so resplendent of the Scottish Highlands.

Heather honey, vanilla fudge, dark fruits.

Splendid.

"At the same time," Spencer said, "I do wonder whether it doesn't also make us look…" He paused as if looking for the right words.

The Meanness of Things

"Heartless?" Hilary offered as he sat on the edge of his desk and took a sip, rolling the liquid in his mouth before swallowing, savouring the way his tastebuds burst into life and rich heat ran down his throat.

Spencer's response was clipped. "I believe 'too aloof' would be more appropriate,"

Hilary stood up straight. "Right. Of course."

Careful son, your tongue's too loose this evening.

"In that vein," he continued, "you'll be glad to know that the police have suggested offering a reward. You know - to encourage people to come forward. We could put it up. Make a show of it. A modest amount but enough to look like we care."

"Won't that only prolong things?"

For a moment, Hilary didn't follow, then it came back to him. "Oh! You mean in terms of providing certainty?"

"Yes. The sooner this matter is behind us, the better."

"Samuel says it won't make much difference," Hilary replied. "Real witnesses tend to come forward anyway, while rewards mostly attract a bunch of chancers."

"All right," Spencer said evenly. "I'll leave that in your capable hands."

Whilst the Group CEO's words sounded like a compliment, Hilary sensed that they also included an embedded threat. He was still contemplating his response when he was saved by a change of subject.

"What's the update on Tate? I don't like the way she keeps catching us off guard."

Good. Back on safer ground.

He relaxed and took another sip of whisky as he perched once again on the desk. "She's a freelancer who, we suspect, has a source in the SA police. The good news is, as the SAPS investigation falters – which we're sure it will - her source will also run dry. But we'll continue to keep close tabs on her, nonetheless."

"Glad to hear it," Spencer said this with so much relish it was as if he was imagining grinding Tate under his heel. "And your other assignment? Have you found out anything about Derrick that could bite us?"

"Not so far. I'm just looking into one more thing and then I should be able to tell you for sure."

"Then I'll leave you to it. Have a good evening and give my love to Grace."

"Night, Spencer."

He put down the phone and loosened his tie. Down the hall, the faint bangs of dinner preparations drifted from the kitchen as Grace beavered away. He could smell the result of her labours, the aroma of sautéed chicken mixed with garlic, chilli, herbs, and tomato making his stomach grumble.

However, since dinner time was still some time off, Hilary turned instead to the file he had brought back from the office. A folder from the money laundering investigation that had caught his eye.

Setting his whisky on a coaster, he opened the folder at the marked spot. The page in question contained the list of transactions Michael and Patrick had been accused of manipulating. It had been alleged that Michael had assisted the parties involved in these transactions to misrepresent their true identities and sources of capital to hide their illicit nature, while Patrick had allegedly deliberately failed to ensure that the requisite checks were conducted to ensure that the transactions were legitimate.

The problem was, whilst he had now gone through all the files from the investigation, he hadn't been able to find any of the documentation relating to the transactions themselves. He also hadn't been able to find any record of these transactions on the divisional server or the bank's main one. It was almost as if the actual transactions and their supporting documents had gone up in smoke. Moreover, the overall report had no conclusion or recommendations and was not even signed by the forensic auditors. This meant that not only had the auditors not pronounced on Michael or Patrick's guilt, their report - being unsigned – also had no actual *locus standi*.

Hence, given the fact that Derrick would have known all this, what Hilary couldn't understand was why he had still pushed Michael and Patrick out and why he had continued to tout the investigation as a major achievement. To his mind, there were only two possibilities. One possibility was that, despite the report itself being incomplete, there had nevertheless been enough evidence to point to their guilt and someone had now gone to great lengths to eradicate that evidence. The second possibility was that the evidence had never existed in the first place, and it had all indeed been just an elaborate sham.

Yet, both of these options still didn't answer the central question. Why? Why would someone want to eliminate the evidence? And why had Derrick needed a smokescreen in the first place? Turning the page, Hilary picked up a highlighter and started going through the witness statements from the investigation, making notes in the margins as he went. The answer had to be amongst those pages. Three statements from three witnesses.

Threads of a tangled web, hiding in plain sight.

16. Risk and Reward

Alexandra Township
Johannesburg, South Africa

It was election season again and the political parties were out in full voice, driving up and down in bakkies with loud hailers, making new promises in the hopes that people would forget the ones they'd already broken. Their bright-coloured party posters glinted in the sunlight, covering every billboard, pole, wall, and even temporary toilet. A joyful, bombastic, multi-coloured canopy hovering above baked-earth streets littered with sewage, dead rats, and garbage.

The way was so packed that they walked in a single line, Thabo at the front, Lucky and Boy in the middle with Innocent bringing up the rear. The crowd around them was a mix of young and old, individuals and groups, some political party faithful and others like them, just going to the rally for free food and entertainment. Party members sang struggle songs as they went, their voices reaching to the heavens, the rhythmic thumping of the toyi-toyi buoying everyone along in unison. Despite being a non-believer, Thabo sang with them, the words long learnt by heart, the camaraderie infectious.

As they got close to the junction where their alley met the tarred road, the air became tinged with the stench of carbon and sulphur, the remnants of last week's protest. Hands and elbows gently pushed him left and right, everyone jostling to avoid the scraps of bricks, burnt tyres and charred party t-shirts that still lay scattered across the road. A ward councillor who had been running for re-election had been murdered three weeks before. The rumours had started immediately, some saying he'd double-crossed a man who had bribed him for a tender and paid the price, whilst others claimed that he was killed by one of his own comrades to get his seat. However, when community leaders had found out that the party was planning to replace the dead councillor with an outsider they didn't even know, the neighbourhood had erupted.

Thabo smiled to himself, remembering the burst of heat as they had set the barricade alight, the orange-red flames rising three metres high into the night sky. For five days and four nights, they had blocked the road, taking shifts, bringing everything to a standstill, all four of them standing shoulder to shoulder with MK and Amabutho alike. And it had felt damn good. Not because it would make any difference. It never did, even when the resulting forked-tongue promises came from the President himself. It was about being seen. Standing together to take back some of their power. Even if just for a moment.

Beyond the junction, they flowed into the main road. Traffic that day was heavy, so the crowd broke up as people squeezed themselves into the narrow pathways on either side. Thabo glanced behind him, signalling to the gang that they should cross to the other side. As they dodged whooshing cars and troves of minibus taxis battling for business, the sound of their neighbours singing grew fainter, muffled by blaring car radios, tooting horns and angry drivers complaining about near misses.

Looking up to the top of the hill, he spotted the stadium where the rally was being held in the distance. He felt the usual tightness in his chest, sadness tempering his excitement at what was to come. After all these years, he could still smell his father's cologne, see the joy on his dad's face as he sprung to his feet whenever the home team scored a goal. It had been one of the best days of his five-year-old life. Little had he known that it would also be one of his father's last.

Pushing away the hurt, Thabo focused on the task at hand, increasing his pace. As they got closer to the stadium, street noise was drowned out by Amapiano music, sporadically interrupted by the voice of the master of ceremonies calling for people to take their seats or not block the entrance and exits. Then they were on the path to the entrance gate itself, tables with different types of party regalia banking both sides, from t-shirts and caps to scarves and wraps. While party members eagerly crowded around each table, they kept going until they reached the stadium gate. Here the crowd swelled, people squeezing together tighter and tighter as they shuffled their way through the narrow tunnel leading into the stadium grounds until they finally emerged on the other side.

Inside the stadium, the music was so loud Thabo felt the vibrations in his chest. The seating was on one side of the pitch while a stage, the main focal point, had been erected on the opposite side. Heading towards the stands,

Thabo picked the third row from the front. A spot far enough from the speakers that they could talk once the boring speeches began but close enough to the entrance that they could get out quickly enough to each get a food parcel before they ran out. They sat in the same order, Lucky next to him, followed by Boy then Innocent. Lucky tried to shout something in his ear, but Thabo couldn't hear most of it, something about a thousand rand. He indicated that Lucky should hold on for a little while and settled in to wait for the show.

They didn't have to wait long, the music abruptly coming to an end as the MC launched into the first "VIIIIIIEEEVAAAA!". After the opening ritual was over, it was time for the first prayer. Head bowed, eyes closed, hands clasped in front of his chest, Thabo leaned to his left and whispered, "What were you saying?"

"I said did you hear about the reward?" Lucky murmured.

"What reward?"

"Some white guy's missing. The police are offering a thousand-rand reward to anyone with info."

White guy? Could it be?

"What white guy?" he asked.

"I don't know. They say a rich, foreign dude. Thought we could take a chance, pretend we'd seen something."

Thabo's mind was whirring. "What does this white guy look like?"

"Does it matter? All of them look the same, don't they? We can just claim we saw him somewhere, give a general description and we can eat for weeks!"

"What are you guys talking about?" Boy hissed.

"A reward" Lucky replied. "For info on a white guy."

"Yeah," Boy said, "I heard about that."

A rotund, middle-aged lady in the row in front, turned and glowered at them. "Shhhhhhhh!"

"Sorry Ma," Thabo replied, hiding a smile.

"You boys should know better!" she said, tutting in approbation, before swivelling back towards the stage and resuming her recitation of the Lord's prayer.

They all glanced at each other, quietly giggling. As Thabo waited for the prayers to end, mumbling along, a myriad of possibilities ran through his mind.

Was this guy the same as his white guy? If it was, he must be important for them to offer a reward. So, he could score twice, getting the money from the backpack and the reward. But if that guy had been important, and he went forward now, wouldn't he be punished for not having done so sooner? And what about the backpack and the phone? If they had belonged to the white guy, wouldn't they say he'd stolen them?

The MC thanked the last priest and called the first speaker to the podium.

He began with the usual chorus. "Long live, our beloved movement, long live!"

Innocent leaned over and asked, "Were you guys talking about the reward for that white guy?"

"Yeah," Lucky said. "I think we should go for it."

"Not so sure about that," Innocent made a face. "Heard that the police aren't the only ones looking for him."

"What do you mean?" Foreboding crept up Thabo's spine. "Who else is looking for him?"

"Not sure exactly. Just that, whoever they are, they're bad news."

Lucky bristled, hating being thwarted, "How do you know it's the same guy?"

Innocent looked at him with contempt, "How many dead, rich, foreign white dudes do *you* know?"

"Could still be someone else," Lucky pouted.

Innocent's nostrils flared. "It's the same guy, ok?! I was over at my cousin's place. The one that's just been initiated into the 28s? Reward announcement comes over the radio. When he hears it, he sneers. Says pigs shouldn't waste their breath. I ask him why and he says the reward is a death sentence. Anyone who goes up for it will be capped."

Thabo's heart skipped a beat. "Was he saying the 28s would kill them?" he asked, careful to keep his voice even.

Innocent thought for a moment then shook his head. "Don't think so. If that was the case, he wouldn't have told me. And he said it by the by, you know? Like it was just something he knew rather than something he was involved in."

That was a relief. Or was it? What if there was someone worse than the 28s? What if that someone was the one who'd been calling?

"If not the 28s, then who?" Boy asked.

"I don't know, do I!" Innocent exclaimed. "All I know is that my cousin doesn't lie."

Yet the caller had been quiet lately. Was that just a coincidence or were the two things linked?

Lucky stuck out his jaw, signalling that his mind was set. "Still sounds like a rumour to me."

Innocent looked at him sideways but didn't comment.

Thabo suddenly felt cold.

What if the phone had belonged to the dead man? What if the caller hadn't been trying to get hold of the dead man at all but hoping to find out who now had the dead man's phone? To find the person who now knew the last numbers the dead man had dialled...

"I'm with Cent," Boy said. "Better to be safe than sorry."

And what if they had heard about the reward and thought that would be an easier way to track who they were looking for? That would certainly explain why the calls had stopped recently.

"What do you think?" Lucky said, looking at him, his eyes imploring.

What should he say? Could be his guy, could be not. The truth was, though, whether it was or wasn't, the question remained the same. Was the reward worth the risk?

Thabo swallowed. "I think we should wait."

Lucky's face fell as Innocent vigorously nodded, feeling vindicated.

"See if anyone goes forward," Thabo continued evenly. "There are bound to be all kinds of people who might have seen something. Then, if nothing happens to them, perhaps we can have a go."

Lucky instantly brightened, giving Innocent a sly, sideways glance. Boy reached over and gave Thabo a fist bump, praise for keeping the peace. Acknowledging the commendation with a tight smile, Thabo then turned and stared at the stage, pretending to be unexpectedly enraptured by the speaker on the podium. All he could think about, however, was the phone in his pocket, now heavy as a rock, and the people desperately looking for its new owner. And, most important of all, what they would do when they found him.

17. Victoria

Chelsea
London, UK

Self-described as "a close, intimate friend" of Derrick Murdoch, Ms Victoria Saint James' social media profile had hinted at impending runway stardom and a distant relationship to royalty. Now that they had met, however, Charlie suspected that this profile was as fake as a shyster's grin. Nevertheless, her tears seemed real enough.

"Derrick and I were in love!" the would-be model wailed, teardrops teetering on her fake lashes as her twig-like hands clutched the lapels of what Charlie hoped was a faux fur coat. Wondering if her companion would ever allow actual tears to spoil her perfect makeup, she got the answer when Victoria lifted her face to the heavens and quickly blinked them away.

Not quite inconsolable grief, then.

They sat in a corner of a crowded French restaurant in Chelsea's Sloane Square. Not to Charlie's taste but necessary given that Victoria had refused to meet anywhere else, saying, "One has to be seen in the right places, darling!" Charlie had already been seated, with bread and wine on the table, when Victoria had made her entrance, pausing at the doorway as if expecting everyone to turn and gaze at her with awe. Realising no one was going to, Victoria had then valiantly tried to do a runway strut to their table, head held high and legs crisscrossing like scissor blades, only to be confronted by the reality of the table arrangement, forcing her to side-shuffle the rest of the way, head now slightly bent, a faint, embarrassed blush rising up her cheeks.

Greeting Charlie with two air kisses as she sat, she had lost no time in making her wishes clear. A piece in Vanity Fair by a confidante, as in she, showcasing the side of Murdoch no one knew. When Charlie had demurred, pointing out that her assignment was currently only for The Torch and her primary focus was finding out the reasons for Murdoch's disappearance, Victoria had been put out but soon rallied, stating that some publicity was better than none. Now, coolly observing her first chronicler, Charlie took a sip of wine and hoped it would all be worth it.

"I knew him better than anyone!" Victoria blubbered. "And certainly, better than *her*."

"By 'her' are you referring to Mrs Murdoch?"

"Who else?"

"I guess this must be hard for you," Charlie said as sympathetically as she could.

"Yeah. Everyone thinks about the wife. The family. But I'm the one Derrick loved." She took out a tissue and dabbed the absent tears on her cheeks. "I'm the one who misses him the most."

Charlie grabbed a piece of complimentary French bread and slathered it with butter. For this, she was going to need sustenance. "How did you guys meet?" she said with her mouth full.

"We were introduced by a mutual friend. At a party in Marble Arch about five years ago."

"And when did you become lovers?"

Victoria blinked. "The same night we were introduced."

Charlie almost choked. *What happened to playing hard to get?* "What about Murdoch's wife? Was she not also at this party?"

"Derrick said she'd left early. Something about a headache."

"And it didn't worry you? That Murdoch was married?"

Victoria's face hardened. "Should it have done? Who are you anyway? The morality police?"

There you go, Charlie. Alienate the source, why don't you?

"I misspoke," she said, looking suitably apologetic. "Why do you think you knew him better than his wife?"

"Because Derrick told me so. He always said he could be his real self when he was with me." Victoria ate some more bread and washed it down with water. She'd said eating calmed her nerves. Looking at the skin and bones that constituted her body, Charlie concluded that she must either have a crazy metabolism or she had to be 'a thrower'.

"His real self being?" Charlie prodded.

"Free," Victoria said with a surprisingly sweet smile. "That's the way he described it. Not having to pretend all the time."

Ok. Now things were getting interesting.

"Did that mean he could be vulnerable with you?" she said eagerly. "Tell you his deepest secrets?"

Victoria smirked. "Derrick didn't believe in vulnerability. Said that was only for the weak."

"What about his secrets?"

"He was pretty open. Never hesitated to tell me what he wanted."

Not that *type of secret.*

Charlie decided to try another route. "And when was the last time you saw him?"

"About one and a half weeks before he disappeared. He attended a meeting in Paris and flew me over to keep him company."

"Did you notice anything unusual?"

Victoria frowned. "What do you mean by unusual?"

"Was he behaving differently in any way?"

"Not really. He was a bit uptight, but I figured it was just the usual stuff. Work stress, you know?" She picked up another piece of bread.

"Did he talk to you about it? The stuff he was stressed about?"

"He never discussed things like that with me and I didn't want him to, either. Who cares about all that corporate drama!"

Keep pushing, Charlie, There's something here.

"So, there was drama?"

"I got that sense. Drama and politics. But, like I said, we didn't talk about it much."

Charlie silently groaned with frustration, but she kept her voice bright. "Then what *did* you talk about?"

"Sport. He played a lot of golf and loved telling me about his golf games." She rolled her eyes, shaking her head. "All the dumb things people were always doing! He was also helping me with my modelling career, so we talked a little about that. And then, of course, us. How we felt about each other, that sort of thing."

Talking to Victoria was like walking through a maze. One dead end after another. Again, Charlie changed tack. "What did you love most about him?"

Victoria's eyes lit up. "That he was bold, ambitious, and driven. Didn't let anything or anyone stand in his way. I like that. A man with power who knows how to use it."

"And how exactly did he use it?"

"To get what he wants, of course. Though, he was always very loving to me. Always telling me how beautiful I was and how he wished we could be together," she said wistfully.

Charlie looked down, pretending to pluck a crumb off the tablecloth.

Why did young, beautiful women always fall for the same, married man crap? Staying with them for years only to end up washed up and used up like a dirty, old rag?

"In your voicemail, you said you agreed to this interview because I was 'the only one asking the right questions'," Charlie said, fishing one last time for a useful morsel. "What did you mean by that?"

"Like you said in your article. Why isn't Lucy making more of a fuss? Giving interviews. Asking people with info to come forward?"

"Yes, but my question was just that. A question. Do you have any other reason to believe that Lucy had a hand in her husband's disappearance?"

Victoria crossed her arms, standing her ground. "I wouldn't put it past her."

"Let's say I believe you," Charlie replied. "Since Murdoch made little attempt to hide his affairs, Lucy must have known about them. Known about you. So, why now? What would be her motive?"

'What Derrick said when we last met."

"And what was that exactly?"

Victoria smiled like a self-satisfied cat.

"He said he was going to leave her."

18. Fry

Hyde Park
London, UK

He had said he'd only speak to her if everything was off the record and she accompanied him on one of his walks, which he undertook every morning, setting off from the day's route of choice at 10 a.m. sharp. That day's route was Hyde Park, the starting point, Speaker's Corner. When Charlie got there at five minutes past ten, however, Mr Kenneth Fry, former Chief Investment Officer of the Yeats Africa Division and now bank retiree, was nowhere to be seen.

It being a weekday, the corner was relatively deserted, a few tourists ambling by, past a handful of devotees listening to an exuberant woman standing on a box, shouting about the creeping Nazification of America. The last time Charlie had been at Speaker's Corner was as a child, trailing along with her brother to watch her parents hold forth on one political topic or another. The experience had been both frightening and fascinating. She had like she was in a chamber full of a thousand, different voices spurred by thundering hearts, each one battling to be heard above the cacophony, until one voice would suddenly breakthrough, mesmerising the crowd, and bringing forth rapturous applause. It was a place where, every Sunday, her parents had turned into something magical, no longer mere mortals but something beautiful and alien, towering above them all, everyone feasting on their words like nectar from the gods. That was why she went there during the week. Some ghosts were just too sweet to endure.

Cursing her tardiness, Charlie was just about to turn back when she heard someone call her name. Pivoting towards the sound, she saw a harried, short, grey-haired man in a tweed jacket speed-walking towards her.

"So sorry, Ms Tate," Fry said when he reached her. "Had a spot of bother with the internal plumbing this morning. Not what it used to be," he rubbed his stomach by way of demonstration. "Hope you haven't been waiting long?"

"No, not at all. Happens to the best of us." Charlie shook his hand in greeting as she silently thanked her ancestors.

Fry smiled ruefully. "Some more than others, I'm afraid. The joys of senescence."

"Sene-what?"

"Old age, my dear, old age," he said with a chuckle, his long, pointy nose and big ears jiggling about like a house elf. Yet, instead of fearful obsequiousness, Charlie sensed kindness underlain by steely resolve.

"Well, shall we?" he said, setting off down the path towards the 7th July Memorial, legs and arms pumping. As he sped away, she struggled to keep up, not used to walking at such a frenetic pace.

"It's all in the arms," he said, noticing her discomfort. "Pump them vigorously with each stride and you'll find your rhythm in no time."

It took a few strides but, surprisingly, it worked, and soon they were walking shoulder to shoulder.

"You said you wanted to talk about Murdoch?" Fry prompted.

"Yes, amongst other things. Can we start broad? To give me some context."

"Such as?"

"How long did you work at Yeats?"

"Thirty years. Fifteen in the Africa division and the rest spread between South America and Asia."

"You must have liked working there, to have stayed so long."

He raised his brows, taken aback. "What I liked had nothing to do with it. It was a living and a good one at that. When I was young, my parents gave me a choice between becoming a doctor, banker, or lawyer. Since I can't stand the sight of blood, being a doctor was out of the question. Between the remaining two, I thought finance was a slightly cleaner profession than the legal trade, so that's what I became. I didn't expect to *like* it."

"And what about Murdoch?" Charlie asked. "Was he a good boss?"

Fry recoiled, his nose wrinkling in disgust, "He was never my boss."

"Oh? I thought you and he -?"

"I transferred out of the division as soon as I heard that Murdoch had been confirmed as the new CEO."

"Can I ask why?"

His face turned grave, the expression in his eyes hidden behind heavy lids. "It was personal."

Charlie felt bad pushing him, but she did it anyway. "Personal how?"

He gave her a strange look. Like he was trying to assess her soul. Then, after a few moments, he said, "Do you have children, Ms Tate?"

"No, not yet."

"Well, when you do, you'll realise it's both the best thing that can happen in your life and the worst. You'll experience a love like you've never experienced before, not even for your soulmate. But, if anything terrible happens to them, you'll feel so much pain, you'll think you're never going to recover. And you don't."

She could relate to that. Not the children part but certainly the rest. However, she didn't comment, suspecting that he knew that already. That was the thing about grief. It was an invisible shroud recognisable only to those who knew its touch.

Fry didn't immediately expand, as if trying to find the best place to start his tale. When he found it, it wasn't the place Charlie had been expecting. "You're doubtless familiar with Murdoch's wife, Lucy?"

"To some extent, yes."

"Lucy was once my youngest daughter Becky's best friend. When they were growing up, they were almost inseparable. It naturally followed, therefore, that when Lucy started seeing Murdoch, they would go on double dates. Lucy with Murdoch and Becky with her boyfriend of the time. After Lucy and Derrick got married, this practice continued until one day it just stopped."

Fry swallowed as if there was a sudden constriction in his throat. "She didn't tell me straight away. When she started losing weight after she and her boyfriend split up, I thought it was just the result of a bad breakup. That she would get over it and be back to normal again. Then she started having massive mood swings, some so violent it was like dealing with a different person. We thought what most parents would think. That she was having some kind of psychotic break or had secretly started taking drugs. But we didn't know what to do. She was in her thirties, financially independent and fully capable of making decisions about her own life. We tried to conduct a family intervention, but it was a disaster, ending with her telling us she never wanted to see us again. At my wit's end, I reached out to Lucy. I knew that she and Becky were no longer close because Becky hadn't mentioned her in a very long time, but I thought, given their history, that Lucy might be able to help. What happened instead was rather a shock."

Despite reciting his story in a calm, methodical manner, waves of emotion emitted from him, part sorrow, part something Charlie couldn't quite identify.

"Lucy refused to take my call," Fry continued. "Then, after about two weeks of trying, she eventually sent me a terse text message saying Becky and her hadn't spoken in six months and I shouldn't contact her again. At first, I thought she had gone through what we were going through. That Becky had done something to alienate her. Turned out, I couldn't have been more wrong."

Again, Fry fell silent, leaving Charlie to wonder whether he was working up the courage to finish his story or waiting for her to ask a question. Experience had taught her that an ill-considered question at a delicate stage in an interview could make someone clam up, so she held her peace, walking calmly by his side until he was ready.

As they passed the white pillars of the 7th July Memorial, Fry shuddered as if the sight of it had jogged him out of his repose. "Do you ever think about death, Ms Tate? I do. And the day that we nearly lost our only child." His voice grew thick, pain seared on his face. "We got the call on a Wednesday. Or I should say, Woden's Day. The Norse god responsible for guarding the dead. Rather apt, don't you think? The call came from one of Becky's few remaining friends, telling us that our daughter had been rushed to hospital. When we got there, the doctor told us that she'd tried to commit suicide. A real attempt, not a cry for help. Luckily, the friend had found her in time." He sniffed. "They'd found traces of drugs in her system and had given her something to flush them out. They'd also found evidence of self-harm on Becky's body. Something that seemed to have been going on for some time. When we got to Becky's room, she was just waking up from a sedative. I don't know what did it. Perhaps it was the sedative that loosened her tongue, or maybe it was the look on our faces, but the floodgates opened, and it all came out."

Without looking at her, Fry took out a handkerchief and wiped his teary eyes with a shaky hand. Charlie pretended not to notice.

"Six months before my daughter tried to commit suicide, about 3 years after Lucy got married, Lucy and Becky had gone out on one of their usual double dates. First to dinner and then on to one of the clubs they frequented at the time. By her own admission, Becky drank way too much that evening. The last thing she remembers is stumbling to the unisex toilets, totally smashed. After that, things get sketchy."

"Sketchy how?"

"She remembers waking up in her flat the next morning, not knowing how she got there and feeling sore. You know – down there. She takes a shower, thinking that perhaps she and her boyfriend just went at it a bit too hard the previous evening and assuming that, at some point, she must have blacked out. But when she texts him, thanking him for taking her home, he says that it wasn't him. Something he had eaten at dinner that evening had made him feel sick, so he had gone home early, leaving her with Lucy and Murdoch just after they got to the club."

Charlie's stomach dropped. "She'd been raped?"

He nodded once, the movement jerky and clipped. "At that point, Becky's still not sure, so she takes the morning off work and goes to the clinic. They find small traces of Rohypnol in her system and bruising in her vagina but insufficient DNA evidence. It was the shower, you see. Still unable to remember what happened, she rushes to Lucy's place to check if her friend knows what happened. Derrick opens the door, and his aftershave triggers a memory. Him pinning her down on her kitchen table, groaning as he…uh… came inside of her. Given how drunk she was, he must have dropped Lucy off and then taken Becky home. Only to…." Fry let out a shaky breath, struggling to control his emotions. "Anyway, realising he's the culprit, she starts screaming at him, hitting him, tearing his clothes. Derrick fends her off but doesn't deny it, almost as if he's proud of it. Lucy, who's just gotten up, comes downstairs to find out what's going on. When Becky tells her what happened, Derrick says she's lying. Claims Becky took a pass at him and got mad when he turned her down. Back then, one thing Becky never did was lie and Lucy knew that, so she expected Lucy to back her up. Her best friend refuses to look at her. Just mumbles Becky must be mistaken before running back inside. Derrick laughs, smug and triumphant, then slams the door in her face."

"Lucy knew she was telling the truth. That's why she wouldn't look at her?"

"Becky says that was the worst part. That when it came down to it, her life-long friend chose to betray her when she needed her most."

Charlie shook her head in disbelief. "What about her clothes, the kitchen table? He must have left traces there, surely?"

"There were no traces of semen on her clothes or the table. They found Lucy and Murdoch's DNA in other parts of the flat but that was to be expected since they went there often, and her lawyer said that's exactly the argument Murdoch would make. In short, there was only one other person who could confirm at least some of what happened that evening, and she refused to talk."

"But why? Misguided loyalty to her husband?"

"Perhaps. Or maybe it was shame. That's the reason Becky gave for not telling us. Shame. Can you imagine? That, somehow, it had been her fault. If she hadn't gotten drunk. If she hadn't let her guard down. And shame because she now felt soiled, unclean, violated."

Charlie frowned, still slightly confused. "So, you're saying Lucy acted the way she did because she was ashamed of what Murdoch had done?"

"That and also what she, Lucy, had done. Later, during the long years of recovery, after she had left the hospital, Becky started putting the pieces together. The lunches cancelled at the last minute, the dark glasses in winter, long sleeves in summer. Make-up suddenly too thickly applied."

The penny dropped. "Murdoch was also abusing his wife?"

"Becky thought so. But Lucy never told her. Never warned her of the kind of man her husband really was. That's why Lucy cut all ties with her after that fateful morning. She couldn't admit the shameful secret of her perfect marriage *and* that she had endangered her best friend as a result."

Charlie looked up as they passed the Statue of Achilles. Seeing the exposed penis, the rippling muscles, and the shield raised in victory, she thought of all the odes to toxic masculinity that pervaded their lives. Had Murdoch been taught to behave the way he did, or had he been born that way?

"But where's Murdoch in all this?" she asked, her tone sharper than she'd intended. "All these women feeling ashamed when the only one who should have been ashamed was him!"

Fry flushed with rage. "He was the only one who felt no shame at all! Not one ounce of remorse. When Becky finally told us the truth, I was so angry I went to the office to confront him. Can you believe he laughed at me too? Repeated the lie that she was making things up just because she 'wasn't his type'. But he knew I knew he was lying. I could see it in his face."

"You must have wanted to kill him."

"I did. Tried to punch him but he swatted me away like I was no bigger than a fly. When I eventually calmed down, I realised that my reaction was exactly what he had wanted. Derrick enjoys crushing people, making them feel small and helpless. I decided there and then that I wouldn't give him the satisfaction. That the best way of getting revenge was to make sure that Becky made a full recovery and became all that she could be. And that's what I've devoted my life to ever since."

Fry suddenly stopped and grabbed her arm, his eyes fierce. "Don't encourage people to mourn this man, Ms Tate. Don't write about him as if he's a saint or a victim worthy of our sympathies. People deserve to know who he really is. *What* he really is. People deserve to know he's the devil."

19. Claudia

Wimbledon Village
London, UK

Charlie had always thought that the adage about people and their pets was a myth, but when she saw Claudia Day across the Wimbledon stable yard, grooming her horse after their morning ride, she couldn't help but notice that the resemblance was unmistakable. The same big, brown, shiny eyes in a long face, the same glossy, brunette mane, and the same prissy air about them. Once the interview began, Charlie soon realised that the similarities between Pebbles and her owner didn't stop there. Claudia had an annoying habit of interjecting her speech with short bouts of neighing laughter, which invariably prompted a similar response from her twin, making it very difficult to concentrate on what she was saying. Thus, twenty minutes in, after Claudia had insisted on regaling her with every minutia of her girlhood adventures with Lucy and Becky, including all their fallings in and out, Charlie had no choice but to intervene.

"That's all very interesting, Claudia, but perhaps we might get back to my original question? You said you had information on Lucy. Related to Murdoch's disappearance?"

"Well," Claudia huffed. "If background and context are not important to you…"

"Of course, they're important, Claudia. I'm just not sure what point you're trying to make."

"Isn't it obvious? When it comes to Lucy, still waters run very, very deep."

Pebbles grunted and pawed the ground, presumably in agreement.

"I thought you and her used to be best friends," Charlie said, hoping to inch closer to her goal. "Before Becky that is?"

"Yes, in primary school. But when Becky joined in secondary school, it was suddenly like I didn't exist. Becky was popular with all the boys and Lucy wanted to be popular too. Didn't need plain old me hanging around anymore. If it wasn't for Becky, I'm sure Lucy would have ghosted me altogether. She was like that. Always trying to cannibalize what other people had. Then, when she had it, she moved on to the next thing."

Charlie thought about what Victoria had said. About how Murdoch took whatever he wanted. And now Lucy too.

Had that been what had brought them together?

"And Murdoch?" she said. "How did he fit into that picture?"

Claudia gave a facial shrug. "He had money and she wanted it. Even though her daddy's a peer, their family fortune was squandered long ago. Besides, by the time we finished Uni, she had tried almost everyone else in our group. They happily took what Lucy was putting out, but no one wanted her for keeps. So, she fell back on Derrick. A poor boy made good." Claudia and Pebbles neighed in unison.

She wasn't sure which was more repugnant, Claudia's venom or her snobbishness. Fortunately, at that point, Pebbles decided to poop, providing ample cover for the look of disgust on Charlie's face. Her companion didn't flinch, carrying on brushing her horse's coat like standing next to a pile of shit was the most natural thing in the world. Musing that animals were cute until you got to the shit shovelling part, Charlie discreetly stepped out of the stable into the yard. Close enough to remain within conversational distance while also enabling her to breath fresh air.

"Tell me more about their marriage,' she said. "Is it a happy one?"

Claudia smirked. "Lucy likes to pretend it is."

Charlie knew what her companion was alluding to, but always it was useful to get corroboration, so she gazed at her innocently and said, "What do you mean by that?"

"Cheating...and other things." Claudia stopped brushing, her air of malicious mirth morphing into a dull sadness. "It all started with Becky. Derrick raped -"

"You don't have to go into the details," Charlie interjected. "I've already spoken to Fry. But I would like to know when *you* found out."

"A few weeks after it happened."

"And what did you do when she told you?"

Fury flashed in Claudia's eyes. "I did what anyone would do, of course! I went to find Lucy. She refused to talk to me. Wouldn't even open the door. Said I was causing a ruckus and threatened to call the police."

"So, you left?"

"What choice did I have? We didn't speak to or see each other for years after that. Not until last year when I bumped into her in there," Claudia jerked her head towards the pub next door. "All lovey-dovey with a man who wasn't her husband. Lucy must have thought she was going somewhere no one would recognise her, so when I walked in, she looked mortified! Then she tried to ignore me altogether. It was only when I took a photo of the two of them and threatened to send it to Derrick, that she agreed to talk to me. Her date then fled, leaving the two of us to have a nice little chat." She resumed brushing her horse, her strokes long and steady, as if the labour gave her comfort. "When I asked her why she had done what she did to Becky, she got defensive. Claimed that Becky had been pretty drunk that night, that it could have been anyone and Becky had just accused Derrick out of spite."

Charlie gasped, genuinely shocked. "Spite?"

"Yep,' Claudia rolled her eyes. "Because she was jealous, Lucy said. Jealous that she had found a husband and Becky still hadn't. But Lucy was just fronting. When I told her that Mathew had told me what Derrick was doing to her, her face crumpled, and she started to cry."

"Who's Mathew?"

"My hubby, of course," Claudia said, shooting her a 'keep up' look which Charlie felt was rather undeserved. "He's a doctor with a practice in Chelsea. One day, he bumped into Lucy at the chemist. Even though she'd tried to cover them up, there were big bruises on her face, and she was cradling her arm. She claimed to have fallen down the stairs, but he knew from her injuries that that was a lie. He urged her to get help and she promised that she would, provided he didn't tell anyone."

Charlie frowned, not quite sure what Claudia was telling her. "Are you saying Lucy confirmed to your husband that she was being abused?"

"Yes. And she said as much to me as well. After her little cry, Lucy changed her story, claiming she'd had no choice but to do what she'd done to Becky that day. That Derrick would have made her suffer, otherwise."

"Do you think she was telling the truth? About her husband making her suffer?"

"At the time, I wasn't so sure," Claudia replied. "I thought she might have done it for more selfish reasons. You know, to hold onto the money, the lifestyle. But when I look back now, I think she might have been. There was real fear in her eyes when I threatened to tell on her. Perhaps that's why she went on to ask me about the Dewani case. Because she was looking for a way out."

Charlie's ears pricked up.

A way out.

"Isn't Dewani the guy who was accused of murdering his wife when they were in SA?"

"The very one," Claudia said evenly. "Specifically, he was accused of arranging the hijacking and murder of his wife whilst they were on honeymoon in Cape Town."

Finished with the grooming, she put away the brush, hugged and kissed Pebbles on the mouth, then closed the stable door behind her and joined her in the yard, enveloping Charlie in eau de horse shit.

Not wanting to cause offense, particularly at such a critical juncture, Charlie suppressed her gag reflex and ploughed on, saying "What exactly did Lucy want to know?"

"Why Dewani had been acquitted. My father's firm was involved in the extradition proceedings, so he had some knowledge of the case. I told her what I knew and asked her why she was so interested."

"And?" Charlie said eagerly.

"The shutters came down. Like she had realised that she'd said too much. So, she faked a laugh and said she'd just been making small talk."

"But you think it was more than that? That Lucy might have been planning something similar?"

"Wouldn't you?" Claudia said in a tone that implied no intelligent person could possibly draw any other conclusion. "Especially, given what's just happened!"

Charlie was quiet for a moment, mulling it over. Then her thoughts turned to Victoria. "What if Murdoch was going to leave her, anyway?"

"Nonsense!" Claudia scoffed. "Whatever makes you think he was going to do that?"

"Someone said he told them so, just before he disappeared."

Claudia's face went from assured scepticism to contemplation. Clearly, this piece of news was something that had never occurred to her.

"Do you think Lucy knew about it?" Charlie said.

Her companion drew in a deep breath, then slowly exhaled. "If she did, that would've only made matters worse."

"Why?"

"Her getting rid of him was one thing. But *him* getting rid of her?" Claudia slowly shook her head, her face sombre. "Lucy would have seen him dead before that happened."

20. The First Witness

The Strand
London, UK

Hilary stood in front of the mirror in the private bathroom of his office, washing his hands and thinking about luck. He'd read somewhere that luck was the intersection between preparation and opportunity. He, on the other hand, preferred to think of it as assisted fate. If you worked for something, willed it enough and were smart enough to recognise the right time to strike, sooner or later things fell into place. Almost like it was written in the stars. Get your timing wrong, however, and years of preparation could be nullified in an instant. Most people never knew which one it was going to be until after the fact. Not him though. He never left anything to chance.

"Hello?" a voice called from his office. "Anyone home?"

Drying his hands and straightening his gold, shark cufflinks, Hilary exited the bathroom to find the Head of Private Clients hovering uncertainly in the doorway. The perfect example of a man who had had all the opportunities but who had nevertheless failed to be adequately prepared.

"Ah, Jonathan," he said, pulling his lips into a facsimile of a smile as he went to sit behind his desk, "come in and have a seat. Has Gertrude offered you something to drink?"

"Yes, but I declined." Jonathan was about to sit in front of him when he paused halfway, his bum in mid-air above the seat cushion, suspended by indecision. "Sorry - did you want one? Shall I tell -"

"No, no," Hilary waved him down. "She knows what I want. Please. Sit."

As his guest perched on the edge of his chair, Hilary couldn't help but notice the remarkable change that had come over the man in the last few weeks. His prediction had indeed been correct. Gone was the brash and combative demeanour. In its place was someone shrunken and small, like all the bombast had been sucked out of him and all that was left was an empty husk, wary of the slightest breeze. It would have been sad if it wasn't so pathetic.

"Gertrude didn't tell me what this meeting's about," Jonathan began, "but, if it's about Mr Sisulu, I did as you advised and he's going to come back to me with a response in two weeks."

"Yes. That's very good," Hilary opened a drawer, pulled out a folder and placed it before him. "But that's not what I wanted to talk to you about."

Jonathan peered at the folder, trying to read upside down. "Oh - sorry. I just thought -"

His words were interrupted by Gertrude's entrance who, after placing a cup of peppermint tea at Hilary's elbow, exited as quietly as she had arrived.

When they were alone once more, Hilary opened the folder and took out a stapled, five-page document. "Remember the money laundering investigation that Derrick conducted?"

"Um…yes," his colleague replied.

"I wanted to talk to you about the witness statement you gave to the forensic team."

Was he mistaken or had Jonathan just become even paler than when he'd come in?

Hilary handed him the document. "Do you remember it?"

"Oh, that!" Jonathan feigned a chuckle as he leafed through it briefly before handing it back. "Seems so long ago now. More than a year, in fact."

"Yes, I'm aware of that." Hilary opened the statement to the relevant page. "I wanted to ask you a few questions about it, if I may."

"Of course. Though I'm not sure why that's necessary. Seems water under the bridge, don't you think?"

"Yes and no." Hilary took a sip of tea, his eyes locked on Jonathan's face. "Please indulge me. I promise this won't take long."

Jonathan opened his mouth then closed it again, begrudgingly nodding his consent.

Hilary looked down at the page before him. He didn't need to. By now he knew the statement by heart. He just thought it looked more officious, like a top inquisitionist about to eviscerate his subject. "You say on page two of your statement that Michael always involved one of his lieutenants in every transaction."

"Yes, that's correct."

"That, even though he would handle all the crown jewel private clients himself, he still got someone else to do the grunt work, yes?"

"Correct again. That was his standard practice." Jonathan's shoulders relaxed and he sat back in his chair, crossing his legs.

He's settling down, thinking this is going to be an easy ride. Well, we'll see about that.

"Hence, you say in your statement that you were surprised when you learnt that there'd been a number of transactions that Michael had undertaken entirely on his own."

"I believe so, yes."

Hilary paused, confused. "You believe so?"

His visitor sighed. "It was such a long time ago. I can't remember everything exactly. But if that's what the statement says…"

"Then how did you know?"

Jonathan blinked. "Know what?"

"About the transactions. Who told you?"

His colleague stared back at him, stumped, then finally said, "Gosh. You know what? I can't remember." He eyed the statement in Hilary's hands. "Does it not say?"

"But isn't that the sort of thing you'd remember?" Hilary asked, ignoring his attempts at obfuscation. "After all, if - as you allege – Michael had been going out of his way to hide these transactions, you wouldn't have just stumbled on them, surely?"

Jonathan pursed his lips and looked at the ceiling, the picture of deep thought. Hilary waited him out, counting the seconds.

How long did you have to pause to convince someone you were thinking?

After eight long seconds, his guest shook his head and looked at Hilary with regret. "I'm sorry. Something came to me but then it went again. Give me a few days. I'll find my notes from that period and come back to you."

"All right," Hilary turned the page. "You say on page three that you confronted Michael about these transactions, but you don't say when this alleged confrontation took place or exactly what concerns you raised. Just that "Michael reacted angrily and told me to mind my own business", quote unquote."

"Was that a question?"

"Naturally. Let's start with the confrontation, as you put it. When exactly did it take place?"

"Come on, now!" Jonathan angrily snorted, a faint echo of his former self. "You surely don't expect me to remember exact dates after so much time! I also don't see why it matters."

"Is that so?" Hilary said archly. "As I understand it, when one makes statements under oath, you usually also have to back them up with some kind of evidence. So, if you allege a meeting took place, then you need to provide the date and time so that it can be corroborated by diary evidence or other witness testimony. In the absence of that, it is not clear to me how the forensic team could have established that you were telling the truth."

"As I'm sure you will appreciate," his colleague said, planting both feet on the ground and folding his arms across his chest like a protective shield. "I can't speak for the forensic team or for how they went about their business. I was just asked to make a statement and I did."

"Asked?" Smelling blood, Hilary leaned forward, resting his elbows on the desk. "Asked by whom?"

Jonathan's eyelids fluttered. "What do you mean?"

"In a normal investigation, potential witnesses are first interviewed. Only then, if they have something pertinent to say, are they asked to make a formal statement. But it sounds like someone approached you to make a statement right off the bat. Is that what you're saying?"

"No – you misunderstood me. I meant…um…after the interview. They asked me to make a statement after the interview."

"You mean the forensic team."

"Yes."

"But there's no record of your interview with them in the report. Just your signed statement."

"Like I said, you'll have to ask them about that." Jonathan pulled at his tie, eyeing Hilary's tea hungrily.

"Are you thirsty?" Hilary asked, following his gaze. "You wouldn't like a drink, after all?"

"No, no. I'm fine," Jonathan gave him a tight smile. "Throat's just feeling a bit scratchy." He coughed as if to illustrate the point. "I must be coming down with something."

"Oh, I'm sorry to hear that. Anyway, as I said, this won't take long." Hilary went back to the statement, turning to another page. "My other question relates to the specific concerns you raised. What were they?"

Jonathan looked at him blankly. "What were what?"

"The specific concerns you had about these alleged transactions."

"Why do you say 'alleged'?"

"Let's leave that for now. Just focus on my question."

"My concerns, you say?" He looked at the ceiling once more as if hoping for inspiration. "Um, as I recall, though I will obviously need to look at my notes, my concerns largely centred on the account information provided given the amounts in question, the nature of the transactions and whether the requisite approvals had been sought. Surely that's all in the statement?"

"Yes – almost verbatim. But that's a very high-level summary that doesn't really say anything about exactly what the problem was. What was it about each transaction that worried you?"

"Each transaction?" Jonathan shot a surreptitious glance at the door. "Again, I'm sorry but I'll have to refer to my notes."

"Fair enough," Hilary replied obligingly. "As you say, it was a long time ago. However, since you seem to have been so meticulous about inscribing the event, perhaps you can also refer me to the location of the records."

"Records?"

Really? Was this man just going to keep repeating his words like a dumb automaton?

"Yes. The supporting documents for each transaction. I'm having difficulty locating them."

"Ah, I see," his colleague made a show of checking his watch. "Oh dear, I seem to have double-booked myself. I should be on a call with John Reinhart as we speak. I would shift it but since he is one of our most important clients…"

Hilary considered this for a moment, tempted to call his bluff, then thought better of it.

Why not let him stew for a while?

"Of course," he said brightly. "I'll ask Gertrude to book a follow-up meeting in a week or so. I trust you will have time to go through your notes before then?"

"Absolutely," Jonathan sprang up so fast he almost made Hilary jump. "I'm sorry I couldn't be more helpful. But now I know what this is all about, I'll be much better prepared next time."

As Jonathan scurried out the door, Hilary put his statement back in its folder and locked it away. Then he sat back, replaying the interview in his mind and wondering what to make of it all.

Whilst he hadn't known exactly how things would turn out, he certainly hadn't expected what had just happened. Had it really been all so amateurish, so simple? Merely smoke and mirrors, sound and fury? Or was Jonathan just a bungling fool?

Though didn't they also say it was always the fool who spoke the most truth?

21. Too Close

Tooting Bec
London, UK

Her heart thudded steadily, echoing the consistent slap of her trainers against the pavement as she ran. A glimmer of sunshine peeked through the noon clouds, a faint wind caressing her cheeks, its freshness tingling her nostrils as her brain got rid of its clutter. Running always helped her think. Helped her plough through the fog to get to the heart of a matter.

First, the facts so far. Murdoch had now been missing for almost five weeks and still no witnesses had come forward. According to Viper's latest report on the SAPS investigation, both the police and Interpol had yet to locate any additional bank accounts, reinforcing the likelihood that he had been taken by professionals. At the same time, neither the bank nor Mrs Murdoch had received a ransom note nor was there any indication that anyone was being pressured in any way, ruling out a kidnapping for money or some other gain. This, combined with the length of time Murdoch had been gone, increasingly suggested that they were now looking at kidnapping and murder. Hence, in terms of suspects, they were looking for someone who had a motive to get rid of Murdoch for good.

She began with Fry. He was clearly a man who held no truck for Murdoch and rightly so, based on his and Claudia's accounts. He'd said that his daughter's recovery was the best form of revenge, but had that been that true? Could his hatred have extended to kidnapping with malicious intent? Charlie thought about the hot, bitter emotions that had raged through him as he recounted his and Becky's story, compared to the cold, calculated planning of Murdoch's disappearance. It just didn't seem like Fry's MO. Moreover, if Fry had been involved, why make himself a suspect by coming forward with his story? That just didn't make sense.

Then there was Victoria. Whether she had had real feelings for Murdoch or not, there was no indication that she would have had a motive to get rid of him. On the contrary, he appeared to have been a very useful benefactor. Her jealousy of Murdoch's wife had also been clear despite her claiming to have had the upper hand over Lucy in their ménage à trois. Had the green-eyed monster led her to lie about Murdoch planning to leave his wife or had she been telling the truth? Or what if her truth was a deceit and it had been Murdoch who had lied to her? Either way, Victoria's story clearly needed further corroboration.

As for Claudia, it was obvious that she still nursed a great deal of antipathy towards Lucy. Not only because of how Lucy had treated Becky, but also how Lucy had treated her all those years ago. In her experience, deep wounds never truly healed, and Charlie sensed Claudia's scars were still very raw. Could her ongoing hurt and anger have prompted her to maliciously incriminate her erstwhile friend? Possibly. There was also the matter of the time delay. Claudia had spoken to Lucy more than eight months ago. If Mrs Murdoch had sought to get rid of her husband by replicating the Dewani case, why had she waited for so long? Unless Lucy had had a change of heart only for the prospect of Murdoch leaving her to be the final straw? Then again, one would think that an abused woman would welcome the possibility of her husband's exit. However, maybe public humiliation had not been the only thing Lucy had been worried about.

A lot of questions and not many answers. Nevertheless, what was clear was that the Murdoch marriage had been on the rocks long before Murdoch disappeared. Plus, the combination of Claudia and Victoria's testimonies and what had emerged from Viper's report, increasingly pointed to Lucy as the prime suspect. The problem was she also continued to be the most elusive. Charlie had to find a way of talking to her face-to-face. Of looking into her eyes, staring into her soul, when she posed the fateful question. Only then would she know who Lucy truly was and whether Victoria and Claudia had been telling the truth about what she was capable of.

Picking up her pace, Charlie turned towards home. Letting herself into her flat, she quickly put on a hoodie and grabbed a cap, some cash, and her tool bag before heading back out the door. In less than thirty minutes, she was on Gloucester Road, her tool bag around her waist, a cap on her head and EarPods in place. Just another jogger carrying out their midday recreational.

The Murdoch residence stood on a quiet, leafy street, set back from the road behind a chest-high wall with an open driveway. Jogging on the other side of the road, Charlie stopped and dropped to one knee as if fixing an errant shoelace. From this vantage point, she scanned the front of the house. Security cameras covered the driveway and porch, all of which seemed relatively new judging from their cleanliness. Now, whilst there was no doubt that the Murdochs had recently received increased media attention, such heightened security seemed a little bit excessive for a few journalists. Particularly given the fact that the media frenzy had since died down, evidenced by the absence of any of her colleagues along the street. That meant the cameras must have been put there for another reason. Perhaps due to something Lucy was afraid of. Or someone.

Interesting.

Though the empty front windows of the residence suggested that there was nobody home, appearances could be deceiving. Deciding to try her luck anyway, Charlie stood up, pulled her cap down even further to avoid facial recognition, and jogged across the road and up the drive. Once on the porch, she pressed the bell long and hard, signalling to the residents that she was a determined and persistent visitor. The sharp 'triiiinnnng!' of the doorbell echoed inside the house but there was no response. She pushed it again. Twice, thrice but still nobody stirred. She felt a pang of disappointment. On the way there, she'd been psyching herself up, readying herself to ring the truth out of Mrs Murdoch. Yet, it seemed she had arrived on one of the rare occasions when her target had ventured away from home.

Or had she?

Charlie jogged out of the driveway and to the end of the road, turning into the cross street. According to Google Maps, the Murdoch property stretched to the street behind it, which hopefully meant it had an accessible back garden gate. When she got to the parallel street, she slowed down and took out her phone, keyed in the Murdoch address then edged forward, careful not to overshoot the speed of the GPS. About halfway down the block, Charlie got to what the map said was the back of the Murdoch's garden. A creeping vine spilt over the top of the wall, running next to a sturdy, wooden door which appeared to be locked. She stopped and mimicked a stretch as she looked around for CCTV cameras along the lane. Unable to spot any, she turned back to her task.

Over the top of the wall, Charlie could see the top floor of the residence, the back of which comprised two bedrooms that were both currently empty. Kneeling to peer into the keyhole, she saw a green, manicured lawn surrounded by sculpted bushes, interspersed with Greek statues. Looking onto the garden was a kitchen cum family room with two box windows as well as cottage pane doors opening onto the patio. The patio doors were closed, and the kitchen looked deserted. As far as she could tell, the garden and patio were also devoid of security cameras. Either Lucy only expected a frontal attack, or she put a premium on her privacy. Charlie waited a beat, checking for any sign of movement or indication that someone was home. Finding none, she got to her feet, considering what to do next.

One option, the safer option, was to go home and come back another day. However, this could just land her back where she was now. Alternatively, she could capitalise on Lucy's absence and see what she could find. A far riskier option for numerous reasons but didn't fortune favour the bold?

Charlie waited for a car to pass, then looked up and down the lane to ensure that no one else was coming. After testing if the vine would hold her weight, she put on gloves and quickly scaled the wall, landing in the garden with a soft thud. She was pretty sure Lucy didn't have dogs, but she paused just the same. When man's best friend failed to emerge, she ran across the garden, got on one knee in front of the cottage pane doors, took out a lock-picking set from her tool bag and got to work.

Five seconds later, the lock clicked open. She pushed the door forward just a smidgen to check if that would trigger an alarm. Silence. Then she walked into the kitchen and closed the door behind her, again waiting to see if her presence would be picked up by the sensor on the opposite wall. Whilst it flashed red, indicating it had picked up movement, the alarm still didn't go off. From this, she surmised two things. First, Lucy hadn't bothered to put on the alarm before she went out and, second, this was probably because she didn't intend to be out for long.

Better get a move on, Charlie!

She did a quick recce of the ground floor. The spacious house was spotless, absent of the usual signs of neglect brought on by despair. Whilst it was furnished with the standard trappings of a family home – bright flowers in key spots, walls painted in warm hues, children's paintings and smiling family photos everywhere - it still felt cold. Like something had sucked all the joy out of it. However, given what she knew about the Murdoch marriage, maybe it had never been there in the first place.

Then she commenced her search, working her way swiftly but methodically through the house, looking for secret stashes and hideaways. The main bedroom yielded no insights, apart from the fact that most of Murdoch's stuff seemed to be in the guest bedroom. Further confirmation that their marriage had not been a happy one. Nothing in the two lounges or the kitchen either, though the latter indicated that Lucy had a distinct disinterest in the culinary arts. By the time she got to the study, Charlie was beginning to lose hope. Then she noticed something odd about Murdoch's book collection. He seemed to prefer the literary greats of classical literature, though the pristine nature of the books themselves suggested that they were more for show than reading. He also sought to have whole sets of each author. Everything that they had ever written. Yet four books were missing. One from Hardy, one from Dickens and two from Dostoyevsky.

Strange.

Charlie slowly scanned the room, taking in Murdoch's antique mahogany desk, the cream sofa in front of the fireplace next to a small drinks cabinet and back to his ceiling-high bookshelves. She started with the chimney and went on to the bookshelves, the sofa, and the drinks cabinet. Nothing. She checked the top of the desk for a secret compartment, rifled through the drawers, and removed the bottom drawer on the left of the desk to check the hollow base. Nada. Finally, she did the same with the bottom right drawer and bingo! The three books lay in a tray within the hollow base. Charlie started going through each book, taking photos as she went.

Far from the Madding Crowd provided the first reward for her efforts, with Lucy's diary lying in its scooped-out innards. However, a quick scan of the slender volume seemed to suggest nothing incriminating. Only addresses, phone numbers and patchy appointments written in a long, slopping hand. The only thing that piqued her interest was that, whilst most appointments were written out in full, one set of appointments was only ever recorded as an initial. M. So, not only had Lucy hidden her diary but she had also gone the extra step of hiding the identity of M should it ever be discovered. Charlie thought about the man Claudia had seen Lucy with.

Was that M or was it someone else?

Dickens's *Bleak House* provided the second bounty, with the summaries of old investigation reports hidden within the book's large carcass. A few years ago, Lucy had hired a private investigator to gather evidence of her husband's infidelity. And there had been many, all captured in terms of dates, and times, along with thumbnail pictures. Given that the reports also spanned a considerable amount of time, it was unlikely that Lucy had simply gathered this info so she could confront her husband about it. Rather, it seemed like she had been attempting to build a case. Yet, whether that was for a divorce or some other leverage, Charlie couldn't tell.

The third book she went through, *The Brothers Karamazov*, suggested an answer to this question. It contained correspondence with Lucy's lawyer regarding grounds for and ideal terms of separation. Mrs Murdoch had sought advice on how to circumvent a water-tight prenup. The feedback from her lawyer had been simple. She couldn't, which meant that if Lucy sought to leave her husband, she was likely to leave without a cent. Charlie closed the book and picked up the last item in the tray.

Amongst the pages of *Crime and Punishment* sat newspaper cuttings from the Dewani case. Claudia had been telling the truth after all. Given the number of cuttings, it was plain that Lucy had researched the case very thoroughly, though whether this was before or after she had spoken to her estranged friend was unclear. She had also highlighted key aspects related to the details of the wife's hijacking and murder, as well as the judge's ruling.

Not quite a smoking gun but certainly heading in that direction.

She had just taken a photo of the last clipping when she heard a car crunching over gravel followed by the sound of an engine cutting off. Lucy was home. Putting everything back as it was, Charlie went to the study door, and sneaked a look into the hall. On the other side of the front door, she heard a thud followed by a curse as if Lucy had dropped something. She calculated the distance she had to travel versus how long it might take Lucy to pick up the object and open the door. Just enough time for her to run to the kitchen and out through the patio doors. Then, as Lucy was walking down the passage, she could head out the way she came.

With no time to lose, Charlie dashed across the passage and into the kitchen, skidded past the kitchen island, through the patio doors and into the garden. Behind her, the front door slammed shut.

Speed up Charlie, you're almost there.

Then, inches from the garden wall, she heard footsteps on the other side, coming down the lane, stopping her dead in her tracks. If she went over now, she'd be caught, but if she stayed where she was, Lucy would see her. Kicking herself for not leaving sooner, Charlie looked around for a place to hide.

Not the vine – too little cover. Not the sculpted bushes – too small. Not the hedges – too little room. How about…

She dashed to the corner, squeezing into a gap between the garden wall and a tall statue of Venus. Once hidden, she realised that there was one problem with her choice. It blocked her view of the house, leaving only sound as her guide. In an attempt to filter out all other noise, she took a deep breath to calm herself and concentrated. In the lane, the footsteps grew louder, while behind her, the house stood silent.

Odd.

Lucy should have been inside already.

Charlie strained her ears, hoping to get a signal of Lucy's whereabouts. On the other side of the wall, the footsteps drew closer and closer until they were parallel to the garden door. Then they suddenly and inexplicably stopped. A sense of foreboding crept up her spine.

Damn.

Had someone tipped off the security company?

Fixing her eyes on the door, Charlie slowly unzipped her tool bag and took out her pepper spray. As soon as the guard opened the door, she'd spray him in the face and make her get away while he was still reeling from the effects. Twisting open the lock, she held out the spray and waited.

One potato, two potato, three potato, four…

Had the garden door just shuddered?

It had to be him.

Charlie tensed, ready to spring, switching to breathing through her mouth for total silence. She heard a metallic jingling like someone had just taken out their keys and raised the spray higher, preparing to strike. Just when she thought she couldn't bear the tension any longer, a car door banged shut and an engine roared to life.

Someone had just left. A visitor who'd parked in the lane.
Had the footsteps been theirs?
If not, what was the security guard waiting for?

As the car pulled away from the curb, a toilet flushed in the house behind her. It sounded like it was coming from the guest toilet at the front of the house. Lucy must have stopped to go to the loo. If she washed her hands, Charlie would have just enough time to climb over the wall before her target got to the kitchen. Yet still, she hesitated, thinking about the guard. Once she started climbing, she'd be more vulnerable, easier to get off balance. If he came through the door at that point, she'd be a sitting duck. Yet, if she didn't go now, she could end up confronting two people instead of one.

Get going! It's now or never.

Putting the spray in her pocket for easy retrieval, she stepped out of her hiding place and grabbed the vine, blood pounding in her ears. When she got to the top of the wall, she would have no choice but to jump the guard from above to maintain the advantage of surprise. Behind her, an internal door creaked open. Lucy was on her way down the passage.

Charlie scrambled up the vine as quickly as she could, her nerves on tenterhooks, imagining Lucy's bloodcurdling scream as she got to the kitchen and finally clocked she had an intruder. Getting to the top, she peeped into the lane, expecting to see the crown of a burly man's head, and beefy, wide shoulders. However, there was no one there. No one behind the door, and no one in the lane.

It had been the visitor all along!

Relief flooded through her as she swiftly clambered over the top and dropped to the other side. Her heart still thumping, she bent over, hands on her knees, and took deep breaths. A car turned into the lane and whizzed past, the driver giving her a disinterested glance. To him, she must have looked like just a normal jogger, pausing to catch her breath after overexerting herself. Which was just as well. When she felt more like herself again, Charlie donned her EarPods and began the leisurely jog back to the tube station.

That had been close.
Too close.

22. Secrets

Alexandra. Township
Johannesburg, South Africa

Lucky sat on the floor, a towel over his head as he leaned over a bowl of hot water, inhaling medicinal fumes to help clear his chest. He and Boy were alone in the shack, Thabo having gone begging in town and Innocent off to see his cousin who'd said he might have a job for him. Innocent had asked Boy to tag along but Boy had opted to stay and look after him instead. Not that Boy was a particularly good caregiver. He just knew how to safeguard his interests, living being one of them. Still, Lucky was glad of the company.

It was roasting in the shack that day, so hot they could barely touch the walls. They had both stripped down to their shorts and Boy had fetched cold water from the river so that they could cool themselves down. With the river being so close, the air felt thick and heavy, like breathing through water and it was even worse underneath the towel.

"That's it for now," Lucky said, lifting his head as he pushed the bowl away. "I'll try again later."

Sitting on the bed, Boy got up and picked up the bowl, careful not to spill it as he placed it next to the washing bowl in the corner. "You feeling any better?" he asked.

"I think so." Lucky replied, standing up on shaky legs and going to lie on the bed. Truth was, he was feeling worse. Had been for some days now. "Can you please open the door?' he said. "While you're up?"

Boy unlocked the latch and pushed open the door. "I thought the heat was supposed to help?"

"Depends on the type of heat." Lucky rolled onto his side, relishing the air that rushed through the door and washed over his sweaty face. It was still warm, but it was cooler than the air inside had been. Trying to ignore the tightness in his chest, he closed his eyes and concentrated on the soothing lullaby of the neighbourhood. Distance traffic and musical drumbeats battling for dominance, excited chatter interspersed with shrieks of laughter and irate mothers shouting at husbands and children alike.

However, Boy, now sitting next to him on the bed, seemed more focused on his wheezing. "Innocent also made some more of that stuff. The one his grandmother uses for her chest. Shall I get you some?"

"Doesn't work."

"But he swears -"

"May work for her. Not for me."

"Why don't we go back to the clinic, then?"

Lucky scoffed, "And wait the whole day only to be sent home with a couple of panado?"

"Maybe they'll have stock this time?"

"They never have stock!" His voice was gruff, part frustration, part anger. "At least, not for us."

Thabo had said there was some kind of racket going on. Public health workers taking government supplies and selling them to the private sector for ten times or more their original price. Always somebody winning and somebody losing in this world. Problem was, they were the ones usually losing.

Lucky flipped onto his back. "What we need is money. So, I can go to a proper doctor for once."

They both fell silent, knowing there was nothing more to be said. Money lay at the centre of everything. All their woes, all their hopes, all their daily struggles. Lucky thought about the reward. He'd heard they'd increased it to two thousand rands. The police, probably having heard the rumours, had also promised to keep the names of those that came forward secret. Imagine what they could do with two thousand? Apart from his medicine, Boy could get those sneakers he'd prayed for, Innocent his boxing gloves, and they could even put a down payment on that DJ turnstile Thabo had always wanted. And food. Food for months!

Lucky felt a tingle at the back of his throat. Sitting up, he coughed, once. Then again and again and again, trying to clear it. It went on for so long, he started to worry it would never stop. Even Boy patting his back didn't help. When he finally managed to cough it up and spit it into the tin cup he kept next to the bed, he tasted metal, the contents of the cup turning red.

Blood.

He and Boy looked at each other.

"Let me get you a cloth to wipe your mouth," Boy said, his face grave.

Lucky put the cup down and lay looking at the ceiling. He should have been overwhelmed with fear and panic but all he felt was resignation. History repeating itself. From grandmother to grandson. He'd heard Gogo's nurses call it TB. Some people got it and recovered. If they had money for proper treatment and caught it early enough, that is. Those who didn't, passed. Just like his grandmother.

Boy handed him a wet cloth. Lucky wiped his lips and was about to hand it back when he changed his mind and placed it next to the cup. Chances were, he was going to need it.

His carer watched his every move, his face pained. "I've thought of a way,' Boy said, sitting back on the bed.

"A way for what?" Up on the ceiling, Lucky noticed a line of ants walking across one of the wooden beams holding up the corrugated iron.

Were they going to a feast? Perhaps he and Boy should ask to tag along?

"Of getting the reward without anyone knowing," Boy replied.

Intrigued, Lucky pushed himself up on his elbows. "You have?"

"Uh-huh," Boy looked particularly pleased with himself. "We phone them! That way, no one will see us going into the station. No need to give our real names. Nothing!"

Sighing, Lucky lay back down and focused on the ants. He should have known it was too good to be true. "With what Boy? You suddenly get a phone or something?"

"No," he replied, insulted, "but I know who has."

"Yeah – right."

"It's true!" Boy shook his leg, demanding this attention. "He usually takes it everywhere he goes and stores it under his pillow at night. He thinks I don't know but I can hear it when it rings."

"And who's this? Your imaginary friend?"

Hurt, Boy turned away. "Forget it. I'm not going to tell you if you're going to be mean."

Lucky immediately felt ashamed of himself. Even if Boy's scheme was just wishful thinking, he shouldn't have been so hard on him. Seeing him sitting there with his back to him at the foot of the bed, Boy suddenly seemed so small and frail. With his head bowed, Lucky could see the bones in his spine while his shoulders blades stuck out like the wings of a bird. He thought of when they'd first found him, so traumatised he cowered at the slightest touch. Boy had come a long way since then. So much so that Lucky always forgot he wasn't as tough as the rest of them.

"Ok – I'm sorry," he said, gently. "I believe you. I do."

Boy didn't budge.

Lucky playfully pushed his bum with his foot. "I'm just grumpy, ok? I shouldn't have taken it out on you."

Boy sniffed.

Shit – was he about to cry?

"Hey…I didn't mean to -"

"I don't want you to die, ok?" Boy blurted out, struggling to hold back the tears. "Everyone always dies and it's just not fair!"

How many deaths had Boy seen in his short life?

Too many it seemed.

Lucky scooted to the end of the bed and gave Boy a hug. "I'm not going anywhere, ok?" he whispered in his ear.

Boy didn't respond, tears rolling down his face. Lucky held him even tighter. "Trust me," he said. "Not now, not ever."

Boy turned and looked at him, his wet eyes as big as saucers. "You promise?"

Lucky held out his pinkie finger, his face solemn. "I promise."

Boy clasped Lucky's pinkie with his own and they shook, sealing the vow.

'There you see," Lucky said, grinning. "Now you got me on the hook. I'll be like that smelly mouse you love so much. No matter how hard you try, you won't be able to get rid of me!"

As Boy wiped away his tears, Lucky tickled his armpits, making him squirm. Boy fought him off, but he was relentless. First, he got Boy to smile, then to chuckle and soon he was giggling so much Lucky couldn't help but join him.

The exertion rang Lucky out, so they sat side by side on the bed, enjoying the breeze from the doorway.

"Now, tell me more about this phone," Lucky said.

"Ok. But you have to swear not to tell Thabo I told you."

He frowned at Boy in surprise. "Thabo?"

"Yep. Like I said, he doesn't know, I know. He gets calls on it late at night, but he never answers them."

That was strange. Ever since they'd met at the orphanage at five years old, they had shared everything. Food, clothes, hopes. Since when did Thabo start keeping secrets?

"Calls from who?" Lucky asked.

"I don't know but one day, when he went out, I followed him and saw him call someone."

"When was this?"

"A few days ago."

"So, it still has airtime?"

"Suppose so."

Lucky thought for a moment. "You said he usually takes it with him. Does that mean he didn't take it today?"

"No, I saw him put it in his pocket when he got dressed this morning. Before everyone else woke up. It's just that he used to take it all the time but now sometimes he doesn't."

"And when he doesn't, where does he put it?"

"I don't know. He just goes out and comes back around 30 seconds later."

30 seconds? That meant that, wherever his hiding place was, it couldn't be far.

"So, are you going to ask him?" Boy prompted.

"Ask him what?" Lucky replied absently, his mind on possible nearby hiding places.

Boy lightly elbowing him in the ribs. "To use his phone, silly!"

Lucky wasn't so sure that was a good idea. Thabo had been very quiet lately. Ever since the rally at the stadium. He'd assumed it was sadness. That going there had triggered memories of his father. Yet, what if it was something else? Especially since, as it now turned out, there was a phone he hadn't told them about. So, it seemed to him that all this secrecy meant that the chances of Thabo agreeing to lend him his phone were zero to none. However, that didn't have to be the end of it.

"I'll see," he said pensively. "Best to wait till the time is right."

Boy's face fell. "But I thought –"

"Don't worry! I said I will, so I will," Lucky said to put him at ease. "And by the way," he continued as he fondly patted him on the shoulder, "thanks for telling me, bro. You're a lifesaver."

Boy smiled bashfully, his face glowing with pride.

23. Interviews 2 and 3

The Strand
London, UK

His face was the picture of bafflement. "I'm not sure I understand," Reuben replied, "I was simply asked if I had seen the transactions before and I said that I hadn't and that they hadn't passed through our standard risk review process. I was never asked to attest as to whether the transactions themselves existed!"

They sat at the conference table in his office, Hilary struggling to hide his impatience as he listened to a less-than-sterling rendition of innocent naiveté.

"But surely, that is the *first* thing that you should have sought to establish?" Hilary replied. "Especially if the result of your testimony was likely to be the loss of employment of two of your colleagues!"

"They said the transactions had been discovered during the forensic team's prelim investigation. Who was I to doubt their authenticity?"

Hilary leant forward, "Who said?"

"Whoever took my statement. I assume a member of the forensic team?"

"And did it never occur to you," Hilary said, making a note to double-check this claim with the investigators, "that the reasons you hadn't seen these transactions, the reason they hadn't gone through the normal risk review process, was because they had never happened in the first place?"

Reuben looked at him blankly. "Again, I can't say whether that's true or not. You're the one who's saying there's no record of them. Despite them being listed in the draft report. So, respectfully, I think you should be asking the forensic team these questions, not me."

There it was. The same old talking points.

"And what about Patrick? Did you not at least attempt to check with your then-boss if he knew anything about the transactions in question?"

"Again," his guest said slowly as if it was *his* patience that was being tried, "my sole duty in this matter was to answer the questions that I was asked. Any further involvement in the process on my part would, in my view, have been inappropriate. Including talking to the Chief Risk Officer, who - as you know - was one of the accused."

It lay just below the surface, faint but present, nonetheless. An air of scorn. Superiority even. Born of someone who was convinced they had the upper hand. Well, we'll see about that, Hilary thought.

Sooner or later, he'd get Reuben to break.

"In the same vein," the CRO continued, "I had no control over what Derrick, or the forensic team, did with my testimony or what the outcome of the enquiry would be. So, I would like to push back on the implication that I was somehow complicit in what happened to Michael and Pat. I think that's very unfair."

Hilary pursed his lips. "And that's all you have to say, is it?"

Reuben squared his shoulders. "I'm afraid it is. Unless there's something else you would like to talk to me about?"

"No," he said evenly. "I think you've told me all I needed to know for now." As his guest stood up to leave, Hilary added one more thing, just to remind him who was boss. "Steven should be here by now so send him through, will you?"

While the door closed behind Reuben's back, Hilary walked to the window, staring with unseeing eyes at the scene before him. When Jonathan hadn't turned up to their follow-up meeting last week on the pretext that he was feeling sick, he had known that his instincts had been right. The three witness statements had indeed been the right trail to follow. Now, Reuben's blame-shifting responses had served as further confirmation that something had been very wrong with Derrick's investigation. The only thing left to ascertain was the depth of the rot.

"I hope I'm not disturbing you?" Steven said from behind him. "Reuben said you were ready for me?"

Hilary turned, rearranging his facial features into a warm and welcoming expression. "Yes, please Steven – come in. Gertrude's at lunch but my new coffee machine makes a passable cappuccino."

"Thank you, Hilary. A cappuccino sounds wonderful." Steven walked to the window as Hilary went to organise the coffees. "Whenever I come in here," the CFO continued, "I can't but help marvel at this view. I think it might be even better than the one from Derrick's office."

"Oh, you think so?" He kept his voice neutral, never sure whether Steven's comments were compliments or hidden barbs.

"Yes. It's absolutely breath-taking. I'm definitely putting dibs on this office when you move upstairs."

Were these words a fishing expedition to tease out the extent of a rival's ambition?
Or, having given up the fight, was Steven merely trying to curry favour?

"Upstairs?" Hilary said with just the right intonation of surprise.

"When you become the next Africa CEO, of course!" his guest winked, his eyes full of mischief. "Don't be coy, Hilary. We all know Spencer is eyeing you for the role. Unless, of course, you think Derrick's coming back?"

He didn't respond, handing Steven his cappuccino before picking up his own and going to sit at the conference table, waiting for Steven to join him.

"Well?" the CFO pressed as he sat opposite him. "Do you?"

"It's too early to tell," Hilary said in a tone that he hoped signalled a supreme disinterest in the subject. "Now, coming to the reason for this meeting," He pointedly glancing at the documents spread on the table before them, "I've some questions about some transactions I was hoping you could assist with."

Steven followed his gaze. "I'll try. Though, as you are aware, as the CFO, my role in the transaction process is more from the Treasury point of view rather than the deal-making perspective. If all this relates to the money-laundering investigation, you'll see that I said as much in my witness statement."

So, Steven had been briefed and come prepared. No matter. The real question was what had been the nature of the briefing? A colleague merely passing on a helpful tip? Or a warning by a co-conspirator?

"Yes, I've read your statement," Hilary replied. "That's exactly what it says. That's *all* you said, in fact. But your role is also to act as our primary accountant, keeping our books straight, isn't that so?"

"Of course."

"Then I assume Derrick spoke to you about the investigation's findings?"

"Yes - to some extent. As I'm sure he did with you." Steven leisurely took a sip of coffee, raising his little finger as he did so.

"So, what exactly did you discuss?" Hilary asked, picking up his cup with all his fingers like any sensible person would.

A brief, ponderous frown puckered his colleague's brow. "Well, if I recall correctly, it was mostly to do with our liquidity."

He couldn't keep the credulity out of his voice. "Liquidity?"

"Yes. He seemed to be worried about cash flow. Wanted to know how we were handling the extremely large cash transactions going through our books.

What quantum could we handle in a day before we took strain, that sort of thing."

"And what exactly did that have to do with Michael and Patrick?"

"Can't say. I didn't see the final report. But that's definitely what Derrick wanted to know at the time."

Hilary was quiet for a moment, trying to figure out if what Steven was telling him was so ludicrous that it must be true or so audaciously false that it could only have been said to hide an even bigger lie. He suspected it was probably the latter.

"I have to say," he said brusquely, "I find it hard to believe that you never discussed the specific transactions themselves or what was alleged to have occurred."

Steven shrugged. "As I said, it wasn't my area."

"Ok. But let's say you wanted to hide something. A falsehood or a reality that you didn't want to be found. How would you go about doing it?"

The CFO did a double-take. "Why on earth would someone want to do that? Is there something going on that I don't know about?"

"No, not at all. I just want to get some things clear in my head."

Now it was Steven's turn to look incredulous. "But why are you asking me? You know our systems as well as anybody!"

"I just want your point of view, that's all," Hilary said innocently. "It's always good to get a different perspective."

Steven took another long sip of coffee, his shrewd eyes gazing at him over the rim of the coffee cup. Hilary kept his face placid, the shadow of a smile touching his lips, determined to give nothing away.

"I see," the CFO eventually said, placing his cup back on the table and pushing the half-drunk coffee away from him as if it had suddenly turned sour.

Had there also been a slight change in the timbre of Steven's voice?
Maybe he was finally getting somewhere.

"So," Hilary said, beginning to enjoy himself. "How would you do it?"

"Me specifically? Or people in general?"

"Let's start with you, shall we?"

Steven cleared his throat. "I'm not sure I'd know how, to tell you the truth."

"And if you were to guess?" Hilary pressed. "Just as a hypothetical."

A vein just above Steven's right eye started to tick. "Well, I've heard people say – though I cannot attest to this myself - that the easiest way would be to simply alter the record."

"Is that so?" Hilary looked at him with wide-eyed wonder. "How could you do that?"

"Again – I'm not an expert."

"How about if you made up a bunch of transactions?" Hilary said eagerly. "Perhaps to hide what you were really doing. Then deleted the entries and files?"

Steven vigorously shook his head. "Wouldn't work since that would impact the general ledger. It would no longer balance."

"Not if you deleted them long after the transactions were complete, and the books had been audited and closed. That wouldn't affect the ledger, would it?

There was a change in the emotional field. Hilary couldn't place the exact nature of it, but it felt as if the air was becoming thicker, the temperature in the room rising.

Or maybe that was just Steven's body heat?

Again, the CFO shook his head. "You know our IT systems make that virtually impossible."

"Not if you have human cooperation."

Steven blinked, his head jerking back as if Hilary had slapped him.

"In fact," Hilary continued. "If you had the right set of collaborators, there are all kinds of things you could do, wouldn't you say?"

"How dare you!" the CFO said, outraged, the tick above his eye now galloping. "Not on my watch! If I found any of my team involved in that sort of thing, I would fire them on the spot."

"If you say so."

"I *do* say so. And what, by the way, does any of this have to do with the money laundering investigation?"

"Maybe nothing," Hilary said coolly, looking down briefly as he picked a piece of lintel off his trousers, before giving Steven a piercing glare.

"Or maybe everything."

24. A Motive

Tooting Bec
London, UK

The tube compartment was rush-hour packed but silent apart from the occasional cough or sneeze, interrupting the steady whoosh of the train barrelling through the underground warren. Charlie didn't know why, but the determination of her fellow commuters not to greet, speak or make eye contact during their collective temporary incarceration always brought on an urge to disrupt. To shout, stamp or find some other means to shake her fellow commuters from their self-imposed vocal internment. Something always stopped her though suggesting, *appallingly*, that she was more of a conformist than she thought.

Today, she had the honour of being squeezed in between the door and a smelly armpit which, judging by the brown underarm stain on the owner's shirt, was probably the result of a congenital sweat disorder combined with poor hygiene habits. To avoid said armpit and any contact with its owner, she had turned until her face was inches from the glass partition between the doors and seating area. The downside of this was that the woman sitting on the other side of the partition kept behaving as if she was being spied on, scowling at her, and shielding her phone no matter how much Charlie tried to make it clear that she was looking into thin air.

She'd just been the reluctant recipient of another searing look from the partition woman when the train finally pulled into her stop. Springing out of the door, Charlie silently said a longed-for goodbye to laser-eyes and armpit man and rushed towards the stairs, pulling out her vibrating phone as she went.

"Have I caught you at a bad time?" Viper asked. "Sounds like you're somewhere busy."

"I'm just getting out of the tube after another horror commute. I don't think human beings were meant to live like this."

"Can't be bad as the New York subway."

Charlie laughed out loud. "Ok – that's true. I'll give you that one."

After battling through an unexpected miasma of Old Spice at the top of the stairs, she emerged out of the tube station into the busy high street, thankful for the crisp night air. Instead of heading straight home, she turned right, thinking a nice takeaway would be just the ticket. "Did you get the photos I sent you?" she added.

"That's why I'm calling. So, you think the wife's in the frame?"

"The documents I found strongly suggest she certainly had a motive." Charlie glanced inside a Chinese restaurant. Despite having opened only a few months ago, the place was empty and forlorn - always a bad sign. She carried on walking.

"What about someone at the bank?"

"Still in my top suspect list. I'm not ruling anything out until I have reason to." She waited for Viper to respond but got nothing. "Hey – you still there?"

"Yeah." Viper sounded unsure, tentative. "Was thinking, that's all."

"About?"

"Well – by most accounts, Murdoch's a piece of shit, right?"

Charlie looked left and right as she crossed the road, "Yeah – that seems to be the case."

"So, why help him? Say Lucy did it? So what? It's not much of a loss, know what I mean?"

"I get where you're coming from, but Lucy is not some innocent victim who killed her husband in self-defence. She seems to be just as selfish as him and willing to subject others to harm, even by omission, when it suits her."

"Yeah, but…" Viper's voice slowly trailed off.

Charlie's mind flashed back to the time when they'd first met. How Viper had looked so scared and fragile. "Look," she said gently, "given the circumstances, if you want to step away from this one, I'll understand."

"I'm not saying that," Viper murmured.

Charlie tensed, sensing what was to come. "Ok," she took a deep breath, "then what *are* you saying?"

"I know you don't want to hear this," her friend said in a sombre tone, "but ever since your family died, you treat each case as if it's some kind of crusade of atonement. You couldn't find their killers, so you have to save everyone else in the world. Or bear witness or whatever way you think about it in your head. Truth is Charlie, not everyone deserves a saviour."

She counted to ten, pushing away their faces, blocking out the pain.

"Charlie? Are you still there? I'm sorry if I overstepped but -"

"No," Charlie swallowed the lump in her throat. "It's ok. I'm good." Another deep breath. "I'm not trying to play the saviour V. I just feel there's something deeper going on here. Bigger than Murdoch, bigger than Lucy. And I have to find out what it is. Yeah, it would make a great story, but it also seems like the right thing to do. Does that make sense?"

"I guess." Viper still didn't sound convinced.

"There are so many people whose stories never get told," Charlie said quietly. "The murder of my family is just one of them. These poor children I've been tracking are another. If *you* were murdered or mysteriously went missing, wouldn't you want someone to try and find out what happened? Attest to your truth, whether you are worthy of it or not?"

Viper was quiet for a moment. "I suppose so," she eventually said reluctantly.

Feeling eyes boring into the back of her head, Charlie glanced behind her. People seemed to be going about their business. There was a man she thought she recognised - from the tube perhaps? – but he was window-shopping at the travel agent.

Must have just been her imagination.

"But the offer's still open if you want to jump?" Charlie said.

"No, no. I get it." Charlie heard nails tapping on a keyboard, "Since you're so determined to go ahead *and* due to the fact that I'm you're do-or-die friend, I suppose you want me to tell you what I found?"

"That would be nice."

Charlie smiled to herself.

What would one do without the Vipers of this world?

"Bien. After I got your photos, I did a bit more digging, eventually finding a way into Lucy's laptop and phone. About eight months ago, she wrote another letter to her lawyer but this time asking what kind of settlement she would get if Murdoch divorced *her*."

"So, Victoria was on the money. He *was* planning to leave his wife."

"Looks like it."

"But why did he only tell Victoria two weeks before he disappeared?"

"Did she say Murdoch was going to leave Lucy for her specifically?" Viper asked.

"No, now that you mention it. Victoria certainly *thought* he was leaving Lucy for her but perhaps that was just her assumption."

"Yep."

"What did the lawyer say? How big would the potential settlement have been?" Charlie spotted an Indian restaurant up ahead. Wafts of masala flitted in the air, guiding her footsteps.

"Minimal. The prenup made provision for alimony in such an instance but certainly well below fifty percent of what her husband was worth. Not only did Murdoch have shares in Yeats but also several other blue-chip companies. Apart from their house in London, he also owned various properties in the UK and abroad. All in all, she would have been a rich woman in a normal divorce but not in this case."

Charlie spotted a chippie across the road and felt a sudden craving for battered sausage and chips in curry sauce. She waited for a car to pass then ran across the road. "What about Murdoch's will?"

"I didn't come across the will itself, but Lucy mentioned in one of her letters that, whilst she got a reasonable sum, Murdoch had left the bulk of the estate to the children, split fifty-fifty. These sums would be held in trust, with Lucy as the trustee, until they turned 25."

"And life insurance?"

"Substantial. On each other should either of them decease the other."

"That's it, then. The best thing for Lucy was for her husband to go. Then she would get the insurance money, what he left her in his will and the ability to dip her hand in her children's trusts if she wanted to. But only if he didn't change anything before she had a chance to act." The chippie was bulging with customers, so Charlie decided to finish the call outside.

"Exactly. Once she found out she was screwed whether her husband left her or she left him, Lucy started researching the Dewani case. Her search history indicates that she also looked at lots of stuff on how to hire hitmen in SA."

"Really?" Charlie felt a surge of excitement. "Perhaps all that research explains the time gap between when she spoke to Claudia and when Murdoch vanished."

"There's only one problem. I couldn't find a paper trail suggesting that she did more than that. Research I mean."

"What about calls?" Charlie asked, buttoning up her jacket. Now she was standing still, she was starting to feel the cold.

"To SA?"

"Yeah. Leading up to and around the time of Murdoch's disappearance?"

"A few. Six months ago. To Cape Town, not Joburg. A landline at the university. I think she was trying to get in touch with one of the authors of a well-known book on SA contract killers. Each call was very short suggesting the calls had gone unanswered. There's also no indication in her phone records that these calls were ever returned. Not from that number, anyway."

"And you're sure there were no more calls since? Either to Cape Town or Joburg?"

"Not that I can see but she could have used a burner."

"True." Charlie paced up and down the pavement in an attempt to keep warm. "I guess I could try calling the Cape Town number. See if anything comes out of it. But…" As she turned, she saw the guy from the travel agent again, now popping into the betting shop four doors down from the chippie.

Coincidence?

"Charlie?" Viper said. "I can't hear you…"

"Sorry – got distracted for a moment. I was saying that even if they did talk to her, it's doubtful she would have told them her true intentions. And a few calls are a long way from proving that Lucy subsequently hired a hitman to commit the crime. So, all we have at this point is conjecture. I can't use any of it."

She heard Viper tapping some more keys. "There's another angle you could try. Lucy's correspondence shows she also had a fair amount of contact with someone with the initials M D. Does that ring a bell?"

"MD? No, I…," Charlie stopped dead. "Hold on – one of the people Murdoch fired is called Michael Develin. Could that be the guy?"

"Could be. Maybe also the M in Lucy's diary."

"What type of contact are we talking about?"

"Text messages mostly," Viper said. "A couple of phone calls too."

"When?"

"About one month after the calls to SA."

"What did the texts say?" Charlie glanced behind her and noticed the crowd in the chippie had thinned out.

"I didn't look at them closely. I was more focused on the kidnapping/murder angle. But the tone of the few I saw was super friendly. Want me to take a closer look?"

"Please." Charlie stepped inside the shop, glad to be out of the cold. "Interesting," she mused. "Lucy and Murdoch and now Develin and Lucy…"

"You thinking another love triangle?"

"Maybe, maybe not," Charlie replied. "But you know what they say…"

"What's that?"

"There's a thin line between love and hate."

25. No Comment

Southgate
London, UK

She had expected that a boxing club that had trained some of the most famous boxers in the UK, some might even say the world, to have a grander entrance in line with its reputation. Not just a small brown door with 'boxing' printed in white capitals overhead, lying in between two brightly canopied street cafés on Southgate's Crown Lane. Yet perhaps that was the whole point, Charlie thought. No need to shout when your record spoke for itself. No need for bling when you were all about heart, grit, and determination.

She was parked about three shops down from the boxing club, sitting low in the driver's seat with a cap shielding her face, drinking coffee, and trying to be inconspicuous. What had brought her here was a series of ignored friendship requests, one eventual 'yes' and then, after searching through mountains of social media posts, a single photo that had told her all she needed to know.

The ignorer or, if she were honest, decliner-in-chief had been Michael Develin. Rather than just waiting for Viper to get back to her, Charlie had hoped Develin would agree to talk on his own. Since he was no longer residing at his last known address in Mayfair and had also changed his phone number, she had had no choice but to try and use social media to make contact. However, whilst Develin had once been very active on LinkedIn, Facebook and Instagram, his last post had been about a year ago, whereafter he had vanished from the digital world.

Still hopeful he might check his messages occasionally, Charlie had DM'd him, explaining who she was and that she wanted to talk about his experiences at the bank. Still faced with a wall of silence, she had then reached out to one of the friends Develin had included in his last Facebook post. Fortunately, being the obliging chap that he was, this guy had accepted her friendship request almost immediately.

Foster was a keen adventurer and sportsman, with a particular passion for boxing. A passion he and Develin shared. One picture, in particular, had caught her attention. Of him and Develin in a gym, shadowboxing in front of a red, blue, and white tiled wall. After a quick query with the guys at the Torch sports desk to suss the photo's location, she had decided it was time for a stake-out.

Charlie didn't know when, or how often, Develin came to the club, but since his LinkedIn profile hadn't indicated any post-Yeats employment, she figured he was now a sleep-in-get-up-at-midday kind of guy. Hence, she had opted for a lunchtime start, thinking she would wait three to four hours every day and see if she got lucky. Now, two days and three hours into her stake-out, Charlie was beginning to think she'd been too optimistic. She had kept her eyes glued on the boxing club entrance since she'd arrived, but, so far, no one matching Develin's description had gone in or out. Just a couple of guys who looked like pros, some scrawny lads and a bunch of ladies who looked like they were heading to a box-fit class.

Feeling eyes boring into the back of her head, Charlie checked the rear-view mirror, scouring the street behind her. Everyone looked innocent enough. An old lady stepping into the flower shop, a young man walking a fat bull terrier, a middle-aged man sitting in his car talking excitedly on the phone and a man, face hidden behind a newspaper, lounging in the window of the coffee shop. In short, no one that screamed STALKER. Which didn't explain why she felt like scaly eyes were slithering down her spine.

Dismissing her foolishness with a swift shake of the head, she turned back towards the club, hoping she hadn't missed anything. Just when she had started to wonder if the gym had a back entrance or if Develin had simply stopped boxing altogether, she saw a blond, plump man carrying a gym bag walk out of the tube station and turn left, heading in the club's direction. Donning a leather jacket that had seen better days, he hung his head low, eyes on the pavement like a man shrinking from the world. And yet there was still a resolute air about him, his steps assured, his stride determined.

Charlie quickly checked his features against the picture she had lifted of Develin from his Facebook profile. The man in front of her seemed older and was certainly meatier, but the brow and nose were the same. Deciding to take a chance, she jumped out of the car and ran up the street, intercepting him just before he reached the club entrance door.

"Mr Develin? Michael Develin?"

He looked up, scowling. "Who the fuck are you?"

"My name's Charlie Tate. The journalist who sent you all those messages? I'd like to ask you a few questions about Derrick Murdoch."

"No comment.' He tried to barge past her.

Charlie blocked his path. "I believe you worked together. At the bank?"

"No comment." He dodged right, attempting to go the other way but she blocked him again.

"Got any light to shed on Murdoch's disappearance?"

The change was immediate. Develin froze, his eyes ablaze. "What're you implying, eh? That I topped him or something?"

Alarmed by the rage in his eyes, Charlie took a step back. "No, I -"

"You bloody media types are all the same." Face red, he jabbed his finger in her face as he advanced. "Always poking your noses where it don't belong!"

Charlie glanced at Develin's other hand as she walked backwards, now balled into a fist, suspecting that he had a mean left hook. "Honestly, I meant no offence. I just thought -"

"Are you deaf?" Develin turned sideways, pinning her against the wall with the force of his fury, his face inches from her own. "When I say, 'no comment', I *mean* NO FUCKING COMMENT!"

With nowhere to go, she flattened her back against the wall to try and put some distance between them, looking left and right for potential assistance if things went south. Passers-by increased their pace and averted their eyes, no one feeling like playing the hero.

"I didn't mean to…" She licked her lips. "…upset you. I just -"

Perhaps it was the slight wobble in her voice or the unease he must have seen in her face but suddenly, as quickly as it had come, the wrath dropped from Develin's eyes, replaced by what looked like anguish.

"Just leave me alone, ok?" he said quietly, stepping back. "I said no comment. Please – let's just leave it at that."

This time, Charlie let him go, watching silently as he hitched his bag on his shoulder and disappeared into the caverns of the boxing club. With a heavy sigh, she stepped away from the wall and dusted herself off, her mind dissecting what she had just encountered.

While she had partly expected to be rebuffed, she hadn't expected his reaction to be so bare, so violent. She also hadn't thought that Develin would be in so much pain or that she would recognise the rawness that she had seen in his eyes. It had almost felt like staring at her old self, during the days when she couldn't bear to look in the mirror, couldn't stand to see her mother's features reflected back at her. However, even though she didn't know how she knew, she had sensed that Develin's grief wasn't due to the loss of a loved one but the loss of a life. His life. The one he had once known. Yet, she had also sensed that, instead of leaving him weakened and diminished, this loss burned like a fire in his belly, his soul baying for blood.

So much hurt, so much animus.
Had Murdoch been its cause and its target?
And if so, what had Develin done with so much hatred?

26. Bait

Lower East Side
New York, USA

Which one was it going to be, Viper wondered as she scrolled through her music collection, Beethoven, Mozart, or her favourite opera compilation? Or perhaps Summer from Four Seasons? Finally opting for Bach Cello Suite No. 1 in G Major, she put her phone on the speaker dock and pressed play. Sitting back in her chair, she rested her hands on the desk, closed her eyes and luxuriated in the opening prelude, feeling its soft strains reverberating in her soul, filling her with peace. Then, after a few moments, she opened her eyes, cracked her knuckles, and got down to work.

She began with the texts between Lucy and Develin she had found in Lucy's phone records. Unfortunately, a closer inspection didn't yield much apart from the fact that they had gone to great lengths to keep their rendezvouses secret. However, the purpose of these liaisons was unclear. Some messages referred to Develin helping Lucy with someone or thing called 'P', whilst others spoke about Lucy helping him find Murdoch's 'Black Box'. The trouble was Lucy didn't indicate who or what 'P' was or explain why she needed Develin's help. Nor did the texts define her husband's Black Box, why Develin wanted it and how Lucy could help him get it. Nevertheless, since both items were obviously very important to both protagonists, Viper made a note of them and moved on to Develin himself.

Charlie had sent her the name of Develin's Facebook friend, Joe Foster, that had led Charlie to the boxing club. However, Viper only planned to use him as her backup plan. First, she would try going directly to the source. Fingers flying over the keyboard, she opened her web browser and clicked on Michael Develin's LinkedIn account. Using a scraping programme, she extracted his email address and phone number. Then, using his phone number, she tried to hack into Develin's phone. Unfortunately, the number was no longer in use.

Undeterred, she turned to his email address. For the phishing mail to work, she would need a good hook. The easiest thing would have been to send Develin an ad for a special at the boxing club. However, since it looked like he went there quite frequently, it wouldn't take much for him to ascertain that it was fake. So, she'd just have to go the long way round.

Whilst Develin hadn't been active on LinkedIn for more than a year, his profile suggested that he took a strong interest in global financial bodies and trends in the global financial system. Yet, since his profile said he was currently taking a work break, would Develin still find such things enticing? Unlikely. Viper moved on to his Facebook page. Even though this had also been dormant, at least it was a better demonstration of his current interests.

Apart from boxing and Italian food, Develin seemed to be very partial to rare whiskeys. Brushing up on her rare whiskey repertoire, Viper picked two that were likely to be in the price range of a man with expensive tastes but scarce current income. Using a design app, she prepared a flier from a well-known British whiskey retailer advertising a special encapsulating thirty per cent off on a bottle of Macallan Ruby or Laphroaig 27. Pleased with her artistic dexterity, she sent a mail of the flier to Develin's inbox. To only watch, with a sinking heart, as it bounced right back with a message saying the address no longer existed. Kicking herself for not having tested this email first, she reverted to the backup plan.

Whilst Viper managed to source Foster's email address from his social media pages, she couldn't get a phone number. So, logged in as Charlie, she went to his Facebook page. Fifty posts in, it was clear that he was the type of guy who liked to travel and brag about where he'd been. She thought of sending him an email inviting him to enter an airline travel competition with the intent of getting his mobile number but decided, given the Develin experience, to check his email address first. Luckily, she got an automatic reply telling her he was out of the office on vacation, which helpfully included his personal cell phone number as part of his email signature.

People never learn.

Now she had Foster's number, it didn't take her long to hack into his phone so she could go through his logs, messages, emails, photos and generally anything he had once considered private. Whilst he had some unusual interests, Viper didn't linger. After all, he was the road, not the destination. And, fortunately, this road led her to exactly where she had hoped. Develin's current mobile number.

The downside was that Develin seemed to be a lot less trusting than his buddy, with Viper's attempts to gain access to his phone being constantly blocked due to some kind of protective software. Whilst this made things more difficult, it wasn't unsurpassable. Adjusting her whiskey flier for mobile, Viper sent Develin a text that appeared to be from Foster with a little something extra. A piece of malware that, once you clicked on the flier, immediately started working its magic, giving her access to all of the target's phone data in seconds. Sadly, however, it only worked if someone took the bait. Not knowing how long it would take Develin to succumb to temptation, Viper got up, grabbed her phone, and went to do some chores.

Four hours later, she returned to find Develin's cell phone data running across her screens. Turned out he wasn't much of a hold-out, after all. Satisfied with her progress so far, Viper made herself baked potato with spicy tuna mayo for lunch, and then got back to work, starting with Develin's emails. His inbox, apart from the usual subscription notifications, personal chats with friends and ever-persistent unwanted spam, largely consisted of job applications, most of them rejected, and some emails from Schuster & Co Chambers, which looked like a legal outfit. With regard to the latter, one email in particular stood out, headed 'Cease and Desist'.

When Viper opened it, it turned out to be a letter from the legal representatives of a Mr DF Murdoch dated a year ago, just before Develin left the bank. The letter referenced several pieces of correspondence that Develin had sent to Murdoch that month and warned that, if Develin continued in this fashion, further legal action would follow. Whilst the emails in question were no longer in Develin's sent folder, Viper did find them in his archives. In one of these emails, entitled 'Witch-Hunt' and sent to Murdoch a month before his lawyer's ultimatum, Develin threatened to rip off his boss' "lying face" and cut out his "forked tongue". In another mail, sent a week after that, he promised Murdoch that he would "send him back to the hell he came from" if he didn't stop the "bogus" action against him.

Needless to say, the guy had beef.

After downloading this correspondence, Viper looked through Develin's call logs. Though several numbers appeared relatively frequently, only one set of calls had significantly increased recently. Six months after Develin left the bank and six months before Murdoch vanished. A quick directory search revealed that the number belonged to a butcher's shop in Brixton, South London. Viper wasn't sure whether this timing was significant or not, but she noted it anyway.

Looking at Develin's texts, she saw that, leaving aside his exchanges with Lucy, most of the other messages seemed unremarkable, but again with one exception. Develin's recent exchanges with this particular contact seemed overly cryptic. Almost as if they didn't want anyone who might see their messages to know what they were talking about. One message, sent on the day of Murdoch's disappearance, was especially intriguing: "The eagle has landed."

What eagle?

And, more importantly, who the hell was Sparrow?

27. The Call

Alexandra
Johannesburg, South Africa

Dawn's grey light seeped through the plastic window, chasing the shadows to the corners of the shack. The air was hot and heavy with the scent of baked dust, stale sweat, and human waste, the latter courtesy of the toilet bucket in the corner. Lucky lay on the bed, rubbing some of Innocent's home remedy on his chest and around his nose. Innocent had said he'd changed the recipe, put more Eucalyptus, and mint this time. Though he still didn't think it would work, it was better than nothing. Outside, a rooster crowed, followed by another then another, and soon bird song filled the sky while, in the distance, the hum of morning traffic gradually grew louder. Next door, Mrs Khoza broke into a hymn, one of his grandmother's favourites, her voice as strident as it was out of tune, the sound still sweet, nevertheless. Down the street, a radio came on, blasting out the morning news, only to be drowned out by a rival, rocking Amapiano beats. Eventually came the cavalcade of thumping feet, rushing down the path. Unlike the brethren they left behind, lost to hope and dead in all but name, these hasty travellers were the unbreakable ones. Those who still had the will to push forward in such an unfair and desolate world.

As Lucky stroked his chest in slow, rhythmic circles, he thought about his friend's new plan. Thabo had come up with the idea of changing his begging routine into a dance act. All the kids were doing it now and the really good groups could bring in a hundred to two hundred bucks on a good day. Boy and Innocent had been super excited about the idea, but Lucky wasn't convinced. After all, how many days of practice would it take to get that good? And, worst of all, what if they never did? No. He preferred to bet on surer odds.

His eyes drifted to Thabo's sleeping form, lying on his back with his makeshift pillow under his head. He could feel it, calling to him, just like it had been calling to him every morning ever since Boy had told him about it. Two thousand rands sitting just a phone call away. His plan was to take the phone, use it and put it back before Thabo knew it was gone. All he had to do was find the right moment.

Lying next to Thabo, Boy let out a long, sloppy, putrid fart. Lucky cursed. The air was bad enough without Boy adding to it. Then, looking at his blissful, sleeping face, his irritation fled as quickly as it had come. He hadn't told Boy about his plan. He wouldn't have understood. He didn't know how difficult Thabo could be when he wanted to. It had been hard, though, ignoring Boy's searching looks, his silent pleadings to "ask him!" whenever they were all at home. Those looks accused Lucky of betrayal, of not making good on his promise, and of stubbornly refusing to take the chance that Boy had given him. Yet that was precisely what he was doing. Taking the chance. Whilst Thabo still had the phone. Whilst he still could.

As Thabo lifted his head, coming out of slumber, Lucky quickly put Innocent's remedy aside and closed his eyes, pretending to be fast asleep. Eyes closed, he heard Thabo yawning then the grass mat shuffling as he got up. Opening his eyes just a touch, Lucky lay on his side and watched him through lash-covered slits. Usually, as he went about his morning routine, Thabo would pause, looking over the others as they slept, a crooked smile on his face like an indulgent father. This morning, however, Thabo was all business, dashing to relieve himself in the bucket before reaching for the water bottle to wash. Realising the bottle was empty, Thabo walked to the opposite wall and changed into a t-shirt, tattered shorts, and flip-flops. Then he picked up the toilet bucket, grabbed the empty water bottle and gently opened the door.

Fresh air flowed into the shack, the odour almost sweet, the usual miasma of dirt and sewage from the street dampened by last night's rains. Halfway out the door, Thabo suddenly paused, his frame silhouetted in the morning light, his head cocked to one side as if he had heard something strange. Lucky squeezed his eyes shut, trying to keep his wheezing as even as possible, fearing Thabo was on to him. At any second, he expected Thabo's hand to land on his shoulder, forcing him to open his eyes, his friend's gaze boring into their depths, revealing his cunning plan. However, after a few painful seconds, the door closed, and Thabo was gone. Lucky relaxed and opened his eyes, his glance immediately shifting to Thabo's pillow and the almost imperceptible bump that signalled what lay beneath.

How long would it take for Thabo to get water and return?

He imagined Thabo turning left, pouring the contents of the bucket into the organic sewer that ran down the side of their street, before heading to the communal tap to wash the bucket and fill the water bottle. Getting to the tap would take about five minutes. If the line at the tap was long, that could take another twenty minutes. So, a round trip would take at least thirty. Plenty of time to take the phone, make the call and put it back before Thabo returned. Yet, if the line was short, Thabo could be back in half that time, perhaps even less. And, if Lucky got caught, that would be it. Thabo would never let the phone out of his sight again.

Eish!

Too risky.

He felt vindicated for his caution when Thabo returned ten minutes later, the clean bucket in one hand and the full water bottle on his head. Still pretending to be asleep, Lucky lay on his side and put his arm in front of his face, observing the room under the crook of his elbow. Innocent sleepily lifted his head, checking what had woken him and rolled over, going back to oblivion. Putting the bucket back in place, Thabo poured some water into the washing bowl on the floor and started washing. When he was finished, he put the full bowl and cloth in the corner, ready for the next person. Drying himself with a worn towel, Thabo donned a sweatshirt and jeans before retrieving the phone from under his pillow and putting it in his front jean pocket. Lucky's heart sank.

He should have taken it when he had the chance!

Resigned to yet another failure, he was just about to roll over on his back to get some real shuteye, when he noticed something was off. Thabo had taken the phone out again and was looking at it in the palm of his hand as if trying to make up his mind about something. Then he went to the door.

Was this it?

Was Thabo going to finally lead him to his hiding place?

As Thabo closed the door behind him, Lucky crept out of bed, tip-toed over Innocent and Boy who grumbled but did not stir and made his way to the front of the shack. Pretending to be taking a pee, he cracked open the door a slither and peered into the street. The neighbourhood was fully awake now, sheets and clothes billowing on washing lines, mothers chatting in doorways and kids in school uniform rushing to the taxi rank. However, there was no sign of his furtive friend. Lucky started to panic, wishing he had gotten to the door sooner. Then something stirred in the corner of his eye, and he turned just in time to see Thabo ducking out from behind a sheet that hung on a washing line between their shack and Mrs Khoza's house.

Got you!

Excitement bubbling through him, Lucky closed the door and pretended to be washing his hands just as Thabo walked in.

"Eta," Thabo said, closing the door behind him. "What are you doing up so early?"

"Needed to take a leak." Lucky looked down as he wiped his hands, masking the lie.

Thabo jerked his chin in the direction of Lucky's chest, his face concerned. "I see you've been trying Innocent's new recipe. Is it working this time?"

Lucky was temporarily non-pulsed. He'd been so focused on the phone, he hadn't realised that he hadn't coughed in a while. Could breathe a little better too. "I think so," he replied, half surprised himself.

"That's great!" Thabo brightened. "Maybe you could even come with us? You know - for moral support?"

Today was the day they were going to try out the new dance routine. Even though he wasn't well enough to take part, under normal circumstances, he would have tagged along, working as a hype man, and helping to bag the cash. Not today, though. Today he had other fish to fry.

Lucky dropped his shoulders and sighed with heartfelt regret. "I would if I could but I'm still feeling kinda weak. Next time, though, for sure."

"Can you two talk any louder?" Innocent growled from his sleeping post.

Glad of the reprieve, Lucky stepped over him and Boy and went to sit on the bed, his back against the wall.

"Finally, he's awake!" Thabo mocked, hiding his disappointment.

"No choice given the racket you two are making," Innocent sat up, stretched his beefy arms, and yawned. "What time is it, anyway?"

"Time for you and Boy to get your lazy arses up!" Thabo playfully kicked their feet. "Come on. Get going and I'll start on breakfast."

Innocent reluctantly stood up and walked to the wash basin as Boy opened and rubbed his eyes. He didn't know how long it took them to wash, dress and eat breakfast but, for Lucky, every second felt like eons. When they finally grabbed their caps, beer crates and juggling balls and tramped out the door, Lucky waved the proud troop on their way and wasted no time shutting the door behind them.

Alone at last.

After spending another ten minutes in bed in case someone had forgotten something, he quickly got dressed, and peeped through the door to make sure the way was clear. The neighbourhood was quieter now, the morning rush over. Mrs Khoza's door was open, but she had her back to him, working away at her paraffin stove. Stepping into the street, he tiptoed to the corner, ducked under the washing line and into the small gap between their two shacks, following in Thabo's footsteps. Standing in the centre was a tall, wooden electricity poll surrounded by brush and weeds. Lucky scoured the bushy undergrowth with his eyes and feet, moving inch by inch. When his foot felt a looseness in the earth at the bottom of the electric pole, his heart skipped a beat. This was where the vegetation was thickest, where disturbances to the undergrowth could easily go undetected. Looking left and right to make sure no one was watching him, Lucky got to his knees and eagerly dug up the earth. When his fingers brushed something hard, he decreased his pace, carefully excavating the site until he got to the prize. A small, blue plastic bag holding within it an electronic ticket to two thousand bucks!

With butterflies in his stomach, Lucky grabbed the phone and went deeper into the enclave, away from the street and Mrs Khoza's open door. Though he'd memorized the number, it took a couple of attempts before someone picked up, a bored female voice saying, "Thank you for dialling the crime-stop hotline. How can I help you?"

Lucky's mind went blank.

"Ello?" the woman said. "You still there?"

"Ummm…yeah," he murmured so Mrs Khoza wouldn't hear. "I'm calling about the missing white man."

"You have information?"

"Huh-huh."

"Which case?"

Shit! There was more than one?

Lucky coughed. "The one with the two-thousand-rand reward."

"Oh. Ok," he heard the click of a ballpoint pen. "Your name and ID number?"

Lucky felt the first stirrings of panic. "Anonymous," he whispered nervously.

"Anonymous?" Her hoot of laughter rang in his ear. "So, you don't care about the reward?"

"No! I do. It's just -"

"Then how are you going to claim it if we don't know who you are?"

Damn. He hadn't thought that far.

"What if I just gave you a phone number?"

"Just a cell?"

"Yep." As the words left his mouth, Lucky suddenly realised he didn't know the number of Thabo's phone.

God! He was screwed!

"Let me check with the officer leading the case and I'll come back to you," the policewoman said. "Can I use the number you're calling from now?"

"Oh – yes," he said eagerly, relief flooding through him. "I'll…uh…wait for your call."

Leaning against the wall of their shack, Lucky wondered what he would do if the officer said no. He still had his grandmother's ID. They couldn't hurt someone who was already dead, could they? If the officer insisted on some form of identification, he'd use that ID and then, if he got the reward, he'd simply explain that he'd lied for his own safety.

Yes – that was it.
Keep calm.
You've got this.

When the phone vibrated in his hand, Lucky almost jumped. "Hello?" he mumbled into the receiver.

"Hello," said a deep, gravelly voice.
This wasn't the woman from the hotline.
Could it be the officer looking after the case?
Possibly, but the caller ID said private number.

Lucky opened his mouth to ask the man who he was, then closed it again. Something didn't feel right.

"Can you hear me?" the gravelly voice said.

"Sorry. You've got the wrong number," Lucky replied, ready to end the call.

The man's laugh sent chills up Lucky's spine. A laugh born of a cavernous mouth with big, fat lips, glistening yellow teeth and a lizard tongue atop a ravenous throat deep and dark as a soulless pit.

"No, my boy," the man rasped like a snake slithering over gravel. "You're exactly who I've been looking for."

28. An Update

Islington
London, UK

Charlie pushed away from the desk in her study and stood up, listening to the crack, crack, crack of her spine as she stretched. Her head felt heavy, pinpricks of pain playing at her temples. For four hours straight, she had been working through her notes, reliving every interview, looking for something, anything she could put in print. According to The Ferret, The Torch's biggest rival, The Evening Sentinel, had also started digging into the Murdoch story and while the News Editor hadn't explicitly said it, Charlie had certainly heard it, in every pause and unasked question. Time, and everyone's patience, was running out. The problem was that was all she had. Time spent and not much to show for it. Nothing solid, nothing she could prove.

Hoping to clear her head, she opened the window, trying to take solace in the rich aroma emitting from the potted trees in her back garden. Outside, a purple and white speckled starling fluttered by, pausing briefly to examine her with a quizzical eye, before zooming up into the rain cloud sky. As she followed its assent, the mid-afternoon sun peaked briefly through the clouds, then was gone like the slippery tendrils of truth hiding behind lies.

Sighing, Charlie turned away from the window, grabbed the phone and dialled. Maybe Viper would have some good news for her.

"Hey, it's me," she said when her friend answered. "I was hoping for an update?"

"Well, you're right on time," Viper said cheerfully. "What do you want first? The good news or the bad news?"

Charlie thought of The Ferret. "Please - start with the good news." Putting the phone on speaker, she laid it on the desk.

Viper's laugh trilled around the room. "Guess you're starting to come under pressure, huh?"

"You might say that." Charlie picked up a whiteboard marker and turned to her evidence board.

"Well – don't worry. Both types of news are…interesting. They just might not be what you expected, that's all." Charlie heard papers shuffling. "The good news is, if Lucy Murdoch did use a co-conspirator to kill her husband, there's a slim chance Develin's your guy. You said he was fired by Murdoch, right?"

"That's right. Figuratively, at least."

"Well, seems like he didn't take it well. Claimed Murdoch was framing him. So, he sent Murdoch a whole bunch of threatening emails. Got so bad, Murdoch got his lawyers to send him a cease and desist."

Charlie wrote 'threats' next to MD on the board. "Were any of the threats physical? Did he threaten to kill him?"

"Not explicitly. Implicitly? Definitely."

She thought about their last encounter, the rage in Develin's eyes. "I can imagine." She gave Viper a brief run-down of what had happened. "So, given that we've both established that Develin hated Murdoch," Charlie continued, "what we now need to know is whether Develin acted on these threats."

"I may be able to help there too. About six months ago, Develin started exchanging cryptic messages with a guy called Sparrow."

"Nickname or a surname?"

"A nickname. As in death omen."

"Nasty!"

"You could say that. According to a friend of mine specialising in international drug syndicates, a leader of one of the largest gangs in London is called Sparrow. Real name, Dwayne Jones. Apparently, this gang started off in drugs but, under his leadership, has diversified into various businesses, some of them legit. Then I dug deeper into Develin's background. It appears that Develin and Jones grew up together, first in foster care, then running the streets. Seems they eventually got arrested but Develin got off with a warning whilst Dwayne was sent to Juvie."

"Why?"

Charlie heard tapping. "Charges were exactly the same," Viper said, "so I guess it was down to racism in the criminal justice system. Anyway, if it's the same Dwayne, juvie's where he perfected his skills and earned a reputation for unstinting ruthlessness. Hence, the nickname."

"Did that affect their relationship? Develin walking whilst he didn't?"

"Doesn't look like it. From their messages, they still seem to be pretty close."

Charlie wrote 'Sparrow – Accomplice?' on a note and stuck it next to Develin's photo. Now she felt wide awake, the fatigue gone, the hunting juices flowing.

"So, Develin seems to have had the motive and Sparrow could certainly have provided the means," she said. "But have you found anything to link their cryptic messages to Murdoch?"

"The timing. On the day Murdoch disappeared, Sparrow sent Develin a message saying, 'the eagle has landed'."

"And Murdoch could have been the eagle? Perhaps arriving at Joburg airport?"

"Possibly."

Charlie was quiet for a moment.

Close but no cigar.

"Or it all could just be a coincidence," she prevaricated.

"If you believe in coincidences."

She didn't but still…

"Does any of this tie back to Lucy?"

Viper's nails tapped the keyboard again. "Her and Develin seem to have hatched some kind of deal. Develin would help Lucy with P and Lucy would help Develin find a Black Box."

Charlie picked up another Post-it note. "And P stands for…?"

"That's the bad news. I'm not sure yet. The only P I can find associated with Develin is his former wife, Portia. Why Lucy would need his help with her, though, is unclear."

Charlie tapped the marker against her lips, thinking. "Could P also stand for the ultimate penalty?"

"As in death penalty, you mean?"

"Yes. Lucy wants him gone. Finding a contractor on her own doesn't work out so she reaches out to Develin. A man she knows hates her husband as much as she does. Surely, that's more plausible than P standing for Develin's ex-wife?" Charlie wrote 'P?' on the note and placed it between Lucy and Develin's photos on the board.

"Mmmm…maybe," Viper said. "But then why would Develin still want the Black Box in exchange? If they were working together on getting rid of Murdoch, surely that would be enough?"

"What's a Black Box?"

"Another part of the bad news. I don't know yet."

Charlie wrote 'Black Box?' on another note and placed next to the 'P?' on the board. "Ok, let me get this straight," She started pacing, her hands laced on top of her head. "Both Develin and Lucy had serious beef with Murdoch but for different reasons. Lucy and Develin were clearly working together on something. He was helping her with 'P' and she was helping him find a Black Box. But we're not sure yet know what those things are or IF and HOW they relate to Murdoch, right?"

"Right."

"At the same time, Sparrow and Develin were also secretly planning something which could or could not relate to what Develin was working on with Lucy. This something included a cryptic message from Sparrow to Develin on the exact same day Murdoch disappeared. Which may or may not signify their involvement in his murder."

"Yep."

Charlie stopped pacing, pulling a face. "We're making progress V, but it's not enough. We need to know exactly what P and the Black Box are and we're still a long way from putting Sparrow, let alone Develin, at the scene of the crime."

"My friend said he would try and get some more intel on Sparrow if that helps? He's only heard of him but some of his contacts specialising in the UK scene may have more intimate knowledge. That may lead to a more solid link."

"That would be great. I'll also ask around. See if any finance journos know what a P and Black Box would be in Murdoch's world."

"Cool," Viper said. "Cycle back in a couple of days?"

"Sure." Ending the call, Charlie sat on the edge of her desk, looked at the board and groaned.

All I need is one piece.

Just one piece of solid evidence that brings it all together.

Unmoved, the photos on the board silently stared back, each face now furtive and smug.

29. A Deal

Canary Wharf
London. UK

The air in the basement was thick with the reek of fish, blood and chicken shit while cock crows and lusty, male cries echoed off bare-brick walls slick with evaporated sweat. Charlie hung back from the crowd, her eyes averted, her hand covering her nose in a vain attempt to ward off the stink. Yet, try as she might, she couldn't avoid catching a glimpse of the carnage as people shifted in the circle in front of her, a single light bulb illuminating the focus of the bevvy's rapture.

Christ!

She hated fucking cock fights.

The location of this particular fight was a disused basement under a fish shop in Billingsgate Market. Reputed for providing some of the best cuts in London, few knew that the Russian owner of the fishery had honed his carving skills in a very different type of butchery. And fewer still that the shop in question was one of a series of businesses fronting for far more lucrative trades. At least, according to Jake.

Meeting in this basement had been his idea, betting on cock fights being apparently one of the favourite pass-times of bankers and such. It was the only diary opening he had at such short notice, just before another meet with a source in the very same place. The upside of this choice apparently was that it would give her a taste of what the London financial district was really like behind all the glinting skyscrapers and fancy business suits. The hunger, the avarice, the cut-throat competition.

Looking around, all Charlie saw was a bunch of little boys desperately pretending to be men, strutting around with braggadocious shoulders, smiling, laughing, slapping each other on the back, gloating each time their bird went for the kill, hoping no one could smell their own fear.

Pathetic.

A dark-haired woman pushed through the crowd and came to stand next to her. "Hiya love, I'm Constance," she said in a broad Jordy accent. "Connie for short."

"Hi," Charlie clipped, not in the mood for company.

"We haven't seen you around before…?"

"No, you haven't." Charlie looked at her watch, telegraphing her disinterest.

The woman was not deterred. "You wouldn't happen to be Charlie Tate from The Torch, would you?"

Charlie inwardly cursed. "And you're from?"

"The Evening Sentinel."

If Connie was expecting a reaction, Charlie refused to give her one, merely nodding politely and once more glancing at her watch.

"You know," Connie continued, "for a finance newbie, you certainly got the scoop on all of us, that's for sure!"

Charlie kept her eyes focused on the bulb hanging from the ceiling, beginning to suspect where this was going.

"And now you're here."

"Meaning?"

"Perhaps you've got something up your sleeve?"

"I wouldn't say that."

"Come now, pet. Don't be coy."

"I don't know what you're talking about." Now Charlie had good reason to check her watch. Jake was late and this woman was beginning to get on her nerves.

Connie's eyes shone, already salivating at the morsel she planned to drag out of her. "How about a little heads-up, love?" she murmured in her ear. "Just between friends…"

Charlie motioned that she couldn't hear her.

Her rival's eyes turned to flint. "You clearly don't know how things work around here, do you pet? On this beat, we look out for each other."

Looking at Connie's thin, angry lips and the greed in her eyes, Charlie very much doubted that. However, she decided that, in this case, silence was the best policy.

"Come on," Connie pressed. "All I'm asking for is a little collegiality! You lot always complain about being excluded but you never learn how to play the game!"

A familiar heat rose in Charlie's chest, but she kept her anger in check. "You lot?"

"Don't get your knickers in a twist, love! All I meant was –"

"I know what you meant."

Connie's face flushed. "Don't you look at me like that. I've always stood up for people like you. Fought for your right to be here. So, don't make me out to be one of them!"

"I have every right to be here. I was born in Hammersmith. Come to think of it, though," Charlie looked her up and down, "*you* seem foreign. Must be the Mediterranean colouring. Is that where you're from?"

"Fine," Connie pursed her lips, tossing her head dismissively. "Have it your way. But it's cold all on your own, pet. Don't say I didn't warn you."

As Connie stormed away like an angry peacock, Charlie slowly shook her head.

"What was that about?" Jake said as he came up behind her, passing Connie going in the opposite direction.

"Just another Karen," Charlie replied, fuming. "Someone should really tell them the days of the empire are over."

"What?" he said with mock horror. "And ruin their world of alternative facts?"

Charlie smiled, despite herself.

"I'd watch out for Connie, though," he said, growing serious. "She can be a real bitch, that one. Cut you without you even knowing it. Got some powerful friends, too."

"Thanks," she said, grateful for the steer. "I'll keep that in mind." Taking him in, she was surprised at how harried he looked, his hair dishevelled, the shirt underneath his coat looking like it needed pressing. "What happened to you? The bosses at Business Today taking you through the wringer?"

"Pulled an all-nighter," he said with a lop-sided grin, straightening up his shirt.

She hadn't noticed before how handsome he looked when he smiled. The effect was slightly unnerving.

Cut it out, Charlie. That's not what you're here for.

A roar came up from the crowd, both of them turning towards the ring just in time to see a blood-drenched, headless chicken falling to the ground. Charlie's stomach heaved.

"Come on," Jake said softly. "Let's get away from all this mess."

He led her to a room off the main basement, a few metres down from the cock fight. It looked like an old, disused ice cellar, four metres square with no windows. Given that the feeding shoot had long been blocked up, the only light, and warmth, came from the doorway. Following Jake into the chamber, Charlie suddenly missed being surrounded by hot-blooded bodies, even ones she despised. So, she stopped just inside the open door, for the light and the flow of warm air from the room beyond, zipping up her bomber jacket and thrusting her cold hands in her pockets.

"So, to what do I owe the pleasure?" Jake said as he buttoned up his coat.

"I need help on the Murdoch story."

"Yikes! You still working on that?!" His eyes sparkled with mischief. "You'd gone so quiet I thought you'd reached a dead end."

She ignored the dig. "Ever met a guy called Michael Develin?"

"The one who used to work at Yeats?"

"Yeah – that's the one. What can you tell me about him?"

"Why? You think he had something to do with Murdoch going missing?"

"Maybe, maybe not. It's too early to tell."

"All right," Jake clearly didn't believe her, but he didn't push it. "Why are you asking me, though? What's wrong with the guys at your own shop?"

What could she say – that they weren't as specialised? Or perhaps she should just tell him the truth? That, apart from Bulldog, the rest of the business team at The Torch were a bunch of racist shits who, already pissed that she'd gotten one over them, would eat their own mothers before giving her any kind of help? No, their relationship was still too new for such bold truths. At the same time, it was also still too precious for lies. Better stick to the grey lands.

"Well," she huffed as she half turned towards the exit, "if you don't want to help, just say so."

"Wait!" He gently grabbed her wrist, then dropped it like he'd been scalded, looking at his hand and her as if he was seeing both of them for the first time.

Charlie looked away, quickly folding her arms in front of her chest, partly to dispel the electric shock that had shot up her arm and partly to mitigate against further contact.

Whatever this was, it was the last thing she needed.

Jake recovered quickly. "I...um...didn't say that. I was just curious, that's all."

She glared at him defiantly, determined not to show weakness.

Taking in her unwavering posture, Jake adjusted his own, becoming all business. "What do I get if I tell you?"

"Not much to share at the mo. Just a whole bunch of coincidences and allegations that may lead to nowhere."

"But you wouldn't be here if..."

"If I didn't think there was something there? True." She scratched her chin, reviewing her options. "Ok - how about this? I cover crime. I'm not that interested in the financial ins and outs of this case unless they relate to my murder, so -"

"Murder?" Jake tensed, his eyes now hyper-alert.

"Isn't that the most likely explanation?" Charlie replied, nonchalant.

"But what makes you…?"

"As I said, I've got no proof. Not yet anyway." She paused, sensing someone hovering outside the door. Signalling Jake to be quiet, she stepped into the main chamber. The area around the door was empty. Everyone was still gathered further up the basement, all appearing to be focused on the latest battle. "Sorry about that," she said as she came back into the room. "Must have been my imagination." Charlie glanced back into the chamber, still feeling unsettled. "Anyway, as I was saying, I'll focus on the murder. Anything not directly related to that, I'll share with you. Along with my guys, of course. That sound fair?"

"Sounds cool but…" his eyes narrowed, "what's the catch?"

He was good. Not many managed to keep up.

"Only if your info delivers. No free lunches."

"And how will I know if it delivers?"

"I'll tell you."

He thought about it for a moment. "That means I have to trust you."

"Yep. Like I'm trusting you now."

He mulled it over once more, looking down, then at the door, before finally returning to her face. Charlie rocked on her haunches, playing it cool, not wanting him to know how much she needed him.

"Ok, I guess you've got a point," he said. "But then you only work with me. No secret deals with anyone else."

She had to laugh. "Like who? Battle-axe Connie?"

"Connie or whoever else." Jake's face said he wasn't playing.

She hadn't anyone else in mind but appearing to make a concession never hurt.

"Sure," she said pleasantly, "you have my word."

"All right, you've got a deal," Pulling his coat even tighter, he started walking the room's perimeter to keep warm.

Wondering why she hadn't thought of that before, Charlie eagerly joined him. "So, do you?"

"Do I what?"

"Know Michael Develin?"

"Oh – right," another boyish grin. "Yeah, but we weren't close. Never quite seemed to hit it off. Though, I know enough if you know what I mean."

"Are you referring to his being pushed out of Yeats?"

"Yep. Develin wasn't a choir boy, but I never thought he'd throw everything away like that." Jake shook his head in bewilderment.

"And if I said 'P' and Develin in the same breath, what would you say?"

"Just 'P'?"

"Yes."

Jake chewed his lip. "The only thing I can think of is his ex - Portia."

"You sure?"

"That's the only P I know. Dumped him soon after Develin got the boot."

First Viper, now Jake. As unlikely as it seemed, they both couldn't be wrong, could they? Anyway, a lead was a lead. Best move on to the next thing.

As they rounded the corner, Charlie didn't swivel fast enough, forcing her to jump away to avoid their shoulders colliding. Jake pretended not to notice.

"That brings me to my other question," she said. "What do you know about Black Boxes?"

His brows shot up in surprise, "As in aircraft?"

"No – as in the banking sector."

"Mmmm…never heard bankers use that term before," he said pensively, "but I *have* heard some other people use it to refer to an anonymous trust."

"And that is?"

"A trust whose ownership can't be traced. Normally set up via lawyers and other intermediaries. They're also usually located in tax havens governed by regulatory frameworks that favour those seeking…shall we say…a high level of discretion."

"You mean for storing dirty cash and tax dodging, that sort of thing?"

He let out a short, half-suppressed laugh, "If you want to be blunt about it!"

Again, Charlie ignored his teasing. After all, she had always thought not beating about the bush was one of her greater virtues. "And are we talking thousands or millions, here? On average?"

Jake shrugged, "Hundreds of millions. Sometimes billions. Otherwise, it wouldn't be worth the cost or the effort."

So, Murdoch had a secret stash after all. Lucy had told the police that Murdoch didn't have any offshore accounts, but what if she'd been lying? More importantly, whilst Murdoch had been paid well, his salary and bonuses alone wouldn't have amounted to that much extra cash. So, where had he gotten that kind of money?

"Do you know if Murdoch has a side hustle?"

"Like what?"

"I don't know. Anything that would bring in some extra cash."

He went quiet for a bit then shook his head, "Not really. I'm sure you already know that he was a bit of a gambler but…"

"Yeah. I know. Unlikely. He would have had to be very, very good to get such a payload…" Charlie's voice trailed off, her mind working overtime.

Murdoch must have been up to something. Something extremely lucrative but which also required a high degree of secrecy. Lucy must have known about it, or at least enough to know her husband had a Black Box. And so had Develin. Yet, if that was the case, why would Develin have needed Lucy's help?

"Coming back to Black Boxes," she continued. "If I wanted to find one, how would I do it?"

"Well, it wouldn't be easy. You'd have to find out where it was and then find someone in the value chain willing to fold. A lawyer or one of the other intermediaries."

"And once I'd found it? What could I do then?"

Jake smiled, "That would depend."

"On what?"

"Your motive."

30. Woodhead

Fulham
London, UK

Patrick Woodhead sounded far nicer on the phone than he was in person. His cyber persona was jovial and self-deprecating, conjuring up images of a jolly, cuddly man who had plainly been misplaced in the cut-throat world of finance. Yet, as Charlie had greeted him at the bookshop entrance, she had realised that Mr Jolly was just an elaborate act. True, on the surface, the warmth in his voice and the smile on his face had stayed firmly in place. The problem was his eyes. Always calculating, appraising, taking your measure.

He had insisted on meeting at his current place of work, a small independent bookshop in Fulham. An unusual request given that most people she interviewed preferred more private haunts. Yet his reasons had become clear when she had walked in to find him alone, dusting the shelves of what was obviously a much loved but infrequently visited establishment.

With still Develin refusing to talk to her, Charlie had opted for the next best thing. A colleague who had left the bank under the same cloud, hoping he could tell her more about the man she sought and what drove him. Expecting to encounter a high level of reticence, she had been surprised to find that the former Yeats CRO had been more than willing to chat. Extremely keen in fact. Like Develin, there was plainly no love lost between Woodhead and Murdoch.

The Meanness of Things

"Thanks for agreeing to see me, Mr Woodhead," she said, starting with the usual formalities.

"Not at all," he carried on dusting, clearly wanting to let her know that she was in the presence of a man whose time was precious. "And please – call me Woody."

She took out her phone and pressed record. "Ok, Woody. I'm -"

He glanced at the phone, his face perturbed. "I thought this was going to be off the record?"

"It is. But I like to tape my interviews, so I don't misrepresent anything people say. Assuming I end up using what they tell me, of course."

"Of course," Woodhead smiled like a man in no doubt that she and the whole world would be dying to hear what *he* had to say.

"All right then, Woody," she said, pressing record. "As I said on the phone, as part of looking into Murdoch's disappearance, I'd like to find out more about how Yeats operates as well as the experience of you and your colleagues there, particularly under Murdoch's leadership."

"You want to know about the bank in general or specifically why I left?"

"Both. If any of your old colleagues also left around the same time, it would be useful to know why too."

"You mean Michael Develin?"

"Whoever and whatever you think is relevant," she replied innocently.

"All right. Fire away." He went up a small ladder to dust the top shelf, forcing her to look up at him.

"How does a private bank like Yeats differ from a high-street retail bank?"

"They don't have walk-in branches and their clientele is almost solely composed of extremely rich private individuals or the businesses of those clients. In addition to state-of-the-art banking, such individuals value privacy and discretion and banks like Yeats give it to them."

Charlie thought of Jake and what he had said about discretion. "Why is discretion so important?"

He rolled his eyes. "The filthy rich don't get filthy rich by playing on the up and up, dearie. And London didn't become the financial centre of the world by doing so either."

"But surely Bank of England regulations prevent -"

"Yes. On the surface. The appearance of probity and the rule of law blah, blah, blah. It's what happens underneath that matters. Why do you think the City of London is not legally part of the United Kingdom?"

"Are you saying that Yeats is a crooked bank?"

"Not crooked *per se*. I'm saying that the global financial services sector *as a whole* is singularly focused on maximising profit and that often means always staying one step ahead of the regulators. I'm also saying that Yeats is a private bank that operates like many private banks across the globe. It just happens to be better at it than most."

Charlie found herself struggling to keep up, "Better at what?"

"Undetectable wealth storage, accumulation, and preservation. Including, naturally, the optimisation of capital and capital flows. The latter, largely from the global south to the global north." The top shelf done, he stepped down and turned his attention to the next column.

"In English?" Charlie said, wishing she could get him to stop dusting and stand still for a minute.

"Just like I said. Helping rich people syphon, store and maximise dirty or stolen money or evade burdensome tax regimes."

The penny dropped, "You mean money laundering?"

He stopped dusting, turning towards her, "Money laundering is just one aspect of it. There's also tax evasion, fraud, evading international sanctions etc. Haven't you heard about the Panama Papers?"

"Of course I have," she replied, irritated at the condescension. "But what *you* are saying is that kind of thing is the rule, not the exception. If that were the case, then everyone would have known that Murdoch's money laundering investigation was a scam. The BoE, Serious Fraud Office, all of them. Is that really what you're suggesting?"

He smiled like a teacher explaining the basics to a rather dull pupil, "Don't get ahead of yourself. A system designed to facilitate capital flows to the benefit of elites is one thing. Individuals going rogue is another thing entirely."

"Really?" she said sarcastically. "So, corporate stealing is fine, but employee theft is not?"

"In a nutshell, yes."

The doorbell tolled and an old lady shuffled into the shop with the air of someone who was a regular. Greeting her with what Charlie assumed was supposed to be a smile, Woodhead put the dust cloth away, told the client to shout if she needed anything and led Charlie to a makeshift kitchen where he sat at a small table in the middle of the room, inviting her to join him.

"Think of every banking scandal you've ever known," he said, plucking an apple out of the fruit bowl in the centre of the table. "It always comes down to 'bad apples', doesn't it? No one ever acknowledges the nature of the system that put those guys in those positions in the first place. The system that created the environment where they were able to do what they did."

Was Woodhead trying to exonerate himself or had his departure from Yeats been more complicated?

"Let's come to you now,' Charlie said, taking out her notebook. "Why did you leave the bank?"

He put the apple back in the bowl. "I was pushed out," he said, his face grim. "By Murdoch."

"Why?"

Woodhead's nostrils flared, "Because he's a conniving little shit."

Use of the present tense. Did he think Murdoch was still alive or was he just pretending to hide what he knew?

"He ran around thinking everyone was fooled by his soft voice and cultivated charm," Woodhead continued, his voice full of scorn, "but I saw through him from the start."

"So, it wasn't Murdoch who appointed you to the Chief Risk Officer position?"

He laughed bitterly. "No way! It was the previous boss – Anthony Phillips. Now he was the real deal. Full of class and smart too. But that was also his weakness – he never saw past Derrick's brilliance into his dark, murky soul. Anthony was the reason Derrick made such a meteoric rise in the bank and when he decided to retire, he anointed Derrick as his successor."

"Who else was on the Exco when Derrick became CEO of the division?"

"Myself, Michael, the Head of Private Clients, Steven the CFO and John Hilary the Chief Operating Officer."

"Was that it?"

"No, there was also the Chief Investment Officer and the Strategy Head. However, when the previous incumbents – Daniel and Fry – heard that Anthony was going to retire, they decided to transfer to other parts of the Bank. Derrick replaced them with two women – Margaret Ashwood and Trudy Dickens."

She had to say it, "Two women in an all-male team. That must have been a first!"

'Surely was," he pulled a face. "Derrick playing Mr Perfect."

Charlie frowned. Something didn't add up. "Wasn't Murdoch appointed about three years ago?" Woody nodded. "And you've only been out of the bank for just over a year?" He nodded again. "Then, if you saw through him from the start, why didn't you leave earlier?"

"Right," he shifted in his chair, "Well, perhaps I exaggerated a bit."

A bit?

"I did suspect from the start that I couldn't entirely trust him, but he started off alright, to tell you the truth. Making everyone feel at home, going out of his way to build relationships with the existing team."

"Then things started to change?"

"Yeah, though I didn't notice it at first. It was only when the investigation started, and he began going after me and Michael that I suddenly realised what had been going on. How he had been subtly grooming the people beneath us whilst getting the other Exco members on his side. You know how it works – giving out extra bonuses, singling people out for extra perks, that sort of thing."

"Playing favourites," she said with a shrug. "Nothing unusual about that."

"No, it was more than that," Woodhead insisted. "He wanted to secure their loyalty. Not to the bank but to him personally. Once they were on the hook, he knew he could ask them to do anything, and they would."

"And did it work?"

"Let's put it this way, nobody spoke up when Derrick went after us."

"What about Hilary? The guy who's now acting CEO of the division."

"Hilary wasn't going to put his neck out for us, but he wasn't a Derrick fan either. He never went against him, but I always got the sense that he didn't trust him. I suspect the feeling was mutual, but Hilary was too close to the Group CEO for Derrick to mess with him. So, I guess they had to tolerate each other."

"What about the people he'd been…" Charlie flipped through her notes, "…*grooming* as you put it?"

His eyes grew stormy. "Total gob-shite back-stabbers, the both of them! Main witnesses in a bloody kangaroo court! Even after all we'd done for them too, nurturing and supporting them! Only for them to fuck us over and get our jobs as their bloody reward!"

Whilst he was prone to exaggerate, his fury was certainly genuine. The question was, was the story that fuelled it?

"You're referring to the investigation? Whose sole purpose was to get you out?"

"Yeah, that's right."

Charlie didn't immediately respond. Again, something didn't add up. "I'm sorry," she said after going through her notes a second time, "but I still don't understand why? Why did Murdoch need to push you out?"

He leaned forward, agitated, "Don't you get it? Derrick knew we wouldn't go along!"

"Go along with what?"

"With what he was planning!"

"And what was that exactly?"

Woodhead looked away.

"Look,' she said softly, "if you want people to believe you were set up, you're going to have to give me something more than this."

Silence.

She waited.

A beat, then another.

When he finally faced her, the anger and hubris was gone, replaced with what looked like sadness and humility. "I know this sounds weak," he murmured, "but I was forced out before I could find out all the details. But he was up to something, I'm sure of it."

Charlie sighed and went to close her notebook.

"Listen!" Woodhead pleaded, "Just hear me out." He glanced nervously towards the main part of the shop to make sure his customer wasn't hovering anywhere nearby. "In the months before he announced the investigation, Murdoch started acting strange. More secretive, guarded. Then Michael stumbled across some large transactions listed against his name. The problem was, he'd never seen them before. He rang me, asking what he should do. A few weeks later, we were both suspended and under investigation for misconduct."

Finally, something tangible.

"Do you remember what those transactions were?"

"No, but Develin would. If you want a better sense of what Derrick might have been up to, you should definitely talk to him."

I've tried.

"And that's it? You don't remember anything more than that?"

"Only what Michael told me. But, like I said, you have to speak to him."

"And he never mentioned a Black Box to you?"

"No," Woodhead said emphatically.

Charlie searched his face, trying to assess if he was holding anything back. Didn't look like it.

Time to move on.

"Talking of Develin," she replied, "I take it, you and he were close?"

"Not really. Being stiffed up brought us closer though. For a time."

"He must hate Murdoch as much as you do. Perhaps even more so?"

"Can you blame him?" Woodhead turned his head towards the front of the store as the bell clanged, his only customer eventually making a purchase less exit.

"Enough to have him kidnapped?" she asked casually.

His head snapped back towards her, "Michael? Kidnapping? Whatever for?"

"I don't know," she said lightly. "Revenge, maybe?"

Woodhead barked with laughter. "Not bloody likely! Michael would have thought death would be too good for him. Nah – if he wanted revenge, he would have planned something far worse than that."

"What could be worse than kidnapping and murder?"

"Taking everything away from him, that's what. Everything and everybody he ever cared about. Until he wished he were dead. Trust me – I know." He looked down at his hands, but not before she had seen the sudden anguish in his eyes.

Either Woodhead was a very good actor, or he genuinely believed what he was saying. She decided to push him a little.

"Ok. Coming back to you. How long have you worked at this book shop?"

An embarrassed blush spread across his cheeks, "A while. Why?"

"It's quite a change from what you were doing."

"I didn't have a choice. Once the rumour mill got going regarding why I left, no other bank would touch me."

"Must have been quite a difficult time for you, then."

Woodhead bristled. "What's that got to do with anything?"

"Nothing. I was just -"

"Hold on," he said, comprehension dawning. "Are you implying that I had something to do with Murdoch's disappearance? First, you accuse Michael and now me?!"

Charlie prevaricated, "No. Not all. I -"

"Listen you…" His voice was clipped, his eyes enraged. "I only agreed to talk to you so I could tell my side of the story. Not to listen to you make stupid, wild allegations!" He jumped to his feet, his chair scrapping across the floor behind him.

Again, Charlie protested, but Woodhead was having none of it. Storming out of the kitchen and to the shop entrance, he pointedly held the door open for her. "I think I've given you enough for your story," he said stonily. "Now, if you'll excuse me, I have to get back to work."

Charlie did as she was bid, thanking him for his time and turning off the recorder as she left. The interview had ended abruptly but that was okay. She had gotten what she wanted.

31. Famished

The Savoy
London, UK

The pavement was packed, people rushing to grab a bite, do some lunchtime shopping or touring the London sights. He hadn't ventured out in the middle of the day for a while, so he'd almost forgotten how busy it got and, more importantly, how uncompromising people could be as they fought for their space in the throng.

"Have you got a minute?" Hilary asked, stepping aside for a young lady as she darted into the chemists.

"Where are you?" Spencer replied. "Sounds like you're in the street."

"I am," Hilary deftly dodged an octogenarian tourist staring at a map who suddenly stopped right in front of him. "Stepped out to pick up some lunch and get a bit of fresh air," as a red double-decker bus zoomed past, he raised his voice and pressed the phone to his ear. "Thought I would give you an update on Murdoch on the way."

"All right. Though I should warn you - I'm about to set out for a quick nine holes."

"Don't worry. I'll be quick." He walked past a clothing store, the shopfront adorned with neon and black like a bad eighties flashback. Whilst Hilary got why the fashion industry kept recycling old trends, he had never understood why everyone fell for it. "I've finished my prelim assessment and I think we need to call in an external team."

"Oh?" For a second, Spencer's voice sounded strangled though it could have just been the connection. "Have you found something?"

"More of an absence, really. Remember Derrick's money laundering investigation?"

"Of course. The one we got all those accolades for."

"Then you'll also remember that, at the time, the people Derrick fingered also claimed it was a smokescreen?"

Spencer scoffed. "They were just saving their own skin like they always do. What of it?"

"Well, I think they might have been right."

"Right?" Spencer's voice rang with measured alarm. "Why?"

"Critical pieces of evidence central to the case are missing. And when I say missing, I'm talking about both electronic and analogue records. As you know, normally, if something goes wrong with one, the other record acts as a backup. For both types of records to go missing in all the six transactions involved is unheard of."

Passing the Adelphi Theatre, Hilary glanced at the latest production being staged and grimaced. Slap-up comedies always seemed so vulgar.

"Didn't the investigation also include witnesses?" Spencer said. "Surely, they can attest to what went on?"

"That's the thing. Without the documents, their testimony is flimsy at best and, at worst, simply not credible. I won't bore you with the details, but I smell collusion."

Spencer's exhale was long and heavy. "How bad?"

"Two, maybe three members of Exco. Perhaps some juniors too."

"Including Murdoch?"

"I believe so."

Spencer was quiet for so long, Hilary began to wonder if the connection had been lost.

"Are you sure?" he finally said.

"Yes. Of course, I'm sure."

"I mean - only those?"

"Yes – as far as I can tell."

"Good. We need to ringfence this as much as possible."

"Agreed," Hilary looked left and right as he crossed the road.

"Do you know why they did it?" Spencer asked.

"Not yet, no. But I intend to call in McIntyre and Faith to do an in-depth forensic probe. Phones, personal bank accounts, movements, as well as scouring our own systems. Get to the bottom of this quickly and surgically."

"Oh, is that really necessary? We don't want to stir up any unnecessary fuss. Can't we just handle this in-house?"

Hilary was so surprised, he stopped dead. "But...um...can our team handle this with everything else on their plate? Surely, an external outfit –"

"No, no. Pass in onto Group Internal Audit. Let them decide if they need external help."

"But -"

"That's settled then," Spencer said airily. "Let me know if they give you any trouble."

Reluctantly, Hilary swallowed his disquiet. "Ok. Will do." Having delivered his update, he was just about to sign off when Spencer took the conversation in an unexpected direction.

"And your colleagues? The ones you think are involved. What are you going to do about them in the interim?"

Hadn't thought of that. Would they suspect he was on to them after just a few interviews? Probably not. Then again, Jonathan's sudden elusiveness certainly suggested that at least one of them suspected something was amiss. Which, come to think of it, could prove to be a good thing.

"Act as if it's business as usual," Hilary replied, setting off again. "Like I've lost interest in the matter."

"You think they'll really be convinced by that?"

"Even if they're not, sometimes the best way of getting people to incriminate themselves is to leave them in suspense. Wait and see what happens."

"That's true," Spencer said slowly, brooding. "I have to say. This is not the best news I've received this morning."

"Don't worry. Whatever Derrick and his collaborators have been up to, I'll get to the bottom of it and clear it up before the press gets wind of it."

"Talking of press, Tate's been quiet for a while. Any chance she's moved on to bigger fish?"

"Not at all. Sam says she's still digging around like a bloody termite. She's spoken to Fry, but he dropped out of the picture well before the money laundering investigation, so no worries there. She's also tried to get hold of Michael and spoken to Patrick, but I doubt that will lead to much either. After all, if they'd had any evidence to prove their innocence, they would have produced it long ago. I think she's going to be more of an annoyance than a real threat. A Chihuahua snapping at the heels of a Rottweiler." As Spencer chuckled in response, Hilary smiled to himself, basking in the wit of his own analogy.

In the background, he heard Spencer's PA chiding him about being late. "Oops – got to go, old chap. My real boss is calling. Keep up the great work. And you'll keep me in the loop, I take it?"

"Absolutely." Hilary pocketed his phone and quickened his pace, warmed by Spencer's praise. Passing an Italian restaurant, he saw a plate of Osso

Bucco being served to a patron sitting by the window and salivated at the sight. Being on the hunt always made him famished.

As Hilary turned the corner and headed for the covered entrance of the Savoy Hotel, the gold statue of the Earl of Richmond looked down at him imperiously, demanding to know his business there. He thought of the peasants who had once charged down the strand and burnt the Savoy Palace to the ground. Even if his ancestors had not been there that fateful day, they would certainly have identified with the cause. Yet, his father had wanted something different for his son. No more being at the bottom of the pecking order railing against the elites but to become one of them. And he hadn't disappointed. Despite not having an old-school tie, despite everything, he had succeeded. The next leg on his journey to the summit was to be appointed as divisional CEO and he was so close, he could actually taste it. Just a few things to square away and the job would be his.

Feeling on top of the world, Hilary raised a mental middle finger at the golden Earl, set his peasant-stock shoulders and strode boldly into the plush hotel lobby.

32. Alone

Strand Temple
London, UK

T he old Tudor pub was packed, body heat and ambition filling the air as city boys laughed, plotted, and schemed, encased in glass, timbre, wattle, and daub. The scene was almost ethereal with the brass lamps sitting on the tables and festooned on the walls, draping the pub's patrons in a warm, amber glow. However, the homely atmosphere offered little respite for the chill in Jonathan's heart.

Resting his elbows on their table, his eyes scanned their surroundings, trying to see if any of their colleagues were present in the throng. Not that it would have made much difference. From afar, Reuben and he must have looked like two friends out for a drink after a long day, huddled over their lagers, engaged in excited conversation. Nevertheless, knowing they were unobserved still made him more comfortable.

"We're being stiffed, I'm telling you," Jonathan hissed. "Now Derrick's gone, the vultures are closing in!"

"Don't you think you're overreacting?" Reuben said, taking a sip of lager. "My meeting with Hilary went fine. And Steven's too, as far as I can tell."

"Have you spoken to him?"

"Steven?" His companion sat back in his chair and stretched out his legs. "Not recently. But he would have warned us if he felt things were about to go south."

"Are you sure of that?"

Reuben looked puzzled. "What's gotten into you?"

"When I last spoke to him - just after Derrick's news broke - he was decidedly offish. Almost as if he wanted nothing to do with me…I mean, with us."

"Well, he's been perfectly normal with me. I really do think you're seeing ghosts that don't exist."

Fine – find out the hard way.

"And from what you've told me," Reuben continued, "the questions put to you seem to have been fairly standard."

"But you weren't there, Reuben. Hilary had that look in his eyes. Like… like a predator eyeing its prey. The questions may have appeared innocent, but I think he knows far more than he's saying."

"But you don't *know* that do you?"

"Doesn't it worry you, though?" Jonathan scanned the room again, leaning in closer. "If they start sniffing around…"

"And they'll find what?" Reuben said dismissively. "You can't disprove a negative or blame someone for their faulty memory."

Jonathan took a large swig of Guinness.

"What?" Reuben looked at him askance, "I assume you were equally careful?"

"I thought I was but now I'm not so sure," He ran his hand through his hair, a nervous habit he had never been able to break. "But without the original records of those transactions, people may say you and I made the whole thing up."

"Don't be silly," Reuben scoffed. "It was all in the forensic report!"

Jonathan shook his head. "You're not getting what I'm saying. Did you study those transactions? I mean in detail. Or did you just go on the list that Derrick showed you in his office?"

"Derrick's list, of course. The transactions he said had been uncovered by the forensic team."

"And he never gave you the prelim report itself?"

"No." Reuben replied. "Did he give it to you?"

"No."

"But we didn't need to study it," Reuben insisted. "I just had to confirm that I had never seen those transactions before. I thought you'd done the same thing?"

"Some. I confirmed that those types of transactions would be irregular, and that Michael had never shared them with me."

"And that's all you said? In your statement, that is?"

"More or less."

Reuben triumphantly slapped the table. "Then, what's the issue? You just responded to the information you were given. If that information now proves to have been false, no one can blame you for that. Just like we discussed."

Jonathan made a face, feeling sick inside. "Maybe Hilary and the top brass will take that view, and maybe they won't. You, Steven, and I are the ones who testified under oath, remember? Derrick didn't. And he's no longer around to explain himself."

And he never would be if what he'd overheard Tate saying the other day in the fish shop basement was true. Murder? He couldn't believe it! And guess what would happen once Hilary took the throne?

"Someone's passing the buck, I tell you," Jonathan continued. "Getting rid of those records to make *us* the fall guys."

Reuben took another sip of larger, eyeing Jonathan over the rim of his glass. "Don't you mean you?" he said quietly.

"What?"

"To make *you* the fall guy."

Jonathan nearly choked on his Guinness, "What do you mean by that?"

"Well, since you're in Private Clients, you would have been more likely than Steven and me to know whether those transactions existed on not. So, I can imagine that -"

He'd never been quick to violence, knowing how one rash altercation could turn your whole life upside down. Yet, for the first time in his adult life, Jonathan actually felt the blood boiling in his veins. Reaching across the table, he grabbed Reuben by the collar and dragged him forward, batting off his attempts to resist.

"Now, look here," he whispered in Reuben's ear. "If you think you're going to save your skin and leave me hanging, you've got another thing coming. I know what you did, and I know what you've *been* doing since. So, if I go down, I won't be going down alone!"

Jonathan let go and pushed his colleague backwards. Reuben landed with a thump in his seat, his face red, his eyes astonished. "Jesus Christ! Chill, ok?" He tried to compose himself, straightening his tie and smoothing down his rumpled shirt as he smiled broadly at those around them, combatting the curious glances thrown their way. "All I was saying is, *you're* the one who's freaking out. I didn't mean anything by it."

"I mean it, Reuben," Jonathan said through gritted teeth. "Don't underestimate me." He inhaled, attempting to get a hold of his anger. As far as he could tell, people were quickly losing interest, perhaps taking their interaction as just a bit of robust banter. Which was just as well.

"I wouldn't dream of it," the CRO replied earnestly. "Let's just keep our heads down and stick to our story, all right? And who knows? If it turns out those transactions were actually fake, perhaps whoever deleted them was doing us a favour. Scrubbing the evidence, so to speak."

Jonathan scowled, "Maybe."

"Cheer up! We musketeers are in this together, remember?" Reuben grinned as he lifted his glass for a toast. "All for one, and one for all!"

Reluctantly, Jonathan clinked his glass against his. He had never felt more alone in his life.

33. 'P' AND THE BLACK BOX

Clapham
London, UK

Viper's email had been brief and to the point. According to her friend's contacts, Murdoch's disappearance was not in line with Sparrow's modus operandi. Not only did he prefer to take care of business on home ground, he also liked to make an example of his kills as a deterrent. Someone simply vanishing into thin air was way too subtle for Sparrow. Furthermore, they insisted that Sparrow only acted with purpose, either to take forward an agenda or forestall a threat. So, as much as Develin and he remained close, they thought it was highly unlikely that Sparrow would get involved in a personal vendetta. Especially, one that carried the added risk of operating in someone else's territory i.e. Johannesburg, South Africa. In short, whilst Sparrow theoretically had the means to help Develin and Lucy kidnap and murder Murdoch, the probability of him having actually done so was close to zero. Which left her stuck with lots of motives but still no means. Hence, Charlie had gone back out on the streets, looking for the one man who could make sense of it all.

Finding out his new address hadn't been easy but, once she had, it had simply been a matter of patience. She hadn't wanted to approach him at home or on the street, fearing he'd wouldn't let her in or simply walk away like he'd done before. So, she'd had to wait until he was in a place where she could corner him, even if only for a little while. Thus, when she'd finally seen him walking across Clapham High Street and into an Indian restaurant, she'd known it was time to make her move.

The place was almost empty when she entered, the only clientele, apart from her target, being a young couple staring into each other's eyes like love-struck puppies. Hindustani music tinkled quietly in the background as two male waiters dressed in white Jodhpuris hovered amongst the tables, ready to meet their guests' every need.

Her quarry sat at a four-seater table in the far corner, sipping a pint of beer and eating poppadoms as he perused the menu. When a waiter approached her enquiringly, Charlie signalled that she was joining someone. Then, trying not to draw attention to herself, she casually wove her way towards him.

Develin must have sensed danger since, when she was nearly upon him, he looked up, the shock on his face turning to a glower. Putting down the menu, his eyes flicked past her to the entrance and then left and right like he was searching for an escape route. Finding none, his body tensed, his eyes stony.

"What the fuck are you doing here?" he asked when she arrived at his table.

"I apologise, I don't mean to intrude," Charlie said with what she hoped was a beguiling smile. "It's just that I really need to talk you."

"I already told you to leave me alone."

"I know but…" Not wanting to tower over him, she glanced at the empty seat opposite him, wondering if she should try and sit down. "I was wondering if -"

"Piss off!" He picked up the menu again, refusing to look at her. "I've got nothing to say to you, alright?"

A waiter anxiously scurried over to them, a second menu in hand. "Is there a problem here?"

"No," Develin said without looking up. "Ms Nosey Pants was just leaving."

"Woody sent me." Charlie quickly interjected. Given how they had parted, she crossed her fingers behind her back, praying he and Woodhead hadn't yet spoken. "He said I should talk to you."

Develin's head shot up, "Patrick Woodhead?"

"Yes."

Some tension eased out of Develin's shoulders, but the hostility and mistrust remained. "And why would Woody talk to you?"

The waiter hovered, looking at each of them uncertainly.

Charlie pressed her advantage. "He said he wanted…no…*needed* to tell his side of the story. Expose Murdoch for who he really is."

Develin didn't reply, searching her face as if wondering whether she was telling the truth.

The waiter glanced at the young couple who were now watching the scene with interest and stepped closer to them, his voice urgent. "If there's going to be trouble, I'll have to call the police."

Charlie ignored him. "I also spoke to Fry. I think I know who Murdoch was, what he did. Help me tell that story."

Develin looked at the couple then back at her before finally responding with a curt nod. "It's ok, Rashid," he said to the waiter, "just a misunderstanding. Please give us a few moments."

Rashid didn't look convinced but he smiled politely, nevertheless. "Please let me know when you're ready to order," he said, placing the menu on the table.

As Rashid left, Develin jerked his head towards the seat opposite him, signalling for her to sit.

"So, did Woody get what he wanted?" Develin said, crossing his arms over his chest, his eyes guarded. "I've checked your stories, love and, apart from those questions you raised at the beginning, I haven't seen anything about the bank."

"That's why I need to speak to you. For corroboration." Charlie put her notebook and phone on the table. "Woody said that Murdoch had been up to something which is why he pushed you both out. He said you'd be able to tell me what it was."

"And Fry?"

"His reason was more personal."

"Then you know about Becky?"

"Yes."

"Why haven't you published it, then? Not like a journo to keep quiet about a salacious story like that!"

Charlie looked at him askance. "Fry didn't tell me because he wanted his daughter's story in the media. He told me because he wanted me to know the kind of man Murdoch was given I'm trying to find the reason for his disappearance. Whilst the nature of his character may be central to that, imposing unwanted media attention on his victims would serve no purpose."

"Really?" He unfolded his arms and sat forward, resting his elbows on the tabletop, mistrust replaced by surprise. "Then you must be one of a kind, Ms Tate."

"Meaning?"

"A journalist with principles."

"Not so rare, if you must know," Charlie said primly. "But I'll take that as a compliment."

Develin ran a hand over his face. For the first time, she noticed how tired he looked. "Ok," he said, "I'll give you the benefit of the doubt. Now, give me your phone."

She put a protective hand over her mobile. "Why?"

"So, I can check you're not recording."

Putting in her pin, she slid it over to him. After he had flicked through her apps, Develin handed it back. "Now turn it off completely."

Charlie obliged and went analogue, going to a clean page in her notebook. "Please also know that anything you say to me will be off the record until you give me permission to publish it."

"Better be." Develin's tone left her in no doubt that he meant the threat. "So, how much did Woody tell you, exactly?"

"He said you came to him asking for advice about some transactions that had been listed next to your name, but which weren't yours. And, shortly after that, you were suspended and pushed out. He thinks those transactions had something to do with what Murdoch was up to. He couldn't remember what they were but said you definitely would."

"That all?"

"Yep."

Develin looked down, fiddling with his napkin.

"Well?" Charlie prompted. "Was he right?"

"I remember it like it was yesterday," Develin said, half to himself. "Six transactions, different types of trades. Shares, property, art. All by one client – Jupta Inc." He looked at her then, his face strained. "Problem was, I'd never seen the transactions before, let alone having heard of Jupta Inc. I went to Derrick first, told him that there'd been some kind of mistake. Asked him if he'd taken on any special clients lately that I didn't know about."

"Special clients?" Charlie asked, scribbling fiercely.

"High-value, sensitive private clients. Those who have an interest in keeping their relationship with a foreign bank secret. I handled many of them, but Derrick looked after the biggest and most sensitive ones."

"What did Murdoch say? When you went to him?"

"Claimed to know nothing about it. Said I should leave it with him, and he would look into it."

"So why go to Woody?"

"Because when I told him about it, he looked shifty. Like he was hiding something. So, I went to Woody, partly for advice but to also cover my back. Make sure someone else knew what I'd found."

"And Woody also knew nothing about them? These transactions?"

"Not a thing. He logged a Control Failure Alert on the system, and we started trying to find out what was going on. About a week later, we were both suspended."

"What's a control failure alert?"

"Controls are a bunch of protocols and processes to guard against wrong-doing. When a process or protocol isn't followed, it means the control has failed and you have to log it accordingly."

"Oh, I see. And did you find anything? During that week, I mean?"

"Yes. Not through the bank mind, but through other …let's say…channels." He drained his larger and signalling the waiter for another. "Turned out that Jupta Inc was a front. Though, a front for whom I never got to establish. I also found out that Murdoch was a bad gambler who owed some nasty, powerful people a lot of money. That meant he could be persuaded to do those powerful people favours." Develin smirked. "Of the cleaning variety."

Charlie tried to take it all in. "Murdoch was doing what he then accused you of – money laundering?" She said with incredulity. "And the transactions were his, which he tried to hide under your name?"

"I think so," Develin replied. "He put those trades against my name but didn't use my code, thinking that I wouldn't pick it up. And he nearly got away with it too since I only discovered the trades by chance. I made a mistake in typing my code into the system one day and had to use a name search to find my recent transactions so I could fix the code error. When I went to ask him about what I'd found, he must have realised I'd discover what he'd done sooner or later. So, he decided to take pre-emptive action."

Rashid returned to their table with another larger and, after taking Develin's order, enquired if she wanted anything. When Charlie indicated she wouldn't be staying, he was unable to hide his disappointment. Feeling bad for him, she ordered some more poppadoms, making a mental note to leave a generous tip.

"Why did he get rid of Woody as well?" Charlie asked. "Why not just you?"

"I think he initially thought he could isolate me. Get Woody on his side. Derrick called him in. Asked him why he'd issued a Control Failure Alert for 'a minor as a clerical error'. Woody made it clear he didn't see it that way."

"But if you knew what Murdoch had done, why didn't you guys speak up at the time? Tell people what you'd found?"

"I tried to but, by that point, we were already suspended, and trumped-up charges laid against us. For six fake transactions, to cover up the first lot. So, all we could both do was deny the allegations and say we were being framed. Needless to say, no one believed us. Then, once Derrick got enough of our colleagues to turn against us, we were toast."

Charlie scratched her cheek with her pen, thinking.

Something didn't sit right.

"But why the hu-ha? The big, public campaign?" she asked. "If he was trying to cover up just six transactions, why not get rid of you guys quickly and quietly?"

"Because he wasn't going to stop at six. Those first transactions were just the beginning. Isn't that how all crooks and conmen work? Making those around them believe up is down and left is right? The bigger the crime, the bigger the lie required to hide it."

"How big?"

"Billions big. After he kicked me and Woody out and put his boys in, Murdoch really got greedy. Instead of just doing favours for his friends at Jupta Inc in exchange for forgiving his gambling debts, he started taking kickbacks from other parties as well, housing the money offshore so no one could trace it."

"In a Black Box."

"You might call it that, yes." Develin looked taken aback by her use of the term, his face suddenly suspicious.

"So, have you found it?" Charlie asked eagerly.

At that point, Rashid returned laden with a tray. Cursing his timing, she reigned back her zeal and waited, silently watching the waiter deposit the spread and Develin methodically dish food onto his plate. However, when Develin still had not answered after taking his first bite, she realised a frontal attack might have been a mistake.

Time to go a different route.

"All right," Charlie said, watching him chew. "At least tell me what's Sparrow's got to do with all of this?"

He tried but failed to hide his disquiet. "What do you know about Sparrow?"

"Enough." Her tone was deliberately smug. "I also know he likes eagles."

Develin's eyes narrowed to slits, his voice cool. "You have been snooping around, haven't you?"

"Isn't that what nosey parkers do?" she said with an arched look. "Now, are you going to tell me what you guys meant or not?"

"What if I don't?" he said defiantly.

"I'll just keep digging until I find out." To emphasise her point, she broke off a piece of poppadom, scooped up an indulgent dollop of humus and took a lusty, sumptuous bite.

"Mmmm…" Develin's gaze was part annoyance, part admiration. "I'm sure you would."

He carried on eating, his eyes focused on the food before him, shooting her surreptitious looks now and then as if weighing his choices up in his head. Charlie kept her eyes locked on his face, not speaking, not moving, refusing to yield. Eventually, it was Develin who broke.

"Murdoch's Black Box is in the Cayman Islands. But we still don't know the name of the bank or the account number. A source on the ground promised to get us both, along with correspondence proving that Derrick set up the account. All in exchange for a fee, of course. Cash only, hand-delivered, unmarked bills. Sparrow lent me the cash and organised the drop. The eagle was the first payment."

"And when you find it?" Charlie asked, watching him closely. "What will you do?"

"What the fuck do you think I'm going to do?" he said, his eyes smouldering. "Clear my fucking name, that's what! Expose the motherfucker and get my life back! Pull that snake down from his pedestal and crush his rep so deep in the shit, nothing and no one will save him. Then, when the authorities close all his accounts and pull all his assets as the proceeds of crime, forcing him to slither out from whatever rock he's hiding under, I'll make sure they lock him up and throw away the bloody key!!"

No false notes. Not even one. And he clearly thought Murdoch was still alive. So, Woodhead had been right. Develin hadn't wanted Murdoch dead, just ruined. But what about Lucy?

"I take it Lucy told you that the box was in the Cayman Islands?" Charlie said.

Develin nodded, reigning in his emotions. "That's all she knew but it was enough."

"Why did she tell you? She wouldn't have been able to take the money for herself if you planned to report Murdoch's Black Box to the police. So, if it wasn't the money, what was in it for her?"

Develin's grunted derisively. "She hated her husband almost as much as I did. At one point she may have wanted him dead. Who wouldn't? But, in the absence of that, a chance to see him get his just deserts was too good to resist. Along with knowing that she was doing something that would drive Derrick crazy if he knew."

She read between the lines, "You also had an affair?"

"Not an *affair*, affair. We knew after the first time, we weren't into each other. Call it revenge fucking. Something we felt driven to do. To get back at him and at *her*."

"Her? Are you talking about Portia – your ex-wife?"

"Yeah. After I lost my job, we lost everything. The cars, the houses and, most importantly for Portia, the social status. Four months later, she moved out. One month after that, she asked for a divorce."

Charlie winced, "That must have hurt."

"Not really," he said with a sardonic shrug. "We'd married for the wrong reasons and we both knew it. That's why I didn't contest the divorce. But when she took up with Derrick, I knew I couldn't let that stand. If he was going to take what had been mine, I was going to take what was his."

"What about Victoria?" she asked. "Wasn't Murdoch going to leave Lucy for her?"

Develin sighed, "Poor Vicky. Derrick really strung her along. We all knew it except her."

"Lucy too?"

"Yep."

"And she didn't mind? Her husband being unfaithful?"

"She never said so, but I got the sense she was resigned to it. Perhaps, even grateful. It kept Derrick busy. Allowed her to enjoy being Mrs Murdoch without the…marital obligations."

He didn't talk about Lucy being abused but he didn't have to. His face said it all. "But wasn't Murdoch just using Portia too?" Charlie asked.

"No. Lucy said Portia was different. She could just feel it. That if Derrick was going to leave her for anyone, it was Portia. Halfway through our relationship, Lucy confessed that's why she'd initially reached out. To get me to convince Portia she was making a serious mistake. To warn her so Lucy could do for Portia what she should have done for Becky."

"And did Portia listen to you?"

Develin laughed.

"Do ex-wives ever do?"

34. Gone

Alexandra Township
Johannesburg, South Africa

The fifteen-seater minibus taxi was so full, people sat in the isles and children perched on their mother's laps. Their hours of practice had finally paid off, offering them the rare pleasure of a taxi ride home. Ukhozi FM blared out from the radio, the base notes reverberating in their seats as jazz, gqom and kwaito jostled with staccato news bulletins and ecstatic football commentators screaming, "LaDDUUUUMAA!". Thabo, Boy and Innocent squashed on the back seat, leaning left to accommodate Scooter's overwhelming girth. They didn't mind though. With three hundred rands in their pocket and Scooter's big-barrelled laugh shaking the whole back seat as he told joke after joke, they were in high spirits.

Pulling into Alex taxi rank, Thabo's eyes greedily took in the stalls around them. As if reading his mind, Boy poked him in the ribs and tipped his head towards a sweet stand.

"How about we take Lucky some koeksisters? Aren't they his favourite?"

"Good idea," he replied. "Then we can also drop by the chemist and pick up something for his cough."

Boy didn't comment. They both knew that cough syrup wasn't what Lucky needed but, with even low-cost private clinics costing more than three hundred rands per consult, for now it was the best they could do.

Having reached its destination, the taxi came to a stop. As people at the front began to alight, they were crushed even more as Scooter pulled himself to his feet, before squishing down the aisle and the minibus steps.

"Can we also get some sunlight?" Innocent said as they got off the taxi, "And some paraffin for the stove."

Thabo ticked the mental list off on his fingers as they walked towards the trading stands. "Anything else? I've already included the usual food stuff: Millie meal, amasi, half a loaf, tomato, onion and morogo. And maybe pilchards or chicken feet."

Boy's eyes lit up, "Let's do chicken feet!"

"All right," Thabo chuckled, "chicken feet it is."

"Nothing more from my side," Innocent said as they passed a busy fruit stand. Quick as lightning, he grabbed two apples, stowing them under his t-shirt before the vendor noticed.

"Hey!" Thabo whispered in his ear. "I thought you said nothing else?"

Innocent laughed. "You know me – never pay for what you can get for free!"

They shopped quickly and efficiently, going for the cheapest prices, making their money stretch as far as possible. As they made their way home, Thabo wondered what Lucky would be like when they got there. He'd had a brief respite for a few weeks, making them think that Innocent's potion might have actually worked. However, in the last few days, he'd gone back to coughing up blood, the potion seeming to only have delayed the disease's progress rather than curing it.

Yet, it wasn't just that Lucky was sick. Something had changed in his manner too. He seemed more distant, cagey even. It was so out of character. Which meant he was either planning something very bad or he had already done something very wrong.

Turning into their street, Thabo stopped short, surprised to see their neighbour prancing towards them dressed for church.

"Hello Ma," he said, wanting to ask where she was going straight away but knowing she would think it rude and disrespectful, particularly to an elder. "How are you today?"

"Hallo Boys!" Smiling, Mrs Khoza peeked at their shopping bags. "I see you had a good day today!"

"Sure did." Boy did his happy dance. "I knew my backflip would be a showstopper!"

"Yeah right," Innocent scoffed, showing off his biceps. "Like you did it all by yourself!"

Thabo cut through their banter, his tone sombre. "Did you leave Lucky alone, Ma?"

"Lucky?" she rolled her eyes. "Hey – that one! As soon as you guys were gone, he told me he had to go out. An appointment, he said." Then she frowned, looking slightly embarrassed. "Though he did ask me not to tell you…."

"Out?!" Innocent exclaimed. "But when we left him, he looked too weak to get out of bed!"

"Well, the Lord must have rendered a miracle because he walked out of that shack looking stronger than I'd seen him in a while."

Thabo didn't like what he was hearing. "What time was this?"

She shrugged, "Eight, maybe nine o'clock this morning."

He checked the position of the sun. "That's seven hours ago! And he's not back yet?"

"I don't know. I didn't check before I left but I didn't hear anything." She waved down a taxi. "Now, you boys will have to excuse me. Otherwise, I'm going to be late for mass."

As Mrs Khoza got on her ride, they raced home, unable to believe what she had told them. When they arrived, everything looked as it always did. The padlock on the door, the bed neatly made, their belongings as they had left them. The only thing missing was Lucky.

"That's it then," Thabo said, perching on the edge of the bed, trying to ignore the disquiet building in his chest. "She was telling the truth. Seems like Lucky just went out."

"Uh-huh," Innocent said, putting away the groceries. "But why didn't he just tell us?"

Boy sat on the floor, picked up a set of stones and started playing with them, his eyes downcast.

Thabo watched him curiously.

Boy hadn't spoken a word since they ran into Mrs Khoza. Why was he suddenly so quiet?

Something propelled him forward, whether it was instinct or foreboding, Thabo couldn't tell. Ignoring Innocent's startled look, he ran out of the shack and turned right, ducking under the washing line. Falling to his knees, he quickly parted the weeds and shoved aside the earth, hoping that the voice inside him was wrong, that he would find the phone exactly where he had left it. It took him a while to realise that he had been digging for far too long, that if the phone was there, he would have found it long ago.

Rage coursed through him.

Why couldn't people leave things alone? Always poking their nose where it wasn't wanted! Was nothing sacred?!!

Thabo jumped up and ran back to the shack. Innocent had started on supper. Boy still sat on the mat, now just staring at the stones, looking defeated.

"You know something, don't you?" Thabo said, picking Boy up by the scruff of his neck.

As their eyes made contact, Thabo saw the shimmer in Boy's eyes. "I'm sorry Thabo. I was just trying to help. I didn't know -"

"Hey!" Innocent shoved them apart. "Break it up, you two!"

Wiping his tears, Boy went to sit on the bed, his head down, his shoulders drooping. Seeing him so despondent killed Thabo's rage in an instant, leaving only shame. Shame at the anger he'd projected onto Boy when he was really angry at himself. And at his own deceit, which had gotten them there in the first place. Sinking to the floor, he put his head in his hands.

Innocent looked at him then Boy, then back again. "What's going on?"

Neither Thabo nor Boy spoke.

Innocent shoved Thabo's shoulder, "I asked you a question."

Thabo looked up, feeling like he'd just run a marathon. "It's my fault," he mumbled. "I should have told you guys about it."

Innocent stepped back, astounded at the torment on Thabo's face. "Told us what?"

Thabo looked at Boy. Boy looked away.

Thabo gulped. "Remember that dead white guy? The one they put a reward out for?"

"Yes – what about him?" Innocent plonked down on the bed forcing Boy to shift sideways.

"Well, I think it could be the same guy I found."

"Found?" Innocent and Boy said in unison, Innocent's jaw dropping as Boy's eyes widened in surprise.

Thabo nodded, telling them the story quickly and concisely, from the day he stumbled on the body to the announcement of the reward and the calls suddenly coming to an end.

Boy gasped, "You're thinking whoever killed the white guy was calling because they were looking for whoever now had his phone? And when they failed to find you and the reward was announced, they thought it would be easier to just wait and see who came forward?"

"Don't you think that makes sense?" he said. "Especially, given what you told us, Innocent?"

"Wait," Innocent said, confused. "Why would these guys, whoever they are, be looking for Thabo?"

"Not Thabo," Boy shot him some side-eye. "The person who had the phone."

"And they needed to find me – I mean, the person who had the phone," Thabo added, "because that person now knew whom the white guy had called just before he died. And why would they be concerned about that? Probably because they're the ones who called him and killed him."

Alarmed, Innocent jumped to his feet. "Ohhh shit! Now I get what my cousin was talking about! This is fucked up, bra! Really fucked up!"

"I know," Thabo said soberly. "At least, I know *now*. If I'd known this would happen when I found the phone, I would never have kept it."

Innocent started pacing, clearly needing movement to help him think. "Even so, I don't see what this has got to do with Lucky. After all, you didn't tell us you had the phone."

Thabo glanced at Boy.

"That was me," Boy said softly. "While he did a good job of hiding it, I found out that Thabo had a phone. So, when Lucky got really sick, I told him about it. I knew he still wanted to go for the reward, and I figured that if we did it by phone, we could get the money without anyone being able to track us. You know – like an anonymous tip."

"And did he make the call?" Thabo asked.

"Don't know," Boy replied with a sad shrug. "I told him he should ask you to borrow it."

"Which he never did," Thabo sighed. "At least that explains why Lucky's been acting so strange lately. He had a secret of his own."

"Why all these secrets?" Boy cried. "Why didn't you just tell us everything in the first place?"

"I…" Thabo fought to find the right words. Suddenly his chest felt tight. Like all the feelings he had been bottling up for years now wanted to explode. "I don't know. I guess…," his voice cracked, "…I just wanted something of my own, you know? I've never had that. Something that was mine and only mine."

Innocent and Boy looked down, their faces signalling that they knew exactly what he meant. Rather than making him feel better, it made him feel worse, highlighting how selfish he was, thinking that he was the only one who deserved something special.

It was Boy who broke the silence. "Even if he called the hotline, he wouldn't have given them his real name, let alone told them where he lived. So how did they find him?"

Thabo had a sinking realisation. "What if it wasn't the police who betrayed him? What if all Lucky did was answer a call?"

"From the killer, you mean?" Innocent said. "But the point still applies. How would they know who he was or where he lived?"

"They wouldn't have had to," Thabo replied. "The caller could have pretended to be the phone's owner. Offered a reward for its return as a way of getting Lucky to go to him. That must be the appointment he went to."

Boy shook his head, "Lucky wouldn't have done that. Gone to meet a stranger just like that to give away something that was yours? Never."

"You don't understand," Thabo got to his feet, the idea spurring him to action. "What if they offered him so much money that he could not only get me a brand-new phone but everything we all wanted? And Lucky would have thought he was being careful, only agreeing to meet in a public place where he felt safe. Then something went wrong."

'Come on!" Innocent said, sceptical. "That much for a phone?"

"To you, it might be just a phone," Thabo replied. "But would it be so hard to believe it could mean the world to someone else? Someone willing to pay thousands for its return. Particularly, if you *wanted* to believe it?"

"Come to think of it, Thabo's right," Boy said. "Lucky would have been willing to take the chance. Not knowing who the caller was, he'd figure he'd have nothing to lose and everything to gain."

"Ok, let's say that's what happened," Innocent stopped pacing and put his hands on his hips. "What happens now? Lucky's gone. How do we find him?"

"How about we try to retrace his footsteps?" Boy offered.

"There might be a quicker way," Thabo countered. "We could try and trace the phone itself. Find the phone, find Lucky."

Innocent scoffed, "How? We don't have the tech to do that."

"No, we don't," he said. "But I know at least one set of people who do."

"Who?" Boy replied. "Surely, not the police?"

Thabo shook his head, smiling.

"The Blades."

35. CLUSTER-FUCK

Farningham
Kent, UK

Hilary was at the gym when the story broke. The first inkling he got that something was off was when a gym instructor interrupted him mid-way through his circuit to tell him he was wanted on the phone. The second, was when he picked up the call at reception and heard Spencer hyperventilating on the other end.

"Where the fuck have you been? I've been calling you for the last thirty minutes!"

"Working out," Hilary said evenly, "My phone's in my locker. Why?"

"Why? Why? Only because we're facing the BIGGEST CLUSTER-FUCK IN HISTORY!"

"What?!! -"

"Get your pants on," Spencer snapped. "And be at my house in an hour."

Hilary ran to his locker. Ten missed calls, six from Spencer, two from the Bank Media Liaison Officer and a couple of numbers he didn't recognise. Cursing, he texted his driver to come and pick him up and was washed and dressed within 10 minutes.

What would constitute the biggest cluster-fuck in history?

Always wanting to be prepared, Hilary racked his brain as he and Mark wove their way to Spencer's country estate. A hostile takeover? The loss of two or three anchor clients? New Bank of England regulations? All three could potentially be disastrous. However, if it was a hostile takeover, it was still probably early days. Early enough to mount a counter-offensive. Same with new Regs. The Bank could be stubborn sometimes but, given the right kind of pressure, rarely did they refuse to bend. However, losing anchor clients was far more difficult to overcome. People would inevitably ask what led to it, prompting others to follow suit and, before you knew it, you had a stampede. Yes, that must be it. Still, perhaps it was not too late to save the situation. The key would be the specific clients in question, the type of secrets they had and which ones they could use as leverage to persuade them to change their minds. Having said that, Spencer would still be pissed that he hadn't seen this coming. So, it would be best to go in contrite but firm. Convince him that he would soon get things back under control.

"Not sure how long I'm going to be, Mark," Hilary said as they sped up Spencer's driveway and parked under the large portico. "No need to hang around. I'll get a taxi home."

"You sure, Sir?"

"Absolutely."

As his driver drove away, Hilary patted down his hair and straightened his tie. Always put your best foot forward, that's what his father had always said. Especially when all hell was breaking loose.

Be the lighthouse amidst the stormy seas.

Composed, he bounded up the short flight of stairs and rang the bell. In response, he heard a dog barking, followed by the sound of footsteps on carpet, then on wood, before the door flew open to reveal a small, bespectacled boy in pyjamas.

"Dad's mad at *you*!" Spencer's son said, his big green eyes blinking up at him from a cherubic face. His dog, Biscuit, an overstuffed bulldog too fond of his sobriquet, stood guard at his feet, its large tongue licking its lips as if searching for runaway crumbs.

"Should you be up this late, Jeremy?" Hilary replied, hoping the boy's mother would soon come to rescue him.

"Not normally but Mum said I could stay up to watch Hamilton break another record. Do you think he will?"

"What?"

"Break -"

"Oh, dear. My apologies. I didn't hear the bell at all!" Spencer's wife, Margaret, fussed up to the door. "Do get out the way, dear, before our poor guest freezes to death on the doorstep." Hurriedly, she ushered him in, shooing Jeremy and Biscuit down the hall at the same time. "Spencer's waiting for you in the den," she added. "Spoiler alert – he's in a foul mood!"

After gently patting his arm with a pitying look, presumably pre-emptive comfort for what was to come, she trotted after her youngest son, leaving Hilary to find his own way. Crossing the large entrance hall, he turned down a passage banked by generations of family portraits and stopped in front of a large wooden door, knocking to announce his presence.

Silence.

He was about to knock again when Spencer shouted from within, "Come in, man! What are you waiting for?"

His boss sat in one of two Wingback chairs in front of a crackling fire, bathed in a miasma of whisky, cigars and burning wood fumes. The room was dimly lit, the only light a brass and green lamp on top of a large sixteen-century desk in the middle of the room, behind which stood ceiling-high bookshelves.

"Sorry, I wasn't sure you heard my knock," Hilary closed the door behind him.

"Of course, I heard it. Been waiting for you, haven't I?" Spencer's face was flushed, though whether it was from the heat of the fire, copious amounts of whisky, or rage was hard to determine.

"Quite." Hilary glanced at the drinks cabinet, looking for some Dutch courage. "May I…"

"Already poured your usual," Spencer pointed to the armchair opposite him. "Come and sit down. Let's not waste time on pleasantries."

As Hilary took his seat, he saw that Spencer had indeed placed a large glass of brandy on the side table next to his chair which, judging by its generosity, suggested that he may have underestimated just what kind of cluster-fuck they were in.

"So, which clients is it?" he asked, picking up his glass to project an air of calm assurance. "If we work fast, I'm sure we'll be able to arrest the situation."

"You know what I hate?" Spencer said softly. "Hubris. At every point in my career when I've stumbled, at every point when I nearly went down, conceit has been at the centre of it."

Not used to his boss displaying such humility, he immediately jumped to his defence, "Oh, I'm sure it can't be that ba -"

Spencer leant forward, spitting, "Not my hubris, you idiot. Yours!"

Hilary took a large gulp of brandy.

"Don't worry, I have it under control, you said," Spencer continued, imitating his voice. "She's not a threat, you said. A Chihuahua sniping at our heels!"

"She? Don't tell me we're talking about Tate?"

"Of course, I'm bloody talking about Tate! Good God, man. What were you doing on the drive over here? Didn't you check the news?"

Hilary had never felt more like a fool in his life. "No. It never occurred…I thought…" He put down his glass and hastily grabbed his phone.

"Don't bother," Spencer said, "I can give you the highlights. According to

Tate's sources and key documents in her possession, Derrick was an obsessive gambler, who began by laundering money to offset his gambling debts. Then he expanded his operation, laundering money in exchange for kickbacks. These kickbacks he hid in a secret bank account in the Cayman Islands via a myriad of shelf companies. Thus, our famous anti-money laundering campaign was a front designed to hide the fact that Derrick was the real money launderer!"

"What?!" Hilary moved to the edge of his seat. "But we were on her every minute. We knew her -"

"Every move?" Spencer said sarcastically. "Well, clearly, you didn't."

"But -"

"It gets worse. Based on further testimony from her sources, Tate theorises that Derrick could have not acted alone. That is why he needed to get rid of Michael and Patrick, replacing them with people willing to help him in his scheme. In other words, Yeats Bank is a den of corruption, and the anti-money laundering campaign was the biggest fraud in recent financial history!"

Hilary shook his head, befuddled, "I still can't work out how she got there before -?"

"It doesn't matter how!" Spencer yelled. "What matters is she did! And what's worse is that the whole story is so wrapped up in disclaimers and anonymous sources, we can't even fucking sue!"

"I'll get on to the Serious Fraud Office," he said. "Tell them that we were already -"

"Dominic has already called, along with the Chancellor's office. The SFO is going to launch an investigation ASAP and the Chancellor has asked to see me and the Group Chairman tomorrow at 10 o'clock."

"Will you need me to attend?" Hilary asked, opening his calendar.

"No, I will not. I think you've done enough damage already." His face full of scorn, Spencer stood up to refill his glass.

In that instant, Hilary saw everything crumble before his eyes. His hopes, his dreams, his power. And, most important of all, Spencer's hard-won, surely imminent anointment, flying away in search of worthier kin. He couldn't let it go. "But I…"

His boss cut him off. "I want you to deal with the press. Do you think you could handle that?"

That was something at least.

"Yes, yes. Of course," he replied.

"Issue a statement cutting all ties with Derrick. State categorically that he's no longer associated with Yeats Bank."

"Absolutely," Hilary took out a pocketbook and began to take notes.

"Emphasise that, as a bank committed to good governance, we'd already initiated an internal audit process investigating Derrick's past activities along with any other bad apples that may have been involved." He unstopped the whisky decanter and poured himself a triple. "By the way, those accomplices you referred to. Is it too early to offer them up to the wolves?"

"We don't have enough yet."

"Pity. Anyway, emphasise that we've got the matter in hand. Add that this is standard bank practice and that our internal controls remain robust. Nevertheless, even the best controls cannot withstand those determined to thwart the -"

Hilary coughed, "Are you sure you want to say that last part?"

Spencer mulled it over, "Mmmm, you might be right. Could be taken as an admission." The contempt in his face remained but, with it, the begrudging return of a slither of respect.

Hilary sat up a bit straighter.

Maybe it wasn't too late to get back into Spencer's good books.

"Instead, remind them of our sterling anti-corruption record," his boss said, sitting back down. "And lastly, end by emphasising that we look forward to cooperating with the SFO and the Chancellor's office as we jointly work to get to the bottom of this matter."

"Got it."

Hilary made a show of putting away his pocketbook, buying time as he wondered how to phrase the next part. He knew he shouldn't ask but he had to know.

"Did Tate say anything about the link between these allegations and Derrick's disappearance?"

"Not specifically," Spencer took an appreciative sip of whiskey. "She posed the question but nothing more than that."

Hilary nodded sagely.

"Why do you ask?" Spencer prompted as he put down his glass and threw another log onto the fire.

Hilary's hands suddenly felt clammy, the one area where he had never been able to stop his body from betraying him. "Do you think…" he began then closed his mouth again.

Spencer stabbed at the fire with a poker, "What? Spit it out, man!"

"It's just that…Given the nature of our clientele…" Hilary let it sink in.

Spencer stopped poking. "Are you seriously suggesting that one of our clients might have had a hand in Derrick's disappearance? In, as Tate puts it, his possible murder?"

He licked his lips, "It's a possibility."

Spencer put down the poker, his face grave. "Which would make us not only financial criminals but a bank of murderers too?"

Hilary thought carefully about his response. He thought of all the new money despots and dictators, oligarchs and oilmen that littered their clientele, joining the body of old-money slave traders, robber barons and colonial thieves that the bank had been built on. A bank of murderers and criminals wasn't an inaccurate description. However, they knowing that, and the public knowing that, were two very different things.

"Yes," he replied. "Unthinkable."

Spencer got to his feet, wagging his finger in Hilary's face. "Even if one of our clients was involved, Tate must never make that link. Do you hear me? Under no circumstances! If she does, it will be the end of us."

Hilary wiped his wet palms on his trousers, "I'll make sure of it."

Yet another thing his boss hadn't thought of. When Spencer calmed down, he would see that he was indispensable. He had to.

With no more to be said, Hilary headed for the door, leaving Spencer standing with his hands on the mantle, staring into the flames.

"And one more thing," Spencer said quietly just as Hilary reached the door. He looked back to meet a gaze that almost withered him on the spot.

"Don't fuck it up this time."

36. A Name

Camden
London, UK

The queue leading to the Camden soup kitchen almost reached the corner of the block, some standing, others sitting on the pavement as they all silently waited, most dressed in thick jackets and gloves to ward off the freezing wind. While the faces around her wore the serene mask of those long accustomed to tarrying, the yearning was palpable. Everyone's eyes were trained on the iron gate next to the Church and, below it, the stairs leading to the kitchen, hoping to catch sight of the first volunteer and proof that the lunch service was finally about to begin.

Charlie stood among them, about thirty people down from the front, hands in her pockets, shoulders hunched under a puff jacket, a well-worn hoodie covering her head and face. It had been three weeks since her meeting with Develin. Two since an unassuming package from 'MD of Clapham Common', wrapped in brown paper and string, had been dropped off at the Torch reception, marked for her eyes only. Not only had Develin's contact delivered on his end of the bargain, Murdoch's Black Box had proven even larger than anticipated. Needless to say, Bulldog and The Ferret had been ecstatic. Another scoop and one that would make international headlines for months to come.

Whilst Charlie had been happy to temporarily bask in the adulation, from the perspective of solving the Murdoch mystery, the confirmation of Develin's story had merely closed one door only to open another. The challenge was that while Lucy, Develin and Sparrow were now off the hook, she had absolutely no clue as to who might be behind door number two. Though Murdoch's Black Box might hold the answer, it was also true that sorting out the myriad of accounts and shelf companies it contained was going to take weeks, maybe months. Hence, she had happily handed over this task to Jake and Barbara and gone in search of a shortcut.

Charlie had started by tracing the owners of the private gambling clubs Murdoch used to frequent. That way, she had hoped to find out whom he might have been indebted to and ask them a few questions. Unfortunately, she had discovered the hard way that many casino owners didn't appreciate her interest, getting tossed out on her arse so often that her whole body had turned black and blue. All of which had forced her back to a familiar face.

Lucy.

After all, if Mrs Murdoch had known about her husband's Black Box, perhaps there were other things she hadn't told the police or Develin about. However, Lucy had still been Lucying, not answering her door, not returning calls, and scarcely venturing beyond her four walls. So, when a photo and address had quietly slipped into Charlie's inbox yesterday evening, she had almost jumped with joy.

All of a sudden, the energy in the queue changed. Those who were sitting stood up and those who were standing stood to attention. She wasn't sure what had happened, but something was up. Like her fellow travellers, Charlie kept her eyes glued on the stairs, not out of hunger but anticipation, wondering how long it would take before her quarry came into view. According to Arthur, she had started at the soup kitchen two days ago, slipping in amongst the group of volunteers almost unnoticed, and had been back every day since. Why Lucy had chosen this particular gig to end her self-imposed confinement wasn't clear. It could have been genuine compassion, though Charlie suspected it was more penitence for her sins.

A loud clang rang out as the kitchen door flew open. People in the queue shuffled forward, bunching closer together, getting ready. Then she saw it, the blond head of the first volunteer as they approached the top of the stairs with a paper bag in their hand and opened the gate. After that, things went quickly, with volunteers running up and down to the kitchen, fetching and handing each guest their lunch and receiving heartfelt gratitude in return. However, as she edged closer to the gate, Charlie started to get anxious, watching the same two volunteers running up and down with no sign of her prey. She was three people away from the head of the line and about to give up when Lucy finally appeared, running up the stairs in a red apron.

Charlie ducked behind the tall man in front of her, not sure that Lucy would recognise her but not wanting to take any chances. If the volunteers kept the same rotation, Lucy would be the one to hand her a meal. If not, Charlie would have to let someone else go ahead until she came up again but that would draw attention to herself and give Lucy prior warning. Crossing her fingers, Charlie took another step forward, then another until she stood in front of the open gate, head down, her face in shadow. A paper bag was thrust towards her, its holder wearing a red apron. She was in luck.

"Hello Lucy," Charlie said, raising her head. "Got time to answer some questions?"

Lucy withdrew the bag back, confused. "Who are you? How do you know my name?"

"I'm here to talk about your husband."

"Excuse me, Miss," the man standing behind Charlie interjected. "I'll take it if you don't want it."

Charlie stood aside while Lucy handed him the bag, her eyes still locked on Charlie's face. "You're that journalist, aren't you? Tate. The one that keeps calling?"

"Yep – that's me."

Lucy's face hardened. "If you don't stop harassing me, I'm going to call the police."

"Oh? Be my guest. I'm sure they'll want to know you've been hiding things from them."

"I don't know what you're talking about." Lucy turned to go but Charlie blocked her way.

"Yes, you do. I've spoken to Fry, Claudia, and Develin. I know all about you, Mrs Murdoch. The question is – how much of it do you want me to print?"

"Everything ok here, Lucy?" said the blond volunteer as she got to the top of the stairs.

Lucy opened her mouth to speak.

"Lassie, do you mind?!" The next man in line pushed forward forcing both Lucy and Charlie to move out of the way. "Some of us haven't eaten in days. So, if you're not here for the meal, bugger off!"

"I'm going ahead, with or without you," Charlie warned, her eyes boring into Lucy's own.

Indecision marched over her quarry's face. Then she turned to the blond. "I've got to step out for a minute, Sal. Family emergency. Cover for me, will you?"

Sal nodded her ascent, handing the man a bag as Lucy turned and followed Charlie further up the road. Charlie chose a spot just on the other side of the church entrance, about five metres away from the soup kitchen queue. Far enough to have a quiet conversation but close enough to raise her voice and threaten Lucy with exposure if she didn't cooperate.

"You've got some nerve, coming here," Lucy said through clenched teeth when they came to a halt.

Charlie shrugged, "Comes with the territory."

"Well, I'll give you five minutes," Lucy crossed her arms defensively. "Nothing more."

She gazed at Lucy's rigid back, her hostile posture, assessing what it would take to loosen her tongue.

"Look," Charlie said, raising her hands in appeasement. "I think we started off on the wrong foot. I'm just trying to get to the bottom of your husband's disappearance. I'm sure you want to know what happened to him as much as we do."

"Of course, I do. That's what the police are for. Doesn't mean I want you lot poking around!"

"Seems to me, I'm already one step ahead of the police. They never had a clue about your husband's little stash, did they? So, if you and I work together, we may be able to get to the answer a lot faster. *And* you'll be able to influence the narrative."

Lucy's face was furtive, a fox trying to work out its next move. "What exactly did Fry and them say to you, anyhow?"

Charlie leant her back against the wall of the church, her hands in her jean pockets, "I know about Becky, that Murdoch was also abusing you, both of you were cheating on each other and your marriage was on the rocks. I know you were working with Develin, that your husband was planning to leave you for Develin's wife, and that you tried to get him to warn Portia off. I also know that when your husband landed in Joburg, he dumped his usual phone and switched to a burner. Which, on reflection, now makes me wonder if your husband was already trying to avoid detection *before* he was kidnapped. What I don't know is who your husband was running from."

A vein jumped in Lucy's neck, "Running from?"

"Develin said that your husband was indebted to some pretty nasty criminals. Do you think they might have had a hand in his disappearance?"

Lucy's face shut down, "He said it, so you'll have to ask him." She lit a cigarette, taking a long drag before blowing the smoke into the air.

As the smoke cleared, Charlie spotted something she hadn't noticed before. Deep in the recesses of Lucy's eyes. Something that looked like fear.

Go gentle now.

"When did your husband start gambling?" Charlie asked.

Lucy's laugh was without mirth. "They never tell you, do they? Probably before we got married but he hid it at first. I found out about six months in. The first time he cleaned out our account. He replaced the money pretty quickly, though. I'm not sure how he did it, but he always seemed to be able to get money from somewhere eventually."

"Develin said things started to get out of hand. Is that correct?"

"Yep. The better he did in his career, the more he took bigger and bigger risks. It was almost as if a part of him wanted to destroy his success before someone else could take it away from him. At one point, things got so bad, I worried we might lose the house. Then two years ago, everything changed. Not only did our financial troubles disappear, Derrick started throwing money around like it was confetti. Said he had found a new benefactor. And, I'm not going to lie, life got very good. I should have known it was too fucking good to last." She took another drag, even longer this time, flicking the ash into the gutter.

"Oh?" Charlie stood up straight, "What happened next?"

Lucy half turned, glancing at the soup kitchen queue. "Look, I've got to go. Spent too much time out here as it is."

Charlie motioned for her to stop, "What are you afraid of, Lucy?"

She pulled a face, "Who says I'm afraid?"

"I can see it in your eyes. Hear it in your voice. Is that why you dropped out of sight? Got extra security around your home?"

Lucy frowned, "How do you kno –"

"It doesn't matter," Charlie stepped closer. "Tell me what's going on. I can't help if you keep me in the dark."

"Help?" Lucy scoffed, "What help can *you* give *me*?"

"Look," Charlie said earnestly, "if we're talking about the kind of guys I think we're talking about, all too often these types have bent coppers on the inside. People on the take at different levels in the force, ready to tip them off should investigations start getting too close. I work outside the system, never revealing my sources and never running with a story until I'm ready to strike."

"Then what?" Lucy replied. "Not like you can put them in jail!" Despite her scepticism, Charlie saw a spark of interest in her eyes.

"No, but I work with those who can. And I also know which cops are straight and which aren't. Here *and* in South Africa."

"South Africa?"

"Yep."

That got her attention.

Lucy didn't respond, staring at the cars driving by for what felt like an age. Then she put out her cigarette, turned and walked into the church, clearly expecting her companion to follow. Inside, Charlie accompanied her to a pew at the very back, far away from the slim scattering of dedicated souls attending midday mass. As she sat next to her, Charlie could feel the waves of anxiety emitting from her body.

"A few days after Derrick disappeared, I got a package," Lucy whispered, hands clasped in her lap, the knuckles white. "A bloody finger with a note telling me to hold my tongue."

"Your husband's finger?" Charlie asked.

"I thought so, at first. Then I realised it couldn't have been. It was too fat, too hairy. But it was definitely a warning. If I didn't keep quiet, something bad would happen."

Charlie's stomach fluttered with excitement, "What didn't they want you to tell?"

"I wasn't sure at first. But after I got the package, I went through everything. Trying to figure out what they thought I knew."

"And?"

"I'm still not entirely sure but the search triggered a memory." She peeked at the people in the rows further up and leant closer to Charlie. "A few months before he went missing, Derrick's behaviour changed. Not eating, staying up until the early hours, that sort of thing. Occasionally, I would wake up in the middle of the night, go down to the kitchen to get some water and hear him talking on the phone in the study. Sometimes, these conversations became screaming matches. Then one night a few weeks before he disappeared, I snuck up and pressed my ear against the study door, trying to work out what all the screaming was about. Of course, I could only hear one side of the conversation but the first thing I heard was Derrick saying 'Back off, all right? Ever since we started, I've done everything you've asked. But this is *too* much!'"

"Was he talking about a money-laundering deal?"

Lucy shook her head, "Don't know. Derrick never spoke about his work. A week later, I heard something else. I don't recall the exact words, but it was something like: 'Don't you threaten me or you're going to regret it!'. Then he slammed the phone down."

"All this just before he vanished?"

Lucy nodded.

"And you think the person who sent you the package is the guy who was on the other side of the phone?"

"Who else?" Lucy's legs started shaking.

Remember. Go gently. You're almost there.

Charlie took a deep breath, "Did your husband say his name?"

Lucy chewed her lip, looking down at her lap.

"I know this is difficult for you," Charlie said, mirroring Lucy's posture, trying to build trust.

"Do you?" Lucy hunched forward, trembling all over now.

"Yes, I do. More than you can imagine. But you have to trust me."

Her voice dropped even further, "He can't know it was me, ok? You can't say a word about me or the family."

"You have my word," Charlie whispered back.

Lucy wrung her hands, still undecided. Charlie kept her peace, afraid of spoiling the moment.

When Lucy finally spoke, her voice was so soft Charlie could barely hear it.

"Jonas," she mumbled. "His name is Jonas."

37. Feelings

Notting Hill
London, UK

Despite the cold, the market was packed, locals and tourists alike pawing through the vibrant, overflowing stalls standing in front of pink, purple, green and blue houses. As he wove through the throng, Jake savoured the heady mix of aromas from the different food stalls, mentally tapping his feet to the jazz, soul and calypso music filling the air from hopeful serenaders showcasing their talent.

His aim was to add a few choice items to his vinyl collection, his route starting at Firebird, past People's and Rough Trade, and maybe stopping by Honest Jon's and Blue Groove on the way home. It was a while since he'd had a whole weekend free to do entirely as he liked, so why not treat himself?

As usual, outside the record shop stood two stands packed with LPs from every genre, overflow from Firebird's impressive stock. Jake walked past these, knowing that the rarest finds were often found in the recesses of the store. As he stepped through the green and glass front, his heart leapt in anticipation, imagining the thrill of finding a favourite he had long been hunting for. As usual, Firebird was jammed, eager shoppers squeezing past each other in narrow channels, between pine tables covered with white, plastic boxes full of greats from yesteryear. Heading for the soul section, an image of the shop's icon - a yellow Pontiac with a black, orange, and red phoenix painted on the hood - drifted into his mind. Then it morphed into Charlie's face, her eyes sparkling with determination. Firebird meets firebrand.

From the moment they had met at the Yeats press conference, he had felt drawn to her. And still did despite all the warnings he had received, claiming she was a ball-breaker who thought too much of herself. Fortunately, he had assessed such advice from whence it came, namely mediocre, misogynistic arseholes not used to competing for the limelight. As someone who made a habit of going against the tide, people who had no time for fools were just his type. Yet, it wasn't only her strength that drew him to her. He also sensed her vulnerability, hidden behind walls of steel and stone.

He knew about her family, of course. The suspicious death, the docket lost, and justice denied. Jake sensed, though, that what lay behind Charlie's ramparts was more than that. In the depths of her eyes, he saw the struggle of someone dying for connection but too scared of the risks and scars that sometimes went with it.

Or was he just talking about himself?

Not finding what he was looking for, Jake left Firebird and wove his way up Portobello Road. He passed a savoury good food stall and then a vintage clothes shop, Adele blaring from the speakers. As she belted out "hello from the other side", again he was reminded of Charlie. He had to find a way to warn her about the potential dangers she was facing with the Yeats story. She probably thought he'd been over dramatic with his cock fighting analogy, but he'd seen the extent to which people would go to preserve their interests. Behind the whitened smiles, slick hairdos and fancy suits were people who'd slice you open and spill your guts without a second thought. Then, in her latest piece, not only did she double down on the suggestion that Murdoch's disappearance was suspicious, but she had also hinted that it might be linked to his work!

Talk about an open invitation!

The problem was, at this stage, he had nothing more than instinct. No rumours or overheard conversations. No explicit threats or potential ticking time bombs. Just a feeling. And how did you convince someone to hold back and trust in your feelings when they'd just unearthed the biggest banking scandal in the last decade? Bigger than Standard Chartered and even the Royal Bank of Scotland!

Impossible!

Yet, something kept tugging at him. Telling him he couldn't, shouldn't let this go. Though, if he was honest with himself, wasn't it really Charlie he couldn't let go? He thought about their meeting at the cock fight, his desperate urge to touch her and her careful avoidance of contact. Had she felt it too? The sparks that flew between them? Or was it just his own wishful thinking? Either way, he wouldn't be able to live with himself if something happened to her that he might have been able to prevent. It was just as simple as that.

Ambling up to the red, yellow, and green storefront of People's Sound, Jake made a decision. He'd get close to her. Use his work on Murdoch's Black Box as an excuse to keep tabs on her progress. Then, if he came across anything to confirm his fears, he could warn her before it was too late. Yes, that was it. And the good thing was that also meant he would see her more often. Then, even if his suspicions proved incorrect, maybe, over time, the attraction would become mutual.

No harm in dreaming, right?

Softly humming Marley's *No Woman, No Cry*, Jake smiled to himself as he stepped inside the reggae store.

38. Breadcrumbs

Lower East Side
New York, USA

Viper sat in Central Park, wrapped in a thick, winter coat, laughing at the first-time skaters slipping and sliding on the ice in the rink in front of her. Two hours earlier, she had decided to slip out for a breath of fresh air, prompted by the smell of fresh bagels that had wafted up from the bakery below and through her kitchen window. Two mochaccinos and two cream bagels later, her conscience had pushed her to walk off the pounds, landing her, via the subway, in Central Park. She had begun as she always did, by paying her respects to Seneca Village, the once proud home of more than 350 African Americans pushed off their land and their former homesteads now buried beneath grass, trees, and lakes. From there, Viper had let her feet lead the way, basking in the fresh breeze and the blazing colours of autumn until she had come to rest at a restaurant near the Wollman rink, otherwise known as the poor man's Comedy Central.

One particularly ungainly and horizontally challenged skater had just fallen on his butt for the third time in a row, the expression on his face causing her to let out a fit of giggles, when her phone vibrated in her pocket. She was still giggling when she answered it, putting her finger on her other ear to try and block out the hubbub. "Sorry – it's a bit noisy here. Can you repeat that?"

"I said, you seem to be in a good mood," Charlie replied. "Can I have some?"

Viper grinned, "Just some autumn cheer. I'll take a video and send it to you." The crowd erupted with applause as a young girl did a perfect layback spin. "Wait - let me find somewhere quiet where we can talk." She walked out of the restaurant enclosure and down a path leading away from the rink, looking for a vacant bench.

"Charlie?" she said when she eventually found one, "you still there?"

"Yeah – I'm here. You got my mail, right?"

Sure did, Viper thought. At least, Lucy was now off the hook. Thinking about all the times she'd fantasised about killing her own abusive husband, she'd have hated having to have a hand in putting her away. Even if she would have deserved it.

"Since Lucy, Develin and Sparrow are now in the clear," Viper said, "you're thinking Jonas is our man?"

"Could be. But I haven't been able to find his name on any casino title deed and none of the owners or managers will talk to me anyway. So, I was wondering if there's another way to find him?"

"Lucy didn't indicate whether Jonas was a first or last name?"

"No, she didn't. While the male toffs in Lucy's circles usually call each other by their last names, Murdoch was an outsider, a commoner. So, he could have gone either way."

Viper smiled as a mother duck and her brood waddled by, heading towards The Pond, gobbling up any crumbs kind strangers threw their way. "What about nationality?" she asked.

"Again - nada. He's clearly very fluent in English. At least, fluent enough to have a rapid, heated argument in the language. But that doesn't mean anything either since English is spoken almost everywhere in the world. He could literally be from anywhere."

Jonas couldn't be totally off the grid. These days, no one was, no matter how hard they tried. There was always a trial of digital breadcrumbs leading right to most people's doors. She just had to find it.

"Well, given Jonas knew Murdoch," Viper said, "the best place to start would be to see if someone called Jonas and Murdoch were ever spotted together. Leave it with me and I'll see what I can do."

"Great. Once we get the right Jonas, I'll reach out to Jake. See if he's come across him in the Cayman Islands money trail. Then we won't just have Lucy's word for it. We'll have concrete evidence connecting Jonas directly to Murdoch."

While she didn't want to dampen her friend's enthusiasm, Viper countered just the same, "A connection, yes. But we'll still need to prove motive *and* that he actually did it."

"True. But the good news is that, even if Lucy doesn't know the motive, someone else might. In my experience, people always feel compelled to tell their secrets to at least one person. Someone they know they can trust. Not sure why. Perhaps it's the weight of bearing a secret alone."

"Like someone he seems to have trusted enough to want to spend the rest of his life with?"

"Exactly. Portia. But I need to find her first. From what I can see, she's no longer living at her London address."

"Then I guess we've both got our marching orders. Me – Jonas. You – Portia."

"That we do. We're getting close V," Charlie said ardently. "I can feel it."

As they ended the call, Viper got to her feet, deciding to circle back via the rink on her way home. Walking by, she saw that the ungainly guy she had seen earlier had finally managed to skate a few metres without falling over. The look of triumph on his face was enough to light a thousand dreams. Viper shook her head and chuckled. That's why she loved going to the rink so much. Not just to giggle as people wobbled about or fell on their backsides. Rather, it was to witness them struggle, overcome, and stand tall, just like she had had to do. A small reminder that tomorrow could be better than yesterday, and the day after that, even better than the last.

And that's what made life worth living.

39. The Jogger

Tooting Bec Common
London, UK

It was already dusk by the time Charlie got home from the office, but she reckoned she still had time for a short run before night fell. She changed as fast as she could and popped in her EarPods, the pulsating music propelling her out the door and down the street, instilling fresh vigour into her tired limbs. She planned to enter Tooting Bec Common via Bedford Hill Road, heading past the cafe towards the tennis courts and lake, then down to Tooting Bec Road before circling back past the Lido to pop out the way she'd come in.

When she got to the common, most people were going in the opposite direction, dogs panting on leashes after their daily walk, joggers anxiously reviewing their performance stats on their sports watches and senior citizens ambling home after their evening constitutional. Seeing the outflux, she briefly thought of turning back. After all, jogging alone at night was never a wise idea, even at the best of times. Then the streetlights came on, casting the park in a warm, golden glow, inviting her in.

Maybe having less people around was a good thing. Fewer obstacles to avoid.

Her stride quickly fell into its rhythm, her breathing steady and even, her feet thumping to the beat. As ever, her thoughts turned to the Murdoch story, but she pushed them aside, trying to free her mind and bask in the joy of being in nature. Passing the Commons Café and turning towards the lake, she thought she glimpsed someone lurking in the trees in the distance.

However, when she got closer and slowed down to get a better look, he or she was gone.

Must have just been a shadow.

It was odd, though, the way she'd been so jumpy lately. First, she'd suspected that the guy outside the travel agent had been following her. Then she'd thought that someone was watching her outside the boxing club. And just the other day in the fish shop basement, she'd been convinced that someone had been eavesdropping. Wasn't like her to be so skittish. Then again, the nightmares had been worse than usual the past few weeks.

Why was that?

Which had come first – the chicken or the egg…?

Charlie reached Tooting Bec Road, cars whizzing past on the other side of the fence, their bright headlights almost blinding. Across the thoroughfare, groups of teenagers shuttled in and out of the entrance to the sports centre, laughing as they shoved and teased each other. Going past, she wondered what it was like having a close group of friends like that. Not that she envied them. She'd always been a loner. Too comfortable in her own skin. And it was only getting worse the older she became. Perhaps she was well on her way to becoming an old cat lady? Which would have been fine, if she liked cats. Hearing a cry, she looked back just in time to see one of the lads punch a friend in the face. As a fight broke out, she was reminded of her favourite maxim.

Things were not always what they seemed.

Focusing back on the jogging path, Jake's face flashed in front of her eyes. Was *he* all that he seemed? And what did he seem, exactly? On one hand, he appeared to be smart, kind and earnest. Yet, he was also a wily negotiator, which made her wonder if he was artful in other ways. Admittedly, not a red flag but certainly a prompt to proceed with caution. However, telling that to her matchmaker-in-chief had been a futile exercise. Now her and Jake were working together, Quicha had made hooking them up her new mission. Charlie shook her head in exasperation. Sooner or later, she'd have to tell her friend that it was never going to happen.

Not now.

Not after everything.

Turning towards the Lido, she realised she hadn't seen anyone else on the common for some time. Which was odd. Usually, there was always someone. Dossers, kids hanging around or cinemagoers cutting across the common after a visit to the Odeon. But not today.

Spooky.

She took out her ear pods so she could hear everything going on around her. Then she slightly accelerated her pace. Not too much but just enough to make her feel she'd be home sooner rather than later.

As she reached a cluster of trees on her left, she heard footsteps someway behind her. They started offbeat then, as they grew louder, slowly settled in to match her own. Charlie looked behind her to find a man of average build and height, his face hidden by a hoodie. Apparently oblivious to her gaze, the man tripped and got on one knee to tie a shoelace. The actions of a harmless stranger. Even so, instead of continuing towards the Lido, Charlie decided to cut her run short, turning left to cut across the middle of the common. The fastest route home.

This section of the park was darker and more isolated, being far from the commons' main paths and accompanying streetlights. As she ran, she tried to focus on the steady rhythm of her feet pounding the earth, each stride edging her closer to her destination, cursing herself for forgetting to bring her mace. Glancing behind her, Charlie had expected to see the man with the hoodie still on the path she had just left, but he had disappeared.

He must have also taken another route.

She extended her stride, her heart rate up, her breathing slightly ragged. On her right, the emptiness of the open common rose in a solid, jet-black mass of menace. To her left, she glimpsed the glimmer of the lake in between the dense trees, imperial in its silence, without even the rustle of a leaf or the croak of a frog to greet her. Up ahead loomed a dead zone, trees lining both sides, casting the area into even deeper shadow. She broke into an outright sprint, knees high, legs pumping, gunning for the other side where she'd be back in the relative open.

Halfway across the zone, her foot caught on something hard and, before she knew it, she was flying through the air, landing on her front with a thud. Winded, her hands and knees grazed from breaking her fall, she began to push herself up when she sensed someone rushing towards her. She turned her head just in time to see a foot rising. Then it slammed into her ribs, pain exploding in her chest.

"Stay down, bitch!" He spat, his breath pungent with halitosis.

The force of the kick flipped her onto her back, where she lay, blinking in shock and pain, trying to catch her breath, her mind in freefall.

What the hell!
Get up.
What's happening?
Get up now.
Who is he?
Move!!!

She tried to sit up, her heart jumping in her chest as she looked at her assailant and recognised the slight tilt of the head, the sloping shoulders.

The jogger who'd been behind her.

"You!" she managed to get out before howling in agony as two sharp kicks cut into her midriff. Instinctively, she rolled on her side and curled into a protective ball. In a flash, he was on top of her, kneeling on her neck, his other leg rammed against her back, pinning her to the ground.

"I said, keep your fucking trap shut!"

Charlie had to think fast. If he exerted more pressure, he could break her neck or choke her to death. Yet, trying to get up would only increase the pressure on her neck and windpipe. In desperation, she scissored her legs, hoping the action would pull her forward, enabling her to scoot out from under him. In response, he flipped her on her back and placed his knee on her chest, using his body weight to keep her down and suddenly it felt like an elephant was on top of her, squeezing her lungs. When she tried to buck, he leaned forward even further, bringing his head close to hers, exerting more pressure. Then, with a loud crack, one of her ribs fractured and fire roared through her thorax, making her cry out loud.

"Shhhhhh," he purred, flicking open a switchblade and brushing the cold, hard metal against her cheek.

Charlie froze, petrified.

"I've got a message for you," he said quietly, "from someone who doesn't fuck around." He pushed the blunt edge of the knife inside one of her nostrils, tilting her nose and head upwards.

"Stop poking your nose where it's not wanted," he murmured, spittle landing on her face. "Before someone decides to cut it off. You hear?"

Disgusted, she looked away.

"Look at me when I'm talking to you!!"

Charlie swivelled her eyes towards his pock-marked face.

"I said, DO YOU HEAR ME!!"

"Ye-es," she croaked, the weight on her chest constricting her breathing, "I hear you."

Without any warning, he twisted the knife and sliced open her nostril. Charlie screamed, pain shooting up her nose and bursting into her brain as warm blood ran over her mouth and chin.

"This is your last warning, bitch," he said, stroking the blood-soaked tip of the knife just under her left eye. "Next time, I won't be so gentle."

She squeezed her eyes shut, fearing the worst.

"Hey!" A woman's voice bellowed from deep across the common. "What's going on there?" Chorusing its master, a dog started barking.

Startled, her attacker sat back up, inadvertently relaxing his hold as he looked around for the intruder.

Charlie took the gap.

"Fuck you, arsehole!" she hissed, pushing through the pain in her chest as she lifted her bum off the ground, then twisted her hips to the right, trying to flip him off. Caught off guard, her assailant lost his balance, arms briefly windmilling in the air as he tumbled to the side. Hawking out the blood in her mouth, Charlie tried to get up, then screamed as a red-hot poker plunged into her side. As she lay back down, the Jogger sat up, his eyes searching for something.

What was he looking for?

Then she noticed something glinting on the ground near her feet.

He had dropped the knife!

Just then, her attacker spotted it too, reaching towards it, but she beat him to it, swiftly kicking the knife into the undergrowth. He glared at her, vengeful fury blazing in his eyes. Then he looked in the direction of the approaching woman, calculating how much time he still had left.

"Hey, you!" The woman yelled again, closer this time.

The jogger scrambled to his feet, while Charlie groped around for something to hit him with. Finding none, she grabbed a fistful of dirt, planning to throw it into his face when he came at her. Still making up his mind, he looked at her dirt-filled fist, then her face, towards the common and then back at her. Defiant, she lifted her arm, ready to attack.

He lunged.

She threw.

The woman screamed.

"Stop!"

Her good Samaritan was almost upon them.

Cursing, her attacker frantically brushed the earth off his face as he stumbled backwards into the trees. A sinister silhouette amongst the oaks, he paused, unable to leave without having the last word.

"You think you've got the better of me," he rasped, "but you haven't. Not by a long chalk. And don't forget, darling! This is your final warning!"

As she watched him run into the night, Charlie's limbs suddenly lost all their strength. All she could do was lie on her back, looking up at the stars as blood ran down her cheek. She focused on her breathing, blocking out the pain, trying to get her heartbeat back to normal. The woman and her dog were now only a few metres away, hurrying across the grass.

'Oh my Gosh!" the woman said, when they finally reached her, her wrinkled eyes widening as she took Charlie in. "Are you all right?"

They stood looking down at her, the dog panting, trying to get closer for a better sniff while his owner yanked back his leash. Too drained to speak, Charlie just shook her head.

Did she look all right?

Getting out her phone with her dog now obediently planted at her side, the woman hastily dialled with shaking fingers, her breathy, elderly voice rising with panic as she asked for an ambulance.

Tuning out the woman's voice, Charlie tentatively felt along her ribs to assess the extent of the damage. One broken rib, the others only bruised. That was something, at least. Then she went over the attack in her mind, her eyes smarting as rage welled within her.

How had she let him get so close?
Had she forgotten so quickly what her family's death had taught her?
Never, ever, be blind-sided.

She closed her eyes, pushing back angry tears as she tried to calm herself, clenching and unclenching her fists.

"Did you hear that, dear?" the woman asked, looming over her. "The ambulance will be here any minute."

Forcing her face into an approximation of gratitude, Charlie opened her eyes and nodded. Sympathy flooded the woman's face as she mistook her shimmering orbs for tears of sorrow rather than fury.

"You're safe now, love," she said in a soothing voice, the epitome of motherly concern. "That horrible man's gone and now you're safe."

Maybe she was, Charlie thought. And maybe she wasn't. Yet, one thing she knew for sure. Whomever they were. However, they came at her again. Next time, she would be ready for them.

40. Jonathan

The Strand
London, UK

The raindrop elegantly curved around a speck of dirt on the windowpane then remorselessly continued its descent, sometimes thickening as it joined its compatriots only to divide again as obstacles forced them in different directions. A troop of water soldiers leading the advance against the window's dirt and grime, bathed in innocent translucence, camouflage for all the pollutants that rose from the city and chocked the heavens. Beyond the glass, the turbulent sky broiled and shook, pouring torrential rain over steel, glass, and concrete skyscrapers, the water bleeding into the churning grey river at their feet. And between the buildings, swarming through the gunmetal streets, ant-like throngs hustled through Convent Garden, hugging their coats around themselves as a bulwark against the freezing sleet. Tiny grey people in a big grey world.

Is that what he was to become?

Hilary exhaled, the warm air fogging the window and partially obscuring his view. He should have been working but he couldn't summon the will, his usual drive drained from his limbs as if exsanguinated by a greedy vampire. So, instead of returning to his desk, he drew a smiley face in the steamy circle, an old trick his father had used when trying to get him out of a funk. As a child, it had worked every time. Used to still work when he had done it for himself.

Until now.

The Meanness of Things

It had been two weeks since that fateful night at Spencer's home. The SFO had set up almost immediately, moving in one Monday morning and commandeering almost a whole wing. The black suited investigators had set about their work quietly and methodically, hunting in packs likes a murder of crows. Their presence was suffocating, sucking the air out of every space they entered, carrying with them looks of suspicion and unspoken accusations, making even innocent people like him feel raw and exposed.

The disastrous press conference that had followed Tate's bombshell had also come and gone but, unfortunately, not the media attention. Every time they thought they might get ahead of the story a new revelation came out. So much so that the press had started calling the whole escapade the Cayman Papers after its Panama predecessor. Luckily, he'd been able to hand off most of the queries to the press office. Crisis comms, they called it. Otherwise known as, fishing your reputation out of the toilet.

Spencer had also barely spoken to him in the past two weeks. And when their paths did cross, his boss acted as if even looking at him was too much to bear. Did his colleagues sense it? The impending loss of all his power? The shrinking of his prospects into nothing more than a dim, distant light? Hilary shuddered at the thought.

And all because of Tate.

At least he had finally found a way to keep closer tabs on her. Who would have thought eavesdropping on someone would prove so difficult? They had tried hacking into her phone and computer but, according to the tech guys, whoever had set up Tate's security system had locked it tighter than the Svalbard Vault. The next option had been putting a bug in her flat but breaking in had proven far more problematic than he had anticipated. Her flat seemed to be guarded around the clock. First, by an old lady on the first floor who seemed glued to her front window and, second, by an incessant birdwatching neighbour at the back. Though the exact type of bird he was interested in was open to question. That had brought him to the third option. Manufacturing a crisis to gain entry, like a power failure or a telephone fault. However, those could also be tricky. Not only would it mean taking out the whole house or even the street, but it also carried the risk of someone phoning the actual repairmen whilst they were on site and discovering they were imposters.

Luckily, the world was full of inspiration, and it had been whilst he was reading the latest crime statistics that the idea had hit him. Something fool proof that no one would question. A little duff up and an old, trusty saviour to get there just in time. Of course, sweet, old Martha had sent Tate a get-well gift after the event with a little something extra hidden in the base of the flowerpot. Now, he had the best of both worlds. Either Tate would take the hint and heed the warning, or, if she didn't, they'd be able to listen in and know what she was up to even before she did it!

Genius!

Spencer, however, still hadn't been impressed. Though at this stage, even dragging a mountain to Mohammed would barely have garnered a disinterested shrug. Hilary let out another heavy sigh. He had to find a way of redeeming himself. Of turning the situation around to win back Spencer's favour.

Turning away from the window, he cast an unenthusiastic eye over the pile of files on his desk. He took one step towards them then pivoted, deciding he needed some fresh air or, at least, a brief change of scene. Grabbing his coat, he exited his office suite and walked down the corridor, heading for the lifts. As he turned the corner, he spotted Reuben and Steven six metres ahead of him, huddled conspiratorially.

How very interesting…

"You can't just brush me off, Steven. I know –" Reuben abruptly stopped talking as Hilary reached them.

"Everything all right here?" he asked, looking from one to the other.

"Couldn't be better!" Steven said with exaggerated jollity.

A veil fell over Reuben's face. "Absolutely. Just catching up, that's all."

"Good,' Hilary replied lightly. "I'd hate to think the SFO investigation is causing any unease."

"No – none at all," Reuben turned back to Steven. "I'll talk to you later then, yeah?"

Steven didn't respond but when Reuben stood his ground and glared at him, the CFO was forced into an affirmative response, giving a nod so slight it was as if his neck would break at the effort.

Hilary bookmarked the exchange in his head. Clearly, there was a storm brewing in paradise.

"Great speech at Exco the other day," Steven said as Reuben walked away, his Adam's apple bobbing up and down like the wattle of a frightened rooster. "Loved the bit about not letting the few bring down the many. Sooo true!"

"Glad you enjoyed it," Hilary replied coolly, proceeding towards the lifts.

Steven fell into step by his side. "I know you started all this. Long before the higher-ups came sniffing around. So, I want you to know that you have my full support. Day or night, I'll be there."

"Well," Hilary said in an off-handed manner. "It's out of my hands now."

"Oh…yes, quite. Still, perhaps I can help you in other ways…?"

Halting in front of the lift, Hilary gazed at Steven's face, suddenly realising that he had underestimated the man. Behind the temperate facade lay a desperate ruthlessness he hadn't before fully grasped.

"Such as?" he asked, intrigued.

Steven leaned closer, dropping his voice, "Anything. Anything at all."

The Meanness of Things

Hilary thought Spencer and his point about throwing some meat to the wolves.

Would Steven be willing to turn on the others?
Or would that also mean incriminating himself?
Either way, it would be interesting to find out.

"Thank you," he replied with a tight smile. "I'll bear that in mind."

As Steven walked back up the corridor, Hilary rode the lift to the ground floor and took one brisk lap around the block, trying to shake himself out of his lethargy. When he got back to his office, Gertrude sprang to her feet. "Michael Develin's solicitors called again," she said as he reached her desk, "what should I tell them?"

"I thought we'd already referred them to legal?"

"We did but they say legal is giving them the brush off. They said we're not going to discuss anything until the SFO investigation is complete. So, they want to speak to you."

Hilary felt a stab of irritation.

What the hell did Michael expect him to do? Go against his own legal department?

"No," he said, vigorously shaking his head. "Absolutely not. Tell them legal is dealing with it."

Entering his office, he hung his coat up and sat at his desk, expecting her to follow. Nobody came.

"Gertrude?" he yelled. "Where the hell are you?"

She popped her face around the door. "I thought you said I should phone Michael's solicitors?"

"Never mind that now. Has Spencer called?"

"No," she looked puzzled. "Were you expecting him to?"

"Yes…no…I just…"

She stepped into the room. "Do you want me to see if he's available?"

"No!" It came out too loud, so he swiftly moderated his tone. "It's fine. I just wondered, that's all. Any other messages?"

"Not so far," Gertrude said kindly, possibly seeing much more than she was saying.

Hilary averted his eyes and turned his attention to his desk drawer, looking for his notebook. When he found it, he quickly started jotting down what he could remember, not wanting to forget any salient points from the exchange with Reuben and Steven.

Gertrude coughed, reminding him of her presence, "Was there anything else?"

"Not at the moment," he said absently, finishing the last paragraph. His PA nodded and turned to leave.

"By the way, have you seen Jonathan?" he added as an afterthought. "He wasn't at the Exco meeting yesterday."

She turned as she reached the door, "Can't find him."

Hilary's head shot up. "What do you mean you can't find him?"

"Jonathan's wife says he told her he was going on a business trip but, according to our records, he's put in leave for two weeks."

"Didn't we cancel all leave due to the SFO investigation?"

Gertrude shrugged, "Perhaps he didn't get the memo?"

Hilary cursed under his breath. "What about his mobile?"

"He's not answering. Mabel – that's his wife - even tried the phone tracker but it's not working. He must have switched it off."

"When did she last speak to him?"

"Yesterday evening."

"And his PA?"

"Isabella? Last week, she said. Before he went on leave."

"Last week? But surely, they would have spoken since? Aren't there always urgent things cropping up?"

Another shrug, "She says Jonathan was quite insistent that he was not to be disturbed."

Hilary put down his pen and sat back in his chair.

What on earth was Jonathan up to?

"So, he takes two weeks off but tells his wife he's on a business trip?" he said ponderously, half to himself. Then a thought occurred to him.

"When Mabel spoke to him, did he sound near or far?" he said urgently. "You know, a strange ringtone, different from the usual?"

"I can ask," Gertrude replied. "Do you want me to do that right away?"

"Please."

As she bustled out of the room, Hilary remained seated, thinking.

There had to be a simple explanation. Something happened to Jonathan's phone, and he hadn't yet had a chance to get a new one. Or maybe Jonathan was cheating on his wife and just hadn't anticipated that he might be called back to work? Yes, that was it. Nothing to worry about.

Derrick's face flashed before him.

Impossible! Lighting didn't strike twice. Anyway, Mabel had spoken to Jonathan only yesterday. Surely, too early to assume something bad had happened.

A sense of foreboding welled up in the pit of his stomach.

Then again, hadn't Derrick vanished in much the same timeframe?

To calm himself, Hilary began organising the files on his desk, dividing them into groups and tagging them with different coloured stickers. Red for urgent, amber for second priority and green for third. He worked precisely and methodically, picking up each file, scanning its subject, sticking on the tag, and putting them in piles. Thinking about everything and anything other than what might come.

"She says it was like calling abroad," Gertrude said as she came back into the room. "Which is obviously in line with what he'd told her – that he's on a business trip."

"But he's not on a business trip, is he?" Hilary replied, shooting Gertrude a look of annoyance. "Otherwise, we would know about it."

"So, what do we do?" She stood in front of his desk, her face expectant.

Do? That was the question, wasn't it? Perhaps they could keep out of this altogether? After all, officially Jonathan was on leave, not on bank business. So, technically, the bank's exposure was zero.

He picked up a tab and rolled his thumb over the surface, the plastic silky and sleek against his skin.

Yet, if this got out, would the media see it that way? Worst still, what if the media linked this to the money laundering mess? If they did, Spencer would be looking for a fall guy and he didn't need to guess who that would be. Unless he got ahead of the story…

"When is Jonathan due to return from leave?" Hilary asked, carefully sticking the tab on a file.

"The end of the month," Gertrude said, critically assessing his ministrations. "I can do that for you if you want."

The end of the month. Less than two weeks away. That would be enough time to organise a leak to the press. Paint Jonathan as a guilty man who'd fled to avoid the consequences of his own actions. But timing would be key. He would need to be sure that Jonathan had actually vanished first. And make sure no one blabbed before his plan was put in motion.

"No – that's quite all right." He placed a file on the urgent pile. "Did Mabel sound worried about not being able to get hold of her husband?"

"I'm not sure." Gertrude made a face. "She didn't *sound* worried but then again, she did also try to track his phone."

"That could have been for reasons other than concerns about his safety."

"Yes, well," her face went pink, "I hadn't thought of that."

"If Mabel wasn't alarmed then I see no reason for us to be either. It could just be a mix-up. Let's keep this to ourselves for now and see what happens."

"All right. I'll let Isabella know. What about Mabel?"

"Tell her everything's fine. No need to be alarmed. But emphasis that if she has any more problems, she must come to us first. No one else. Understood?"

"As you wish," Gertrude said, taking her leave.

Hilary waited for the door to close before picking up the phone. He answered on the second ring.

"Head of Security speaking."

"Samuel? Hilary here. I need a favour."

41. The Blades

Hillbrow
Johannesburg, South Africa

Standing on his right, Thabo felt Boy nervously assessing the beefy, heavily-armed men loitering outside the entrance of the office building. If the building had been a posh hotel or shopping mall in the heart of Sandton, the guards might have not looked so out of place. However, for a filthy, crumbling, four-storey building in the centre of crime-infested Hillbrow, they looked like they were there as much to keep people in as to keep them out.

"Are you sure this is the place?" Boy whispered.

"Yes," Thabo said, trying to sound more confident than he felt. "She said we should just give them her name and they'll let us in."

The truth was his friend hadn't said any such thing. In fact, she hadn't responded to his message at all. Not on the day Lucky vanished, or on the next, and the next, and the next day after that. So, he'd decided to take a chance. After all, what was the worst that could happen?

As he stepped towards the guards, a Bond villain uncoiled himself from the beer crate he had been sitting on and blocked their path. He shoulders were the width of a Casspir and he had a livid scar running from his temple, through one unseeing eye, to his chin. "What do *you* want?" the guard asked, his voice full of disdain, his good eye sizing them up and finding them wanting.

On his left, Thabo felt Innocent puffing out his chest, getting ready to take him on. He quickly grabbed his arm, holding him back.

"I'm sorry to disturb you, Sir," Thabo said, respectfully bowing his head in greeting. "My name is Thabo Zwane. I'm an old friend of Nolu Mhize. I believe she's expecting us?"

"Nolu who?" One Eye replied as he took the safety off his shotgun.

Never a good sign.

The four guards sitting behind One Eye came to stand next to him, flexing their biceps as they tightened their grip on their rifles. Again, Innocent tensed while Boy stepped behind Thabo, the anxious heat of his body pulsating onto his back.

"Nolu Mhize," Thabo said firmly. "But you probably know her as Cleaver."

One Eye's face shifted slightly but whether that was a good or bad thing, Thabo couldn't tell. He murmured something in the ear of the guard to his right, who promptly turned and disappeared into the building.

Then they waited, engaged in a silent standoff, the guards looking at them with dead eyes, rifles cocked, Thabo and Innocent staring back, determined not to back down. Boy, perhaps the wiser of the three, focused on the guards' shoes.

When the guard came back, he was carrying a phone. He whispered something in One Eye's ear, who then turned his glacial gaze to Thabo, saying in a clipped voice, "She wants to talk to you."

The guard thrust the phone in Thabo's face, the call on speaker.

"Hello?" Thabo said uncertainly.

"Who told you my name?" a female voice shot back.

Boy and Innocent looked at him with surprise and accusation, their faces saying: *You said she knew we were coming!*

Ignoring them, Thabo licked his lips and said, "You did. When you were seven years old. You said that when you got out, you'd pick a name that would strike fear into the hearts of everyone who heard it."

As he waited for her response, Thabo's pounding heart echoed in his head, every second suddenly feeling like a lifetime.

"Let me speak to MK," she eventually said.

The guard snatched away the phone and held it to One Eye's ear. As the guard took his instructions, Boy pulled at Thabo's shirt, indicating that this would be a good time to make a run for it. Even Innocent seemed to agree, his eyes darting around as if looking for escape routes. Thabo kept his eyes locked on One Eye's face, knowing that, if she didn't say yes, he only had one last, desperate card left to play.

When the call ended, One Eye stepped put his safety back on and turned towards him, the veins in his neck pulsing like they were about to burst. "She said I should escort you in personally and…" his mouth twisted as if he'd just eaten something bitter, "…to apologise if I offended you in any way."

"Uh-huh!" Innocent exclaimed, pushing past the guards as he pranced and preened his way to the door.

"Thank you. I would appreciate that," Thabo said, waiting for One Eye to lead the way. "And no – I wasn't offended. You were just doing your job."

As he led them to the entrance, Boy murmured, "That was close."

You don't know the half of it, Thabo thought, glaring at Innocent as they caught up with him at the top of the entrance steps.

Stop mucking around!

Innocent simply shrugged, his face blank.

What are you talking about?

In the lobby, One Eye turned left towards a brand-new-looking lift that hadn't been visible from the street. Instead of pressing up, he touched the down button, the lift opening so swiftly it was as if it had been waiting for them. Innocent rushed to get in first, but Thabo held him back, whispering, "Don't get it twisted. Just because we got in doesn't mean we're *all* getting out. Cleaver will kill you if you piss her off. Got it?"

Innocent's body went rigid, his eyes wide as he quickly nodded.

The ride to Basement Two took less than three seconds, and soon One Eye was ushering them into a vast, brightly lit, rectangular room the size of half a football pitch. On both sides of the room sat rows of whirring computer servers, their lights busily flickering. In the room's centre was four concentric rows of workstations arranged like a horseshoe, and at each desk sat a teenage girl dressed in red, furiously typing away. The horseshoe faced a wall on which hung a bank of huge screens, some with lines of code, others with drone shots of live action or what appeared to be transcripts of live speech. A short, curvaceous girl stood in the centre of the horseshoe, dressed in all black leathers, a black pouch slung across her back, her crown of long blonde braids rippling around her as she walked up and down, shouting instructions above the din.

Cleaver.

"Dagger," she said, looking at a blue-braided girl to her right. "Status report."

"Target en route," Dagger replied. "Intercept ETA two minutes."

The Blades were a gang of techs for hire. Developers, hackers, and security system specialists. Their name arose from two things. One, their reputation for being able to cut through any digital security system; and two, from the fact that their leadership team, chosen through a rigorous selection process that tested both tech and vicious fighting skills, had all adopted the names of different kinds of knives. Cleaver, the gang's leader and founder, was the most skilled and merciless of them all.

Their clientele comprised those who had something to find or something to hide and who also had big enough pockets to pay for undetectability. In practice, this meant that most of their clients were either corrupt corporates, politically exposed persons or members of local and international crime syndicates. From what Thabo could tell from the screens, today they were working for a cash-in-transit gang. The target, a money van that had just picked up its load.

One Eye waved to get Cleaver's attention and pointed at Thabo. She turned towards them, looked Thabo up and down, then dismissed One Eye with a flick of her wrist. While he headed back to the lift, she slowly strolled towards them, her face inscrutable. Innocent and Boy stepped back, sensing Thabo and her needed space. Everyone else in the room kept working, ignoring the scene.

As she approached, Thabo sucked in his breath, his mouth suddenly dry. He had long thought about this moment, but he hadn't expected that she would still affect him so much. He remembered her smell, like Jasmine, and the way a little dimple formed in her cheek when she smiled.

Did she still smell the same?
What would be her first words?
In all these years, had she thought about him at all?

When they were close enough to kiss, she looked down bashfully, shielding her eyes, then lifted her face as if to peck him on the cheek. He inhaled, breathing her in. The same scent, the same curve of her jaw. His heart racing, he leant down to receive her kiss. Then he doubled over, pain ripping through his abdomen as the punch landed right on his solar plexus.

"That's for lying to me," Cleaver said through gritted teeth, raising a knee to meet his descending face. "And *that's* for leaving me behind."

The blow sent Thabo tumbling backwards and onto the floor, blood trickling from his nose. Looking up from his prone position, he saw Innocent and Boy's startled faces to his right and, in front of him, Cleaver walking towards him with balled fists, her eyes shining with ice-cold fury.

"I didn't lie," Thabo blubbered. "I did love –"

"Liar!"

He rolled away as she kicked him, managing to get away fast enough to make it just a glancing blow. Innocent and Boy looked at each other, not sure what to do.

"Why do you think I let you come down here?" she said, reaching behind her and pulling out a giant, gleaming cleaver from her pouch. "Only so I could kill you myself!"

"Wait!" Thabo crossed his arms in front of his face. "We didn't mean to leave you. We had to get out that night because Father Gibbons was after

Lucky. He'd nearly got him once and we knew if we waited, it might be too late!"

Cleaver paused in mid-stroke, her eyes uncertain. "Father Gibbons hurt Lucky?"

"He would have done if we hadn't gotten out." Thabo sat up, wiping the blood from his nose on the back of his hand. "We went to find you, but you weren't in your dorm. When I went back a week later, your friends said you'd already left."

She straightened, putting the cleaver back in her pouch. "Once you'd gone there was no reason for me to stay," she said flatly.

Innocent and Boy exchanged a knowing look.

"It took years before I finally found you again. Heard what you were doing," Thabo got to his feet and brushed himself off. "Then Lucky told me he had heard you were now with someone else. Which made sense given how much time had passed."

Cleaver stuck out her chin and crossed her arms in front of her chest. "If you think that, why are you here?"

He took a step towards her, his eyes imploring, "I…" Thabo glanced at Boy and Innocent. "*We* need your help. Lucky's disappeared and we think some bad guys took him."

"Bad guys?"

Thabo told her the story, keeping things concise but not sparing himself and what he had done. "So, you see," he said in conclusion, "it's all my fault. I have to make it right."

Whilst Cleaver's demeanour had thawed as he had recounted the tale, her eyes remained wary. "And you want me to do what? Try and trace him?"

"If you can," Boy said, drawing closer to them. "Thabo's wrong. It's my fault too." He pulled Innocent next to him. "We *all* need to make it right."

Cleaver pursed her lips, scanning all three of their faces before ending back at Thabo.

"You do know what you're asking, don't you? The people you're up against?"

"Only that they're killers," Innocent replied.

She looked at Innocent with contempt. "If the rumours are true, these people are more than just killers. In fact, if they took Lucky, death would be the least of his worries."

Thabo gasped, "You mean you know who they are?"

Cleaver shook her head. "Not *know*. Suspect. And before you ask me, I can't tell you who they are."

"But -"

"What do you mean, 'death would be the least of his worries'?" Boy interjected, cutting Thabo off.

The Meanness of Things

"Their interests are wide and varied." Cleaver's voice was calm and detached. "But one of those interests is children. Specifically, kidnapping and selling them. Mostly to slave and paedophile rings in the Middle East and the West."

Boy, Innocent and Thabo looked at each other, horrified.

"But what if he was sick?" Innocent said eagerly.

"Sick how?"

"His lungs," Boy said. "He has TB. Bad. That's why he took the phone, to get -. Anyway, the point is they wouldn't take someone who was sick, would they?"

"Well," Cleaver said slowly, "if he was of no use…"

Thabo's stomach dropped. "But surely, we still have time? Lucky's been gone less than a week. Perhaps they haven't decided what to do with him yet?"

She looked at the floor.

"We've got to try," Thabo touched her arm. "Please."

She gazed at the hand on her arm then at his face, her eyes softening. "Ok," she said, sighing. "I'll see what I can do."

Turning towards the nearest desktop, she signalled for the current occupant to give up her seat and sat at the keyboard. Thabo went to stand behind her, looking over her shoulder, flanked by Boy and Innocent.

"Ok." Cleaver opened up a new programme. "Give it to me."

Thabo's mind went blank. "Give you what?"

"The phone number, dummy. The number will tell me the network. The name of the network will lead me to their towers and hopefully, that will lead us to Lucky. It also would be good to know when the phone was last used – to your knowledge."

Thabo hastily told her, hoping against hope that she was right. They all watched as she worked her magic, collectively holding their breath. Since The Blades had already created a backdoor, it only took a few seconds to get into the network. The challenge seemed to be locating the phone through the towers. Five minutes later, she took her hands off the keyboard, her face resigned.

"The only location I can find is on the day that Lucky disappeared. The tower nearest your home. Since then, nada."

Thabo's chest tightened. "What does that mean?"

"One of two things," Cleaver replied. "The phone could have just been switched off at that point. In case, I've already set up a tracker so that we get pinged if it ever comes back online. However, that's unlikely given that the guys who might have taken him are sharp enough not to leave a trail. So, it's more likely that they destroyed the sim or even disposed of the phone in its entirety."

She stood up, giving the station back to its owner, and turned towards the lift, ready to show them out.

"We can't trace him at all?" Boy asked forlornly.

"Nope," Cleaver said. "Not via a phone signal anyway."

Thabo's heart sank.

Without that, what else did they have?

"But if a miracle happens and the phone does come back online," Cleaver continued, "I'll let you know ASAP."

She began walking towards the lift. Looking defeated, Boy and Innocent followed her. Thabo remained rooted to the spot, a terrible thought having just occurred to him.

"It could also mean something else though, couldn't it?" Thabo mumbled glumly. "The lack of signal. It could mean…"

Cleaver stopped and turned towards him, her eyes full of pity. "I'm so sorry, Thabo."

42. The Photo

Lower East Side
New York, USA

Viper sat at her desk in her sanctuary, Stevie Wonder blaring through the speakers, her fingers whizzing across the keyboard. When you knew that you had a tedious job that would take hours on end, there was nothing better than Stevland Hardaway Morris, otherwise known as Stevie Wonder, to get your mouth humming and feet stomping. Her other secret was her favourite tipple. A long glass of wooded chardonnay with five ice cubes. No more than one every two hours interspersed with strong black coffee. After all, you didn't want alcohol dulling your senses. Glancing at her watch, Viper realised she was coming up to hour number two. Time for a stretch and a top-up.

As she sidled up to her mini wine fridge, her mind turned to Charlie. She hadn't said much and, if Viper wasn't one of her emergency contacts, she probably wouldn't have said anything at all. A mugging, she'd said. Her own fault, running alone on a dark night. Viper tutted to herself. Why did they, as women, always do that? Blame themselves for somebody else's violence? For not being careful enough when these days you couldn't even go on a date without giving your friends the location and the man's details in case you never returned. Ridiculous!

What was worse, as soon as Charlie was fixed up, she'd been off again, whizzing around as if nothing had happened. Or, at least, pretending to. As far as she was concerned, it was clear that the incident had affected Charlie more than she cared to admit. She hated feeling weak. Couldn't stand the idea of losing. This meant that Charlie would now be more determined than ever to prove that she couldn't be bested, no matter the risk. Refilling her glass, Viper made a mental note to message Quicha. Tell her to keep a close eye on their mutual friend.

Sitting back at her desk, Viper took a sip of wine and reviewed the progress she had made so far. Or rather lack thereof. She had started with two keywords - Jonas and Murdoch – and had received tonnes of individual hits for various people called Jonas or Murdoch but none for a Jonas tied to Derrick Murdoch. Then she had tried Jonas and Yeats Bank which had also resulted in zero matches. Thereafter, given Murdoch's geographic area of work, she had opted for Jonas and Africa which, conversely, had yielded too many matches. In order to filter the hits she had received, she had then chosen two elimination criteria: Money (indications that they had substantial amounts of it), and age (all those in nappies or with spots had been taken off the list). That had landed her with ten rich guys called Jonas between the ages of 25 and 60 who had business on the African continent.

Next, she had introduced a third set of criteria, looking at the sectors the ten men were involved in to cross-check these with the sectors funded by Yeats Bank. Unfortunately, this had also led to a dead end. As a private bank, Yeats didn't divide their clientele into sectors. Their only qualifying criterion was that the bank's private clients needed to have a net worth of greater than one million pounds. All ten Jonas's on her list more than met that criterion.

So, what now?

Waking up her computer again, Viper decided to widen her search parameters to include associates of the bank or Murdoch and not just the bank or Murdoch himself. She typed in the list of associates and then used a specially designed search programme to cross-reference the names on the list with the social media posts and news articles of all ten men.

Nothing.

Then she imported the images of each associate on the list into the programme and tried again, using facial recognition and not only names this time.

There was one hit.

It was a two-year-old article from a Kenyan newspaper headlined "Maharaj Splurge Shock". Beneath the headline was a photo of what appeared to be a very fancy dinner party. The strapline beneath the photo read: 'Controversial businessman, Jonas Maharaj, wining and dining Kenya's elite at the Nairobi Palace'. One table was the focus of the photograph, with several tables in the background but it was the background that caught Viper's attention. One man had tried to shield his face, not wanting to be caught on camera.

THE MEANNESS OF THINGS

Now why would that be?

Her facial recognition programme had flagged the photo as including a partial match with one of two people on her associates list. However, given that the man's face was partly hidden, she still needed to confirm which one it was. Hence, she searched for every photo she could find related to the Nairobi event. It was the same in each one. Wherever this man appeared, he was either looking away from the camera or attempting to mask his face. As far as she was concerned, anyone trying that hard not to be seen must have something to hide. So, she went through each photo inch by inch, hoping to get lucky. She struck gold with a wide-angle shot. Even though she had to blow it up, which messed up the pixilation, she still managed to get what she needed. An image of the man's face reflected in a mirror as he turned away from the camera. Now she had a 100% match.

"Well, hello Spencer Dovecroft," Viper murmured to herself with a note of satisfaction.

Now she was getting somewhere.

She pasted the photo into her report and added an explanatory note. The photo was an irrefutable link between Jonas Maharaj and the Group CEO of Yeats Bank. And the fact that Dovecroft had wanted to keep this link quiet, meant that their association was probably pretty strong. Not just a friendship but something more. Nevertheless, Viper thought soberly, the photo was just a baby step. It didn't prove that Maharaj had been a client of Yeats. Nor did it suggest, since Dovecroft wasn't Murdoch, that Murdoch and Maharaj had known each other.

Perhaps working backwards would yield more conclusive results?

Fortifying herself with another sip of wine, Viper moved on to focusing on Maharaj himself. Google revealed that Jonas Maharaj was the Chairman and CEO of a company called JM Enterprises. This company had started out in the import/export business before branching out into casinos, property, and construction. Furthermore, according to the South African press, whilst JM Enterprises had long had a presence in several countries on the African continent, they had been virtually unknown in South Africa before the advent of the country's third democratic president. However, when this president came to power, the company's South African fortunes had improved significantly. And so had their notoriety, with JM having allegedly been involved in numerous major scandals involving the misappropriation of state funds.

Viper ticked off the boxes in her head. Casino owner – check. Shady businessman – check. Stolen funds in need of cleaning – check. In terms of the kind of guy they were looking for, Maharaj certainly seemed to tick all the boxes. And having a corrupt banker like Murdoch on your side, able to transfer money surreptitiously to any location around the world, would have been worth more than gold for someone like Maharaj. Again, however, this was still not conclusive proof that Maharaj was the Jonas they were looking for. Plus, Develin had spoken about Jupta Inc, not JM Enterprises. She still needed to find an indisputable link between Murdoch and Maharaj. Only then could they go about determining whether Jonas Maharaj had been involved in Murdoch's murder.

Luckily, there was one more place she could look. The spreadsheet Charlie had forwarded from Jake based on what they had found to date in Murdoch's Cayman Islands account. There were thirty sheets so far, each of which represented a depositor. A keyword search across all the sheets, produced no results for Jonas, Maharaj or Jupta Inc. There was, however, a match for a company called JM. JM was linked to a depositor named Reginald Capital. According to the organigram Jake and his team had pieced together, Reginald Capital was a subsidiary of Siya & Associates which, in turn, was a subsidiary of JM.

Viper punched the air in triumph.

Finally, she'd found a provable link!

However, her excitement had barely left the harbour before she discovered the first problem. When she clicked on the JM link to examine the company's details, she discovered that JM stood for JM Holdings, not Maharaj's JM Enterprises. Moreover, given Jake had not yet been able to find any info on the company's owners or Board of Directors, she had no way of establishing if the two companies were somehow linked. She found the second problem when she scrolled through the list of Reginald Capital transactions. The last deposit they had made had occurred one year before Murdoch vanished, which was not in line with what Lucy had said about Murdoch doing business with Jonas right up until he had disappeared.

Damn.

Viper sat back and looked at the data across all her screens, trying to make sense of it. Option one: Jonas Maharaj wasn't the Jonas they were looking for and the connection between him and Dovecroft was just coincidental. Option two: Jonas Maharaj was their guy but had transacted with Murdoch through various companies, not just Jupta Inc or JM Enterprises. The first option meant she was back to where she had started, the second that Jake's team still had a long way to go. Viper shook her head in exasperation. There had to be a quicker way. All she had to do was find it.

Resting her head against her chair headrest, she closed her eyes and tried to clear her mind, hoping free association would come to her aid. Just then the throbbing beats of Superstition filled the room. Unable to resist, Viper started singing along, "Very superstitious…Writing's on the wall. Bum-da-da-bum-bum…Very superstitious…Ladder's 'bout to fall…" As sang, she pictured a ladder in her mind. All of a sudden, her eyes flew open, and she sat up straight.

Ladder, rungs, connection.

Murdoch hadn't acted alone, had he?
What if someone else had known about Maharaj?
What if there was another witness?

Viper quickly began typing, thinking about what Charlie had said about the weight of bearing secrets.

There had to be someone in Murdoch's inner circle desperate to unburden themselves. And who was she to turn her back on someone in need?

43. Two-Step Rule

The Strand
London, UK

Reuben exited the boardroom and stepped into the corridor. Only his first interview with the SFO investigators and it had felt like they were strangling him one question at a time. In fact, everything now felt cramped. The lift, the corridor, the toilets. Ever since the investigation had started, there seemed to be eyes everywhere, watching and wondering. Waiting for him to give himself away and reveal whether he was 'one of them'.

A conspirator.

That's what Hilary had called the people the investigators were looking for. "Derrick's conspirators". Even now he remembered how his laser eyes had drilled into each and every one of them around the boardroom table. When Hilary's gaze had landed on him, Reuben had felt the sweat breaking out on his back and slowly oozing down his spine as if his own body had been determined to dissolve any strength he had left. Still, he had held firm, staring back without even blinking. Even as Jonathan's empty chair had screamed abandonment and Steven had studiously avoided his eye.

Jonathan had been right. That man really was a piece of shit.

Now walking down the corridor, Reuben also kept his shoulders straight, smiling and joking with those he passed like today was like any other day. It wasn't until he got to his office and closed the door, that he realised he was shaking. Stumbling to his desk, he opened the bottom drawer and pulled out a bottle of vodka. Hastily unscrewing the cap, he took a large swig, then another

The Meanness of Things

and another, liquid dribbling down his chin. Then, wiping his face with the back of his hand, he plopped down on his desk chair, waiting for the alcohol to flood his veins and for warmth to spread over his body like a wave of calming water.

As the vodka took hold, Reuben's thundering heart returned to normal, and the ringing in his ears came to a stop. Hiding the bottle back in the drawer, he gripped the edge of his desk and took a deep breath. It was now or never. He couldn't stand any more of this. He had to take decisive action.

Popping two mints in his mouth, he straightened his tie, smoothed down his shirt, and phoned his secretary to ask her to bring him an empty box. When Trisha came in, box in hand, he thanked her politely and shooed her back out the door, ignoring her enquiring look. He didn't want any witnesses for what he was about to do next.

Getting to his feet, Reuben took a moment to look around his office, marvelling at all the things he had once so coveted. Hand-picked pieces of modern art; bookshelves full of business best-sellers or the leading texts in his craft; a wall dedicated to his certificates and awards; and most importantly, prominently positioned pictures of him hobnobbing with all the right people. All designed to project an image of the person he had thought he had wanted to be. Needed to be. Now, apart from photos of family, his certificates and the documents secreted in his safe, he was surprised how little of it he wanted to keep. He smirked, silently laughing at the absurdity of it all.

Was it time to stop pretending?
Time to show the world the real Reuben Stott and see how it reacted?
Or was that just the vodka talking?

He packed quickly, filling the box. Then he asked Trisha to run down to the canteen and get him his favourite sandwich for lunch. Once the coast was clear, he threw his jacket over the box, picked it up and hurried to the executive lift, hoping to make it to the parking garage without bumping into any of his colleagues. Luckily, only junior staff crossed his path, so focused on their phones they barely noticed his existence, and he made it back to his office just in time to head off his secretary at the door. Grabbing the sandwich, he quickly closed the door in her face so that she wouldn't see the office's altered state. Then, throwing the sandwich in the bin, he rushed to his desk and turned on his computer.

The resignation letter was brief. The reason put forward - personal health. An unnamed illness he could no longer keep hidden blah, blah, blah. The gratitude he expressed for the years of collegial support he'd received was probably overly generous but, for the most part, sincere. When it was complete, he printed it out, put it in a sealed envelope addressed to John Hilary and placed the letter on his desk.

Leaning back in his chair, Reuben took in the moment. He could still remember the day when Derrick had held out his hand and made him the offer. A fast-track to the top of the professional risk ladder and riches he otherwise could never have dreamed of. Later, perhaps even CEO. All in exchange for a little blindness and the odd tiny, special favour now and then. That didn't sound like too much to ask, did it? People did it all the time. Totally legit.

And it had been.

Until it wasn't.

He should never have accepted it. Quit there and then and tried his luck somewhere else. Now, years of cow-towing to get by had been wasted. Decades of painfully building his professional credibility obliterated in an instant.

How could he have been such a fool?!

Sighing, Reuben stood up and walked over to grab his coat off the stand near the window. The grey roofs of the city glinted in the meek winter sun, and, in the distance, he almost thought he saw a rainbow. He paused, staring at the view.

Could it all still be all right? There was a slim chance that the SFO would brush it all under the carpet. Conclude that the scandal was so big that the best thing for the bank and country was to make it all go away. Pin everything on Murdoch the nowhere man and let the rest out to pasture with exuberant reference letters. Isn't that how the old boys did it?

For a brief moment, he could see it all in his mind's eye. The drunken farewell party, the manly handshake from Hilary as he gave him his parting gift, people waving to him in the corridor as he made his exit and, a few weeks later, him putting his feet up on his new desk after landing a better-paying position in the City. A fresh start, a fresh challenge. Then the image warped and flickered, black-ringed holes appearing in the frame before it all burnt to ash.

No. Hoping for a reprieve was just wishful thinking. Too much had already become public. Now, there had to be an accounting. A blood sacrifice.

Slowly he buttoned up his coat.

Even if that hadn't been the case, there was also the not-so-small matter of the anonymous messages he'd been receiving. One every hour, on the hour, over the past two days. Taunting him, telling him that they knew about Reginald Capital and pushing him to "come clean". So what if he'd done a few personal deals on the side? Stashed away a few million, or two, or ten of his own? Was that so wrong given the billions Murdoch had been making? What he'd taken wasn't even worth a footnote in the Murdoch story. Yet, there they were, hounding him day and night.

He turned away from the window and headed to the door.

What he couldn't understand was how they'd found out. He'd been so careful. Even the SFO investigators hadn't yet pegged. That meant that, whoever these people were, they had gone to great lengths to find him out. And you didn't do that unless you were serious. It was only a matter of time before they made their next move. All in all, therefore, no matter which way, he was out. Better to go out on his own terms.

Reuben walked out of his office and closed the door behind him for the last time. His PA, seated at her desk, stopped typing and looked up, surprised.

"I'm afraid I've got a family emergency," he said by way of explanation. "Please cancel my meetings for the rest of the day, would you?"

"Oh?" her brow puckered with concern. "Nothing serious I hope?"

"They're not sure yet. Fingers crossed, eh?"

"Ahhh," she cooed, "I'm sorry to hear that. I hope everything works out. Can we call you on your mobile if something urgent comes up?"

"Best not," he said with forlorn. "I'll let you know once I'm back on air."

"No problem." She opened her mouth as if she was about to say something, her eyes searching his face, then appeared to change her mind. "I'll check in with you later then," she said, turning back to her screen.

"Yes…" he swallowed a sudden lump in his throat. "Later."

After a few steps, Reuben felt the urge to turn back. "Trish?"

Her eyes found his, "Yes?"

"Um…thank you. For everything."

That question again, spoken this time. "Everything?"

"I mean…" *How to say goodbye without giving himself away?* "You know. Your kindness and concern. It has meant…it means the world to me."

She smiled shyly, "Thank you. I appreciate you telling me."

"Take care now."

"You too," she half turned away, then looked back. "But I'll see you tomorrow, right? If all goes well?"

"Of course!" A weak smile. "Of course, you will. Tomorrow."

The journey to his car was excruciating, every moment filled with dread that he'd be denied a dignified exit. It was only when he was driving away from the bank that he allowed himself to breath normally again. Apart from the pool of sweat on his back and torso, thankfully disguised by his coat, step one had gone without a hitch.

Now it was time for step two.

The Two-Step Rule was something that his mentor had drilled into him from the day they met. Step One: Always maintain the power of surprise. Step Two: Attack is the best form of defence.

Turning into a side street four blocks away from Yeats, he parked, googled the number, and dialled. As he waited for the receptionist to track her down, he drummed his fingers against the steering wheel, trying not to think of the letter on his desk or Trisha finding it before he'd had the chance to strike.

The receptionist finally came back on the line, "I'm afraid Ms Tate doesn't seem to be in today. Can I take a message?"

"Yes. It's Reuben Stott from Yeats Bank. Please ask her to call me back. I have some information she may be interested in."

44. A Plausible Theory

City of London
London, UK

The brightly lit, open-plan newsroom was buzzing, journalists typing frantically, talking on the phone to a source, or huddled in groups exchanging takes on a story. In the old days, the air would have been laden with cigarette smoke, the tinge of cheap coffee, and stale body odour from too many all-nighters. Now, thanks to anti-smoking laws, modern air conditioning and in-house upmarket cafés, the dominant bouquet seemed to be processed air beige occasionally peppered by the whiff of a passing expresso, café mocha or the fast-food choice of the day. From what Charlie could tell, today that seemed to be pizza.

She found Jake in one of the glass-fronted boardrooms that lined one side of the floor, huddled over a laptop at a six-seater table, surrounded by walls plastered with enigmatic scribbles, mind-maps, organigrams, red arrows and post-it notes. Apart from two other laptops, whose owners she assumed were temporarily absent, the table was laden with bottles of water, takeaway coffee cups and a somewhat forlorn, half-eaten burger meal.

When she entered, Jake's haggard face brightened, his eyes sparkling with warmth and something that looked like admiration. "They let you in, then?" he said with a cocky smile.

Whilst her ribs were healing fast, it still hurt to laugh, so Charlie proffered a smile instead. "Yeah – they must be slipping!"

All of a sudden, he frowned, "What happened to your face?"

Charlie put a hand up to her nose, "Oh, that! Just a silly accident at kick-boxing class."

He still looked perplexed but didn't press her. Since standing was less painful than sitting, she slowly ambled around the room, studying the walls. "I see you've made more progress."

Jake ran a hand through his hair. "Yep. Still a long way to go, though. We'll get there but finding all the players is going to take some time and, in some cases, we may not even be able to do that."

Looking at his rumpled look, she wondered if that's what his girlfriend saw in the mornings.

Not a bad sight at all.
Wait - did Jake have a girlfriend?
Stop it, Charlie.
Focus.

"Looks impressive, nonetheless," she replied.

"Well," *was he blushing?* "it's you who got us here. Wasn't sure you would, but you really came through."

Charlie didn't respond, seeing no need to emphasise the obvious. She stopped next to a wall with an organigram on it. At the head of the chart was a circle with a question mark in it. Ten tentacles flowed out of the circle, each of which had about 5 to 6 levels. Tentacle number three had JM Holdings at the top of it, from which flowed another set of tentacles, some of which were already known whilst others remained a mystery.

"Well, you'll be glad to know I've got some more info," she said, pointing at the chart.

"Oh?" he asked, tipping his chair back and rocking on its back legs.

"Through a well-placed source, we've managed to establish that, in addition to Reginald Capital, JM Holdings, JM Enterprises and Jupta Inc - the company that Develin initially confronted Murdoch about - are all linked."

"How well placed?"

"A deep throat," she said with a grin.

No doubt about it. Viper had pulled the cat out of the bag on this one.

The front legs of Jake's chair landed with a thud, his face incredulous. "Don't tell me you're talking about a current Yeats employee?"

"Yep. Though technically, an ex-employee. They've just resigned."

"And this person knows because…?"

"Let's just say he has intimate knowledge of Murdoch's dealings. He's ready to go public with his side of the story."

"Mmmm," Jake murmured, "you mean an accomplice. Then how do you know he's telling the truth and not just covering his own arse?"

Charlie gave a facial shrug, "I don't. At least when comes to the arse-covering parts. We're going to run it as a tell-all and let the readers decide. As for the rest, I asked for back up and he gave it to me. Proof that all three companies are located at the same address in Dubai – street, postal, everything. And, more importantly, a copy of transaction documents showing regular, large transfers between Jupta Inc and JM Enterprises to JM Holdings."

"All right," standing up, Jake picked up a marker and joined her by the organigram, erasing the question marks on two tendrils under JM Holdings before he began adding Jupta Inc and JM Enterprises on each respectively.

Distracted by his cologne, Charlie went to stand on the other side of the conference table. "The man behind JM Holdings and its subsidiaries is a corrupt businessman called Jonas Maharaj," she added, gazing at his handiwork.

He wrote 'JM = Jonas Maharaj' on the organigram.

"Another source told me that they heard Murdoch and someone called Jonas arguing just before Murdoch vanished, wherein Jonas threatened him. We think there's a good chance it's the same Jonas. So, we might be getting closer to finding Murdoch's killer."

"A threat is a long way from murder," Jake said as he put down the marker. "Unless you know what the quarrel was about?"

"Not yet. But, from what we know so far, it looks like Murdoch had reached his limit about something. My guess is, for whatever reason, he suddenly wanted to turn off the money laundering taps. In Maharaj's eyes, that would have immediately transformed Murdoch into a dangerous liability rather than an asset."

"Oh, I get you," he said, sitting back at the conference table. "That's certainly a plausible theory, given the billions involved." He pulled his laptop towards him and woke it up. "So, I suppose you want me to look for some kind of pattern. See if there was any kind of decrease in the flows to his Cayman Island account before he disappeared?"

"If you can. According to Develin, Murdoch started laundering larger and larger amounts as time went on. If my theory is correct and Murdoch did call time out, we should be able to see a steady increase followed by a sudden drop."

Jake tapped some keys as she walked around the table towards him.

"Well," he said, "there definitely was a significant increase in the number and value of transactions going through Murdoch's secret account from the first transaction in the data. At first, the increase was gradual and then it really ramped up, which means that Develin was right. There was also a decrease in flows in the month before Murdoch went on his fateful trip to Joburg and, thereafter, the flows reduced to a trickle then stopped altogether. However, you could interpret this decrease either way. Murdoch could have turned off the taps as you suggest. But the flows could also have stopped just because he dropped out of the picture."

"And the trickle after he went missing?" she said, peering over his shoulder whilst still maintaining some distance between them. "Why would that be?"

Jake shrugged his shoulders. "Probably deals that had already been transacted and the payments committed. Since Murdoch wasn't around to maintain the deal flow, additional payments eventually dried up."

Something caught her eye and she had to bend down to take a closer look, her face close to his own. "What's that?" she said, pointing at a transaction halfway down the screen.

"The payment to DM Trust? I assume Murdoch must have transferred some of his money to a trust account. Why?"

"Look at the date of the payment. One day after he disappeared."

"So? He could have instructed the bank to make the transfer before he vanished."

"Possibly." She gently chewed the inside of her cheek, brooding. "Are there any other transfers to DM before or after that?"

His hands flew over the keys. "No. Just this one."

"Still seems odd then, don't you think?"

"I really don't think it's significant. Look at the amount. One million pounds is minuscule compared to the billions that flowed in and out of this account!"

He turned towards her, emphasising his point, and their faces almost collided. Instinctively, Charlie jerked upright and then winced as sharp pain shot up her side. Jake jumped to his feet and reached towards her.

"You sure you're ok?"

"I'm fine," she clipped, backing away from him.

"You don't look fine," he insisted as he dropped his arms and stuffed his hands in his pockets, trying unsuccessfully to hide his chagrin.

For a moment she felt bad, then she reminded herself it was better this way. "By the way, please don't say a word about Maharaj. Not yet. Not until we're sure."

"Don't change the subject."

"I'm not," she countered, making a show of looking at her watch. "Gosh, look at the time. I better run or I'm going to be late." Without waiting for a response, she turned towards the door.

"All right!" he said urgently, delaying her departure. "You don't have to tell me if you don't want to. But given the stakes in this story, stakes we know people are willing to kill for, shouldn't you think about how far you're willing to go?"

First Viper and now Jake!
Why was everybody suddenly treating her like a child?

"You think I haven't thought of that?" Charlie said sarcastically, as she opened the door. "I've been doing this for a while, Jake. I know how to look after myself."

"I know you do," he said, following her as she stepped out of the room. "I'm not doubting that. But you can't take them on alone."

Determined to put as much distance between them as possible, she increased her pace, her back rigid.

"No one can," Jake yelled as she sped towards the exit. "Not even the great Charlie Tate!"

45. Out in the Cold

Kensington
London, UK

The house was deathly quiet. Hilary sat in his study in the dark, his desk chair swivelled round to face the window looking onto the garden. Outside, darkness had fallen, bringing with it a bone-piercing winter chill, the windows touched by the first signs of frost. He should have been shivering but, for some reason, he felt hot. Maybe it was the two bottles of whisky sloshing around inside him. Or maybe it was the rage, coiling and twisting in his intestines, demanding to be unleashed.

He looked at the empty whisky tumbler in his hand. He should have been drunk by now. Better still, unconscious, dead to the world, cocooned from reality. Was that really too much to ask? Just for a few fucking hours? Yet evidently, he couldn't even get drunk properly. At least, that's what Spencer would say.

Swivelling his chair to face the desk, Hilary reached for the next bottle. There were four remaining in all, standing with military precision on top of the blotter. Another five in the cellar if he needed them. Filling his glass to the brim, he took a large sip and turned back to look out the window. Not that he could see anything. Just his own reflection. Dishevelled, old, shrunken, and miserable.

He'd been mulling over the interesting timing of Reuben's resignation when he'd seen the story and put two and two together. They'd withheld the source's name, but he knew it could only have been him. The article had all the hallmarks of Reuben's particular brand of lily-livered venom. Dodging the blame, smearing everyone but himself. "Coerced by a toxic culture of corruption", he'd said, claiming he'd had no choice, as if someone had put a bloody gun to his head! What a load of crap! "A culture driven from the very top" he'd said. Imagine? Implying that he, John Hilary, had also been part of it. PART OF IT! Like they hadn't all plotted and schemed behind his back!

The little shit had tittle-tailed about Jonathan too, claiming that yet another member of the divisional Exco had disappeared under "suspicious circumstances". Suspicious, his arse! True - Samuel had been useless. No info on Jonathan's last movements or what the fucker was up to. Yet did that make his absence suspicious? Not bloody likely. The weak bastard had done a runner, no doubt about it.

Worst of all, Tate had given the strongest hint yet that Derrick's disappearance and possible murder could be linked to a conflict with a Yeats client. A CLIENT! The one thing he had promised Spencer would never happen. And he hadn't even known it was coming.

NONE OF IT!!

Luckily, he'd been alone in his office when he'd read it. No need to hide his shock, warding off startled looks with hasty goodbyes or fumbled apologies. His first move had been to call Spencer, not only to agree on a strategy but also to show that he was abreast of things this time. Not getting through on his mobile, he had called his office only to be told to leave a message. He should have sensed it then, but he'd been too blind, too eager. At least the Media Office had picked up. It had only been when the Head of Media Relations had told him, in that condescending tone she reserved for only the lowliest of species, that all divisional comms were now being managed by the Group CEO's office, that he had finally understood. They were freezing him out. Pushing him away from the life raft, ready to watch him drown. Alone, out in the cold.

Still, a part of him had been confused, convinced there must be some kind of mistake. A miscommunication that would be easily resolved once he and Spencer had had a chance to talk. Thus, when his mentor had finally deigned to call him back, he had tried to explain what had happened. After all, how was he supposed to have known that Tate did most of her sleuthing in the streets, rendering the wiretap useless? He wasn't bloody clairvoyant! As for keeping Spencer in the dark about Jonathan, since when was taking initiative a crime? And was it his fault that Jonathan hadn't the balls to face the music? That Reuben had squealed before he could spin the story? Of course not! Yet, had his boss wanted to know? No, he fucking hadn't!

Nevertheless, the starry-eyed boy in him had at least expected Spencer to agree with him on one thing. To come out fighting, ready to trash Reuben's story and the tissue of lies it was built on. He hadn't expected to be thrown so completely under the bus. To be told in such clear terms that he was finished. Just like that! After all the shit he'd taken. All the times he'd been in Spencer's corner, even when his boss had crossed the line. Only to be rewarded by being tossed out like yesterday's garbage.

The bloody nerve!

Special leave, Spencer had called it. Until they had finalised the investigation. Or so he said. More like fucking purgatory. No – jail if Spencer had anything to do with it. Do not pass go, do not collect £200. Truss him up with the rest of the alleged conspirators and throw away the key. Is this what Michael had gone through? One day flying high, the next day 'the accused'? And by the time he was exonerated, it would be too late. Tainted, that's what they'd call it. Persona non-fucking-grata!

Hilary drained his glass, fire coursing down his throat and exploding in his chest. Drinking like a man, his father had called it. Letting everyone know you could take it, handle whatever shit life threw at you. Not that his father could, in the end. Cancer shrivelling him up into a quarter of the man he once was. "I've always got my Johnny," he'd say, right up until the very end. "No matter what, they can't take that away. My Johnny, up there with the best of them, looking down on all those toffy bastards!" He let out a bitter laugh.

Look at me now, Da!

Aren't you proud of your little Johnny now?

His grip tightened on the glass as a sudden urge to grind it into dust overwhelmed him. He felt like pounding and bludgeoning everything with his bare hands. Smashing the world into smithereens. He'd start with Tate. She was the root of it all. Send her a calling card that would make the event on the common look like a Sunday school picnic. Then he'd move onto Spencer, pummelling him until he was black and blue, his cheeks bashed in, his nose bloody, his sneering lips gashed, and his arrogant glare masked by puffy, black eyes. And there he would be, standing above his prone, battered carcase, one proud foot planted on Spencer's chest, shouting, "I did it! I killed the Giant!"

A splintering sound brought him out of his reverie. Looking down, he was surprised to find that it was from the glass in his hand, a trickle of blood already forming where a shard had pierced the skin. Tutting to himself, he wrapped the wound with a handkerchief, creaked to his feet and wobbled to the drinks cabinet to fetch another one. Back at his desk, he tried to pour himself a refill, but it was taking longer than usual. For some reason, his hand struggled to align with the location of the bottle. Instead, he ended up tipping the bottle over, spilling whisky all over the place. Cursing, he righted the bottle with both hands, carefully poured the amber liquid into his glass and left both the bottle and full glass in a puddle on his desk as he teetered to the kitchen to get a cloth. Unable to find one, he opted for a tablecloth, dragging it back to the study and daubing up the spilt liquid with as much care as he could muster.

Should have moved faster, Hilary thought as he soaked up the whisky with the fine cotton. Should never have allowed Spencer to talk him into using the fucking useless internal audit team instead of externals. If he'd stood his ground, he'd now have the upper hand. First, demonstrable proof that he was not one of them and, second, possibly some real dirt on the culprits. Instead, he had nothing. Nothing but a tattered reputation.

Fuck! Fuck! FUCK!!!

His sloppy succour complete, Hilary dropped the tablecloth on the floor and fell into his chair. Never trust them, that's what Da had said. You can walk amongst them, smile with them, dine with them, but you'll never be one of them and they'll never be part of you.

Why, oh why, hadn't he listened?

He reached for the whisky glass with shaky fingers and downed it in one go before pouring another, thinking about the day his Da had died. As he had lain in bed, fighting for each breath, he had reached over and grabbed his arm with a surprisingly firm grip, pulling him down towards him. His eyes rheumy, his face haggard, his body a shell of what it once had been, he had inched his head from the pillow and whispered, "Never let them know what you're thinking, laddie. Always stay one step ahead. One step ahead and ya'll be awright."

Hilary's throat constricted and his eyes started to sting.

How could he have been so blind? To have ever thought Spencer would be on his side? Stupid! Stupid! Stupid!

Tears brimmed over his lashes and trickled down his flushed face.

Now he'd let everyone down. Grace. The family. Even Da from beyond the grave. How could he have been such a FOOL!!!

The pain in his heart was unbearable, so much so he thought he was going to pass out. Then he felt it. Starting below his diaphragm, forcing its way up his oesophagus, growing and swelling, stamping down his tongue and beating open his lips until the sob burst into the room. And once one broke through, the rest stormed the barricade, rendering it asunder like a gushing torrent. His body shook and his chest grew tight, his breaths coming short and fast as he wailed with the awful ache of rejection.

"What's going on here?" Grace said, flicking on the lights as she threw open the door.

Mortified, Hilary cringed and twisted away from her as he quickly swallowing down a sob and brushing the tears off his face with trembling hands.

Not looking at him directly, his wife took in the room, her brow furrowed below her perfectly coiffed blond hair, her red lips slits of cold disapproval. "Really, darling – what have you been doing? This place smells like a brothel!"

With two long strides of her lithe limbs, her black cocktail dress shimmering and swaying as she moved, she was at his desk, standing imperiously above him. "And look at this! What are all these whisky bottles doing here?!"

Then she blinked in shock as she noticed something on the floor. Her face horrified, she swiftly scooped down to retrieve it. "Oh my God! My mother's tablecloth!" As the smell hit her and whisky seeped through her fingers, she grimaced in disgust. Putting down the tablecloth, she grabbed both arms of his chair and screeched cold fury into his face. "WHAT THE FUCK IS WRONG WITH YOU? DON'T YOU KNOW THAT WAS MY MOTHER'S? THE ONLY THING OF HERS THAT I HAVE LEFT?"

Unable to hold them back any longer, more hot tears streamed down his face. "He said I'm finished, Grace," he mumbled. "Spencer. Said my career is over. I tried everything but…," he sniffed, wiping his nose with a clammy hand. "I'm sorry. I'm so, so, sorry." Snivelling and crying, he buried his head in the nape of her neck, part out of shame but also desperately longing for comfort and understanding. As he felt her stiffen and partially pull back, a part of him nearly broke. Then, suddenly her arms were around him, enveloping him like a balm.

He couldn't say how long they stayed like that. He bent forward in the chair, gushing, his shoulders shaking. Her on her knees, cradling him as she rocked back and forth, soothing away his pain. At some point, the tears slowed, the pain ebbed and, at last, he was able to lift his head.

"There now," she said. "Better?"

Hilary nodded, not yet trusting his voice. Now that he'd calmed down, he steeled himself for the inevitable bombarding questions and scolding recriminations, but none came. Instead, she ran a gentle hand across his wet cheek, wiping away his tears, and then gave him a loving smile, igniting a warm glow all over his body. What a blessing to have a wife who knew that some things were better left unsaid.

Grace got to her feet, turning to practicalities. "Why don't I clear all this away, dear, whilst you get yourself cleaned up, mmm?"

As she gathered the remaining whisky bottles in her arms along with the soaked tablecloth, Hilary pushed himself to his feet on unsteady legs.

When she got to the door with her load, she turned and flashed him a mischievous grin. "You know what Papa used to say, darling?"

He fought to string the words together, his mouth feeling like it belonged to a stranger. "No, dear. What?"

"If you're a great striker, stop playing cricket."

46. The Landfill

Turffontein
Johannesburg, South Africa

Musa pointed to the other side of the road, his eyes sombre, "This is the place." Thabo's eyes followed the direction of his finger, taking in Joburg's biggest landfill, the mountains of rubbish stretching to the horizon, and beyond it, the steel and concrete skyscrapers of the inner city. Dozens of waste-pickers, some in soiled, protective clothing, others with no protection at all, trawled through the trash, looking for recyclables and other discarded treasure. And all around them, fighting for purchase, hovered a wedge of hungry sacred ibises, their wide, white wings blotting the sapphire sky.

"Ok," he replied without enthusiasm. "Which way?"

"Over there," Musa jerked his head towards the far, right corner of the landfill, "about two k in."

Tying a cloth around his face to guard against the stench, Thabo nodded and motioned for Musa to lead the way. A seasoned waste-picker, Musa cast an amused glance at Thabo's scarf, then marched across the road, through the entrance and up the first mountain, his footing sure, his back proud and straight. Scrambling after him, Thabo kept his mind focused on not falling over, pushing aside any thoughts of what they might find once they reached their destination.

It had been three weeks since Lucky had vanished, seventeen days since they'd seen Cleaver, and there had still been no sign of the phone or Lucky.

Leaving Boy stationed at home in case their friend returned, Thabo and Innocent had also been making daily treks to the group's favourite haunts, hoping to find Lucky waiting there, but he was nowhere to be seen. Hence, desperate, they had asked their friends and neighbours to put the word out to everyone they knew, hoping that, maybe, someone, somewhere had seen something.

The news had come yesterday evening. A cousin of Mrs Khoza had found something in a landfill. She hadn't said what it was, but her eyes had given her away. Thabo had agreed to take a look, leaving Boy at home whilst Innocent once more set out to search their usual hangouts. None of them had spoken as he'd left that morning, all words seeming inadequate. Yet, Thabo carried what was unspoken with him, drawing on their strength, knowing he would need it if he found what they all feared he would.

Musa at the lead, they waded through the muck of waste, filth, bird shit and swarming insects, ducking garbage trucks, anxious pickers and pecking birds. On Thabo's far left, a fight broke out between two pickers who had simultaneously seized on what looked like a metal tray.

"What's that all about?" he asked, pointing to the altercation with a jerk of his head.

Musa shrugged one shoulder, not giving the fight any attention, or breaking his stride. "Any kind of metal fetches a higher price. More than paper, cardboard, or plastic." He spat on the ground, his face sour. "The rich take everything and leave us to fight over their scraps."

One of the pickers took out a knife. "Looks like it's about to get ugly," Thabo quipped.

"A little bit," Musa looked dismissive. "Some like the entertainment. But Guilty will be around soon enough to break it up before anyone gets really hurt."

Thabo didn't ask who Guilty was and Musa didn't explain. A few moments later, out of the corner of his eye, he saw a man over six feet tall, dressed in waste picker fatigues with biceps the size of beer barrels, lumbering towards the scene.

That must be Guilty.

While Musa carried on walking, Thabo stopped to watch what would happen next, part out of interest, part out of the desire to delay having to face what awaited him. Whilst most pickers had carried on with their work some also paused to watch the contest, talking excitedly to each other as if betting on who would be the victor. However, as soon as Guilty reached the duelling duo, the fighting stopped. The strongman looked from one fighter to the other, his face grim. Then without uttering a single word or indicating how he had arrived at his decision, he picked up the tray they had been fighting over and handed it to the man without a knife. Thabo expected the other man to protest but he just smiled and nodded at his rival, acknowledging defeat, before picking up his bag and going to excavate another part of the landfill.

Maybe one day he'd be like that. A man so respected that explanations were unnecessary.

"Are you coming or what?" Musa shouted from the top of the next mound.

"Sorry!" Thabo rushed down the mound and up the next, his breathing short and shallow with exertion by the time he caught up with him.

"Down there." Musa pointed at a black shape lying in a valley between the next two garbage hills. Besieged by ibises and vultures, the forlorn package shook each time they pecked at it.

"We covered it up as best as we could," Musa said, beginning the descent. "Just hope the birds haven't done too much damage."

Thabo's stomach heaved.

They walked on in silence, Musa in front, Thabo behind. Down their mound, up over the next heap and down towards the valley. With each step, Thabo was filled with increasing dread, his heart quickening, his mind trying to quell his rising panic.

His first memory was of death. The sisters at the orphanage had said they had found him as a baby crying in his dead mother's arms. He couldn't remember the details, just the sensation of being smothered by icy cold skin. He had never been able to stand the cold ever since. Never been able to think of death without shivering all over. And he felt it now. The goosebumps creeping across his skin, the growing numbness in the tips of his fingers and toes. Like death was reaching out and smothering him all over again.

"You're very quiet," Musa said, glancing behind him. "You, ok?"

"Mm-mmm," Thabo replied. "Just thinking, that's all."

He tried to accompany his response with a reassuring smile only to give up when he remembered that half his face was hidden by a cloth anyway. Musa nodded in response, taking him at his word, and they trudged on.

Focus Thabo. Focus on what you can control.

Your fault. If it wasn't for you, none of this would've happened!

Just put one foot in front of the other. The rest is out of your hands.

Lucky was your brother. Why didn't you protect him?

It wasn't my fault. I didn't know…

Yes, you did. You should have told them about the phone. You should have told them everything!

"Watch your step," Musa warned as he came to an abrupt stop. His reflexes frozen, Thabo bumped into his guide's back before the meaning of Musa's words landed.

They had arrived.

He dragged his eyes away from his feet and looked over Musa's shoulder at a shape lying a few feet away, wrapped in black bags. While most of the birds scattered upon their arrival, a determined few remained, pecking at the bundle with their long, sharp, curved beaks, the plastic ripped and torn in the areas where they had succeeded in getting to their prey. Though much of the body remained covered, through the rips he glimpsed deep, bloody gashes in dirt-smudged, brown skin, some so large he could see pink muscle and white bone.

Thabo's breath locked in his throat and his teeth started to chatter.

Run, Thabo. Run and never look back.

"Ready?" Musa asked, his face concerned.

He didn't respond.

He couldn't go through with this.

Couldn't face it.

But if he ran, what would he tell Boy and Innocent?

He owed them the truth.

Straightening his spine, Thabo pulled his jacket more closely around him, trying to get warm, and reluctantly nodded.

"Sure, sure?"

He forced the words out, "We have to know."

"All right."

Musa cast around for a stick and began shouting and waving it to scare the birds away. Then, standing next to the body, Musa used it to lift the plastic sheeting so they could see the person's face. With more of the body exposed, the stink of rotting meat was almost unbearable. Breathing through his mouth, Thabo took gulps of air so he wouldn't throw up. Forcing his feet forward, he went to stand next to his companion and looked down.

A boy, his face all smashed up and swollen. Possibly around Lucky's age. And he had the same jawline, the same slope in his shoulders.

Oh God! It's him!

Unable to stop himself, Thabo started hyperventilating. Seeing his reaction, Musa began to lower the plastic cover back in place, assuming the worst.

Wait!

Thabo grabbed Musa's arm.

Was that a faint scar, between his left upper lip and nostril?

Or just a dirt-encrusted crease?

His eyes.

He'd know right away, once he got a better…

Thabo bent down. Looking into his lifeless eyes felt like falling into a desolate abyss. He jerked upright then inhaled sharply as something burst in his chest, stinging his eyes, squeezing his throat.

"Is it him?" Musa said. "Is it Lucky?"

Tears welled in Thabo's eyes, his voice thick with emotion.

"Not this time."

47. Rats in a Barrel

Kensington
London, UK

Hilary put his key into the front door lock of their home and sighed. The door was stuck again. Giving it a hard push, he looked over his shoulder and said to his wife, "We really need to get this wretched door fixed."

Grace, coming up the stairs behind him, clutching about her shoulders a black fur stole as a bulwark against the chill, heartily agreed. "Yes dear, Jay's working on it. Beginning of this week, he said."

Hilary snorted.

He wasn't going to hold his breath for that to happen.

Walking into the entrance hall as she closed the front door behind them, he glanced at the answering machine sitting on the French side table. Four messages. Curious, he paused in front of it as he pulled open his black bow tie and shook off his black tuxedo jacket.

"Nightcap?" Grace asked, grabbing his jacket as she passed him on her way to the kitchen.

"Yes, please. Um… the usual."

Play or ignore?

Hilary made up his mind and pressed play. Two of them were from old friends he hadn't spoken to in a while. He'd get back to them in the morning. One was from the old bat next door complaining about his brother-in-law parking in her spot again. He'd leave that to Grace and, thankfully, stay out of *that* mess. The fourth one was from a journalist. Connie, on a fishing expedition disguised as a friendly 'just checking up on you'. He pressed delete.

At least the call hadn't been from *her*. The woman at the centre of his misery, dogging his dreams, tripping his steps, curtailing his ascent with every vicious syllable. He had hoped listening to his favourite Beethoven overture would clear his head and lift his mood, but every beat and stroke had seemed to resound with her name. Mocking him, tormenting him.

The bloody bitch!

The muscles in Hilary's jaw clenched, thoughts of his nemesis bringing on the usual dread.

What if Tate had been up to something new?

"Grace darling?" he yelled down the passage, "I'll join you in a few. Just got a few urgent things I need to attend to."

His wife popped her head around the kitchen door, a glass of Irish cream in her hand. "Mind if I go on to bed?"

"No, not at all. I'll be up in a sec."

Hilary dialled Samuel's number as he walked to the study. After the Reuben fiasco, the bank had doubled Tate's surveillance, including managing to put a tracker on her phone. If that rubbernecking tosser had been up to mischief, the bank's Head of Security would know about it. Getting through to voicemail, he decided not to leave a message. Samuel would see his missed call and respond soon enough.

Waking up his laptop as he sat at his desk, he began by looking through the day's news. Nothing. Then he scrolled through the transcripts from the bug in Tate's flat. At least the wire had finally started yielding results, including a useful morsel he would never have anticipated. One that had proved very handy indeed. Today, however, apart from another visit from an annoying girl whose name reminded him of Quiche Lorraine and several calls by Tate looking for a woman called Portia, the read-out included nothing of significance. The meddling worm must have had a slow day, Hilary thought as he closed the window.

Thank God for small mercies!

He then went on to check for any new developments at Yeats. In addition to Samuel, his other ally, Trudy – who had been appointed to act in his absence – had also kept him in the loop. Thanks to the two of them, over the past week, he'd come to appreciate that special leave had an upside. Plenty of time on his hands whilst still having full access to everything he needed. Today, however, Trudy also had nothing new to report. So, he logged off, sat back in his chair, and let his mind wander.

As always, Hilary's thoughts turned to Spencer. He still didn't know how he was going to rebuild their relationship. However, if the rumours were true that the Group CEO was now planning to bring his retirement forward, perhaps that was no longer such an issue. By all accounts, Spencer's likely replacement was a far easier chap to manage so the sooner his current boss left, the better. Yet, even if that was the case, his new boss's pliability would matter nought if he still hadn't clear his name. And to do that, he needed an inside man. One of the conspirators. Which brought him to the matter of the CFO.

Despite his former pledge of allegiance, now the bloody fool didn't even pick up his calls! Fortunately, there were other ways of guaranteeing someone's loyalty. It had taken a while to find something he could use, but when he had finally found it, he realised it had been in front of him all along. A little bird called Samuel had reported that Steven had been a busy bee, erasing tonnes of documents from his computer and the bank's servers. Whilst he had tried to erase them permanently, that action in itself had left what the Yeats tech guys called a 'ghost print'. Now, all he had to do was convince Steven that the tech team had found a way to retrieve these documents. Then the coup de gras would be assuring the CFO that he still had the power to make sure the matter never saw the light of day - given the right incentive, naturally. And voilà, the man would be putty in his hands!

Hilary smiled to himself, feeling better already.

After that, it would be as easy as counting one, two, three. First, once Steven's rep had thus been washed spotless, he would get him to rat out his co-conspirators, putting all the blame on Murdoch, Jonathan, and that cunt Reuben. Second, in doing so, Steven would make it clear to the SFO that he, Hilary, had had nothing to do with the scandalous scheme, instead working arduously to uncover it and put an end to the corrupt cabal. Third, with a clean bill of health from the SFO report, his ascendency to the top job in the division would once more be assured and all would be back as it should be. The natural order of things.

Then, if he was feeling very generous, he might even consider making Steven his right-hand man. After all, given the CFO's predilections, it was wise to keep turncoats close. Thereafter, once he had had time to win the trust of Spencer's successor, he'd start preparing the ground for the Group CEO position. His strategic moves sublime, his steps steady, his eyes always fixed on the prize. And with that trophy won, he would be in line for everything he had ever dreamed of. If not a knighthood, certainly an MBE and, if he played his cards right, a spot on the Prime Minister's honours list.

"Lord John Hilary," he mumbled to himself as he stretched out his legs and entwined his hands behind his head.

It certainly had a nice ring to it!

Nevertheless, he shouldn't get ahead of himself. For all this to succeed, he would need to work the press. Shape and control the narrative. Given he was on 'leave', going through the Bank's media office was out of the question.

However, he still had some close contacts in the Fourth Estate. He'd start some rumours, promise them an exclusive and before you knew it, everyone would be portraying him as a fucking hero!

Naturally, he would need to target the ones less fussy about the facts. Now who would that be…? Another woman perhaps, striving to make it in a male-dominated world? Not what's her name from the Times. She had eviscerated Yeats in her last piece. Nor that ball-breaker from the Telegraph.

Hilary jerked upright, the answer coming to him in a flash.

The phone call!

He quickly checked his watch. Nearly one in the morning.

Damn - too late to call her now. He'd have to wait until morning. No doubt about it, though, Connie would be perfect for the job. Formerly from a top rag, she had dropped a peg or ten in the past few years and must be itching to get back to the heydays of being the scoop queen of Fleet Street. Maybe her call tonight had been serendipity after all? Fate pulling him towards his destiny. Yes – that was it. And he was more than ready to meet it!

Feeling pleased with himself, Hilary got to his feet.

To think that merely seven days ago he'd been blubbering in this very study, behaving like the world was coming to an end? What foolishness! Only losers thought small. Wept when they should be fighting back. And he was no loser.

Switching off the light, he went to double-check that the front door was locked before heading for the stairs. As he stepped on the first rung, his father came to mind. Da had told him a story once. During a hot August summer just before his eighth birthday. About how, as kids, they used to put scraps of food at the bottom of a barrel to draw out the rats in the neighbourhood. A barrel large enough that once they were in it, the rats would struggle to climb out. As they ran in, they'd dab each rat with a different colour of paint. Then, once the barrel was full, they'd take bets on which rat would be the victor, desperate enough to chew its kin for freedom.

At the top of the stairs, Hilary switched off the passage light and walked to the main bedroom. Grace was already asleep, her nightcap half-finished. Thankfully, she'd left his lamp on so he wouldn't stumble around in the dark and, next to the lamp, a glass of brandy. Sitting on the edge of the bed, he slowly undressed, letting his clothes fall to the floor. That was another first. The old Hilary would have neatly hung up his suit and put his dirties in the laundry basket, ready for Beatrice to collect in the morning. Not anymore.

Who said old habits die hard?

Pulling back the duvet, he ignored the tipple and flopped into bed, suddenly feeling exhausted. As he turned off the light, his thoughts drifted back to his father.

When his Da had finished telling the story, he'd looked at his eight-year-old son with a strange glint in his eyes, eagerly awaiting his response. Not realising what his father had been trying to say, his oblivious younger self had thanked him for the story and then gone out to play. Now, all grown up, he finally understood that his father had been teaching him the ways of the world. Showing him that, whoever you were, whatever you thought you had, we were all just rats in a barrel fighting to survive.

48. A Match

Balham
London, UK

Pow! Pow! Pow! Charlie's jabs were lightning-fast, focusing on what she knew was her combatant's weak spot – her face. Her opponent blocked well, arms tight, boxing gloves a solid shield. They were both breathing hard, sweat running between the guards on their shins and arms. Charlie stepped back and pivoted into a low roundhouse kick, going for her legs. Again, she was ready for her, fading back and countering with a high-spinning kick to Charlie's head. Charlie ducked but too late, the glancing blow sending her staggering backwards.

"Hey! You, ok?" Quicha said, rushing to her side and cradling her in case she fell.

"I'm good," Charlie replied, even though her ears were ringing. "My fault – my evasion was off."

They were on the mat in a corner of a martial arts studio in Balham, surrounded by the grunts and shuffles of their counterparts. After learning of the attack, Quicha, a Muay Thai Blue Belt, had introduced her to the gym and offered to be her sparring partner once her ribs had healed. Now, Charlie was a regular, attending lessons once a week and sparring with her friend on the weekends. When they had started that morning, the gym had been deserted apart from a few other dedicated souls, willing to sacrifice a few hours of sleep to pay homage to the exercise god. Now, one hour later, the place was full, the air dense with competitive zeal.

Quicha led her to a bench by the wall, releasing her as she lay down. Charlie closed her eyes, trying to get the room to stop spinning.

"Girl, you look like you're about to faint."

"I'll be fine in a sec. Just give me a minute, then we can carry on."

"No way," Charlie heard the rip of Velcro as Quicha took off her gloves. "Me? I'm done for the day."

"Wait. I –" Charlie opened her eyes and tried to sit up.

"Slow down, girl!" Quicha gently pushed her back down. "Just cos you got all beat up doesn't mean you now need to go cray cray getting in shape. You gotta give yourself time to breath, ya know? Meditate. Contemplate. This shit is about the mind, not just the muscle."

Charlie made a face as she lay back down, "Yes boss."

Quicha burst out laughing, "That's right. And don't you forget it!" "Now, rest up. I'll come and check on you in a few, awright?"

Charlie nodded and closed her eyes once more. Secretly, she was glad her friend hadn't let her get up. Damn room wouldn't stay still. Seeking to centre her thoughts, she focused on her breathing, blocking out the world around her. Yet, always the traitor, her mind kept returning to the Murdoch story.

She still hadn't been able to locate Portia, even after hounding every relative, friend, ex-lover, and colleague that Portia had ever had. At least Viper was making progress. Her latest update had centred on feedback from a fellow forensic hacker specialising in African criminal syndicates. It turned out that Jonas Maharaj was a pretty familiar figure in such circles, especially due to his import/export business. For years, the authorities had been investigating him regarding his possible involvement in trafficking African women and children to the Middle East and Europe. The problem was the police hadn't yet been able to build a solid case against him. Each time they thought they were making progress, a key witness was murdered or suddenly refused to testify.

Charlie sighed, thinking the pattern sounded all too familiar. When she'd first started reading Viper's report, her heart had skipped a beat, her thoughts immediately going to the girl she'd found by Regent's Canal. Could the two cases have been linked? Halfway through, however, she'd realised that the link lay only in form, not substance. According to the authorities, Maharaj would never have dreamt of being so 'wasteful'. If the 'cargo' couldn't be sold into some sort of slavery, they were 'harvested'. Their skin, their organs, their hair. Even their bones and teeth.

Utter barbarism!

Viper's friend had also given them a list of Maharaj' key associates. For her, one person in particular had stood out. A South African called Jabu Mabasa, Maharaj's head of muscle and general fixer. Jabu had begun his criminal career at the tender age of nine, killing his parents as they slept. Yet, that hadn't been what had caught her attention. It had been his eyes, cold and barren as the Gobi Desert. The gaze of a man capable of anything and everything.

"You feeling better?"

Charlie opened her eyes to find Quicha staring down at her, showered, changed, and smelling of coconut butter.

"Um…I think so," she said as she pushed herself up.

At least the room had started behaving itself.

"Just give me a sec."

Yanking off her gloves, she rushed to her locker and quickly changed into her sweats, opting to shower at home.

"How was the meditation?" Quicha asked as they headed out the door and towards the bus stop.

"Meditation?" Charlie was confused for a moment then she remembered. "Ah, yes," she replied, deciding that a white lie was better than having to explain herself. "I sure did…At least, a little."

"A little is good," her friend replied earnestly. "Once you start, you'll realise Zen is the shit!"

Charlie nodded noncommittally, wondering how to change the subject. Fortunately, she was saved by the bell, her phone buzzing in her pocket. After checking the caller ID, she cut off the call.

She'd chat to Vusi later.

"Who was that?"

"Just my cousin. I'll -"

Her mobile rang again, cutting her off.

God!

What was up with this guy?

Tapping her screen, she signalled to Quicha that she'd just be a minute.

"What is it, Vus? I'm busy."

"Didn't you get my message?" he whispered.

Charlie frowned, "No. When did you send it? And why are you whispering?"

"I emailed it two hours ago. Look – I don't have much time. Serg is watching me like a hawk today. I heard the guys talking. They've found a body."

"What do you mean? What body?"

"At first they thought it might be Murdoch but when -"

"Wait - Murdoch?!" she looked at Quicha, her voice rising in excitement. "Are you saying they've found Murdoch's body?"

"No," Vusi said, elongating the word like he was talking to a dunce. "They thought it might be him, but it turned out to be this other guy."

"What other guy?"

"They didn't say his full name. Jonathan something."

Charlie sucked in her breath, "Jonathan Murphy? From Yeats?"
That couldn't be right.
Quicha mouthed, "Who'd would want to kill him?"
She shrugged her shoulders, wondering the same thing herself.
"I guess so," Vusi replied. "But get this – they found a hair. On the body. They're still analysing it. For age and all that. But they think they've got a DNA match."
What if the DNA match was for Maharaj or his associates? That would certainly prove that Maharaj was willing to kill those involved in the money-laundering scheme if he wanted to. So, why not Murdoch himself? Perhaps, finally, they had found the link they'd been looking for!
"Who's the match?" Charlie asked eagerly.
Vusi chortled like a child who'd just discovered Christmas.
"Derrick Murdoch."

49. Alive

Tooting Bec
London, UK

She sat at the kitchen table, rubbing her temples, trying to ease the dull throbbing in her head. The story had spread like wildfire, her phone ringing off the hook from the early hours, forcing her out of slumber. Putting it on silent, she had quickly dressed and snuck out to grab the morning papers, fearing the worst. Needless to say, none of them had spared her, their headlines broadcasting "MURDOCH LIVES!!", "ALIVE!" or "BUNKER BANKER!". Connie's piece in The Sentinel had been particularly shady, in more ways than one.

> *"The body of a British man in his late thirties was recently found dumped near the roadside of a busy highway in Johannesburg. The body is believed to be that of Jonathan Murphy, the Head of Private Clients at Yeats Bank who was recently reported missing. In a surprising twist, the police also discovered DNA evidence at the scene which could point to Mr Murphy's killer. This DNA has been matched to Mr Derrick Murdoch, the former CEO of the Africa Division at the Bank, who disappeared five months ago. Whilst some less established rags have implied that Mr Murdoch might have come to an untimely end, it is now clear that is he alive and well. Not only that, but it looks like he might also be a murder suspect..."*

Charlie had grown angrier and angrier with each word she had read.

The Meanness of Things

Less established?! Rag?! Then, halfway down the page, she had gotten to a quote from Yeats Bank.

"John Hilary, a colleague of both men, suggested that these new revelations meant that The Torch owed Yeats an apology for falsely claiming that Murdoch was dead and that his death might involve one of Yeats' clients, calling for the Independent Press Standards Organisation (IPSO) to look into the matter. On the question of Mr Murphy, Mr Hilary said that, if it turns out that Murdoch is indeed the killer, the murder of Mr Murphy in his prime was particularly tragic given that he had been one of Murdoch's proteges. "To have groomed someone, to have taken a young, innocent man under his wing, only to introduce him to a life of crime is heinous enough", Hilary said. "However, to then lure him to South Africa and cold-bloodedly murder him just before he was due to be interviewed by the SFO is truly unconscionable." Hilary added that "whilst the SFO investigation is still underway, the revelations over the last month have left everyone in no doubt that Murdoch is a master manipulator who not only seduced gullible colleagues under his care but also managed to fool us all, including financial regulators. I am sure Yeats Bank will continue to work with the SFO to unearth and bring to book all those involved in the Murdoch scheme and to ensure that such a thing can never happen again."

Innocent, young man? Master manipulator? Fooled them all? What a bunch of horse shit! And not a single fact to back any of it!

Her headache still raging, Charlie gave up on home remedies and got up to grab some painkillers. As she popped the pills and washed them down with water, she mapped out her game plan. She'd stand her ground. Write a rebuttal. Show them what real journalism looks like. Heading to the study, she picked up her phone and then gasped. Fuck! Six missed calls from the News Editor. She quickly dialled.

"I've been trying to call you all morning!" The Ferret roared.

Charlie silently groaned. Impatient Kathy was a pain, pissed Kathy was torture. "Sorry. My phone was on silent."

"That's no excuse." In the background, she heard the editor giving instructions to a sub-editor, then she was back on the line. "I take it you've seen the papers?"

"Been going through them all morning."

"So, what have you got to say for yourself? What happened to your sources? Why didn't you find out Murdoch was alive before everyone else did?"

She thought of telling her she had, then decided against it. "There's no proof that Murdoch is alive. They just found a hair, that's all. On Jonathan's suit. It could have gotten there anytime."

"What?" Kathy scoffed, "The hair survived for months on a suit that was regularly cleaned? Pull the other one!"

"Once they've done the age analysis it could turn out -"

"Enough! Stop trying to save face and focus on getting back ahead of this thing!"

"Save face?" Charlie fumed. "I was just following the evidence!"

"Yada, yada, yada! If IPSO gets on our arse, I'll have your head. In the meantime, follow *this* piece of evidence and get your sources working!"

"But -"

"No more buts! Unless you've got facts to support your theory, you better start trying to track Murdoch down. I want an exclusive!" Kathy briefly broke off to reprimand an underling for bringing her a cold cup of coffee before saying, "Or is that too much to ask, Ms Tate?"

Charlie considered her options.

Should she stick to her guns? After all, she was right about the hair, she was sure of it. Then again, despite all she'd been told, despite what all the evidence suggested, she didn't have any actual proof *that Murdoch was dead, did she?*

"All right," she said between clenched teeth. "I'll get on it right away."

"That's my girl!" Kathy said brightly before slamming the phone down in her ear.

Defeated, Charlie flung the phone on the kitchen counter then trudged to the study to check her messages. After getting Vusi's call, she had sent Viper an urgent mail asking her to check in on the Hawks' progress. Doubtless a 'Be on the Look Out' notice for Murdoch would already be out. They had probably also started interviewing witnesses near where they had found Jonathan's body as well as trying to trace his movements on the days leading up to his death. Then there were the results of the hair age analysis that still had to come in as well as of the other forensic evidence they had picked up at the scene. All critical pieces in determining whether Murdoch was alive or dead and what role, if any, he had had in Jonathan's murder. However, getting all that info was going to take some time, and, as she had half expected, a quick review of her inbox confirmed that Viper still had nothing new to report.

Rolling her head around to get the tension out of her neck, Charlie turned to the Murdoch file. While she waited for Viper to work her magic, there was no harm in trying to do what her boss had asked. Though her gut still insisted that she'd been on the right path, prudence dictated that she re-examine all her assumptions, all the data, and try to look at the Murdoch story afresh. As the CCTV footage of Murdoch's arrival at Joburg airport filled her screen, a new mail landed in her inbox. Not from Viper or Vusi but an address she didn't recognise.

Read or ignore?

Deciding on the former, she clicked it open and quickly read its contents. Then she ran to the kitchen to grab her phone.

50. Swallowed

Botany Bay
Kent, UK

Charlie accessed the beach via a curved path running down from the grassy chalk clifftops of Botany Bay to the golden sand below. Trekking across the sand towards her target, she watched the waves crashing upon the shore, a gusting wind making her eyes water as the pale winter sun hid amidst a canopy of cotton wool clouds. On this side, the beach was deserted save for an old lady, sitting wrapped in a blanket on a scuffed deck chair, gazing at the sea and smiling as she sipped steaming hot tea. Charlie nodded a greeting as she passed, marvelling at how some people always managed to find joy in life, no matter the circumstances.

I'll take a cup of that!

The girl at the hotel reception had said she'd find her standing on the far side of the beach, close to the chalk stacks, dressed in red wellingtons, a black parka coat and a green beanie. And true to form, when she finally reached her, there she was, bending to sift pebbles from the shore before skimming them across the choppy water.

"Portia?" Charlie asked, "Portia Develin?"

At the sound of Charlie's voice, the woman's body stiffened. Warily, she turned, her eyes guarded. "Eyup," she said with a tinge of broad Yorkshire. "What brings you here?"

"We spoke on the phone," Charlie flashed her ID card. "Charlie Tate?"

Glancing at the card, Portia nodded and seemed to relax. "It's Maddox now. Went back to my maiden name." Her face was pale, her eyes red, as if she had spent the whole morning crying. Turning up her collar, Portia started walking, inviting Charlie to accompany her.

Portia's email had been short and to the point. The reason she had reached out to Charlie was to help prove that the man who would have been her new husband wasn't a murderer. When Charlie had rung her back, asking where she'd been all this time, Portia had explained that when Murdoch had vanished, she had retreated to a place where nobody knew her, a place where she had hoped to be able to make sense of it all. They had planned to run away together but something had gone wrong. As time had passed, she had become more and more convinced that her lover's silence could only have meant one thing. So, how could you kill someone when you yourself were already dead?

"When was the last time you spoke to Murdoch?" Charlie asked as Portia led her through a tunnel of giant chalk stacks.

"When he landed. He called to confirm he'd arrived and said he would ring me later." Her eyes clouded over. "That call never came."

They emerged from the tunnel into a secluded alcove, uninhabited apart from a couple of seagulls. Sitting on a rock, Portia invited her to join her. As Charlie sat, she activated her voice recorder. "Did he use his usual phone or another number?"

Portia shook her head, "No. A burner."

At least their suspicions had been correct.

"Do you have the number?" Charlie asked.

"He hid his caller ID. D thought it was better that way."

Damn. Without the number, finding the phone and thus Murdoch would be hopeless.

"Then what was the plan?"

"He was supposed to check into the hotel, then go buy some clothes and stuff to change his appearance. Once in disguise, he was supposed to leave the hotel and go to a safe house."

As she spoke, Charlie observed Portia's body language, her phrasing and inflexion, looking for signs of deceit. Nothing.

So far, so good.

"Given that some people are now suggesting that Murdoch might still be alive, do you think there's any chance that he wasn't taken at the garage? That, instead, he hired professionals to help him disappear, faking his own kidnapping, and then went to the safe house thereafter?"

"No," Portia said emphatically, scowling. "Like I said on the phone, if he was still alive, I would have heard from him."

Charlie decided not to push it.

By the look of things, Portia certainly believed what she was saying. However, she wouldn't be the first woman to be left standing at the proverbial altar. The safe house was the key. If they could determine whether Murdoch had been there, that might help settle the matter.

"What was the address?" Charlie asked. "Of the hideout?"

Portia gave a glum, facial shrug, "Don't know. D said it was best if I didn't know all the details."

Charlie silently groaned.

God save her from passive, incurious women!

"Ok. Do you know what he was going to do once he got to the safe house?"

"Lay low for a while until they gave up looking for him. After that, he was going to cross overland to Mozambique using a false passport before flying to the Seychelles where he'd already bought a villa through a trust. Then he was going to transfer the Cayman funds to a local account, get himself established under his new identity and let me know when it was safe to join him."

Well, that hadn't happened. Murdoch's funds remained firmly in the Cayman account. Yet was that proof of his death or simply a change of plan?

"You said when we spoke over the phone that things had fallen apart?" Charlie said. "What did you mean by that?"

"In the months before we decided to run, D began to get worried that they were becoming increasingly reckless. He -"

"Sorry to interrupt. I just want to check what you mean by 'they'. Are you talking about Jonas Maharaj?"

"He was one of them. Kept pushing for larger sums and more frequently. At first, D was into it but then things got out of hand. He was the one taking the risk, see? So, D started to push back, and they didn't like that."

Charlie tried to hold it in but failed. "I'm sorry, I have to ask. Didn't it bother you? What Murdoch was doing? The money laundering?"

"Why should it?" she said, piqued. "Everyone screws other people over to get what they want, don't they?"

"But -"

"Everyone's clutching their pearls, banging on about Derrick being a common criminal!" Portia's voice rose with indignation. "What a load of bollocks! Especially when the biggest criminals are strolling around Parliament and the City in three-piece fucking suits!"

Charlie took a breath.

Careful.

Keep her on side.

"All right," she said placatively. "I guess you've got a point."

"Whatever," with a sullen toss of her head, Portia got up, headed to the shoreline, and stood looking out to sea, her back stiff. Charlie gave her a few moments to calm down, then went to stand by her side.

"Is that when Murdoch put a stop to things?" she said softly. "When things got out of hand?"

Portia looked down. When she finally responded, her voice was flat. "Not at first. Not completely. But when he found out about Pied Piper, that's when the shit really hit the fan."

"Pied Piper?" Charlie's heart skipped a beat, an image of the dead girl by the canal flashing in her mind, body unclaimed, identity still unknown. "Are we talking about…?"

"Trafficking children?" Portia nodded soberly. "When Derrick told me about it, he was so angry, I thought the veins in his neck would burst. One of Jonas's friends got blind drunk at a poker game one night. Turned out he was also one of Maharaj's regular clients. Started complaining about how the latest kid Jonas had sold him was no good. Wouldn't do the things he wanted. Derrick started putting two and two together and began to realise where part of the money he was cleaning for Jonas came from."

Charlie turned her back on her, her muscles tensing with rage, her face growing hot. She thought about all the victims of the paedophile ring, their sweet faces, and broken bodies. She felt like shaking Portia, screaming at her, punching her until she felt just a fragment of the horror and pain that those children had gone through.

Or had people like Portia long lost the ability to care?

"I know what you're thinking," Portia said to her back. "That D was a monster. That we're all monsters. People tell you to work hard, be the best you can be, and the world will be your oyster. But oysters are never free, are they?"

Realising she had instinctively balled her hands into fists, Charlie relaxed her hands and crossed her arms over her chest, reigning in her emotions. After all, her fury would help no one if the story never got out. "If we live in such a Hobbesian world," she said quietly as she turned to face her companion once more, "what was different this time?"

Portia shivered but Charlie didn't think it was from the cold. "D had been abused as a child. That's why he had so much rage inside him, such a strong desire to lash out. He'd blocked out most of the memories but when we got together, he started getting therapy and it all came back. So, when he found out what Jonas was doing, he just couldn't take it. Felt he had to stop it if he could. But, to do that, he needed proof of what they were up to."

As Charlie was about to reply, music drifted from the tunnel. Soon, a group of teenagers emerged through the chalk stacks, some carrying wine or beer, others blankets or firewood, the hallmarks of an afternoon beach party. Their solitude broken, Portia and Charlie turned and retraced their footsteps, walking in silence, each caught up in their own thoughts until they were alone once more.

"And did he get it?" Charlie asked as they reached the path to the clifftop and began their ascent.

"Yep. When they were together on a business trip. D plied him with alcohol and pretended to be dead drunk himself. When he wasn't paying attention, D added some extra to his drink to help loosen his tongue. After that it was easy. Got everything he needed on tape."

"What did Murdoch do with the recording?"

"He made two USB copies and gave one to his lawyer as insurance."

"Then why didn't the lawyer release the recording when Murdoch disappeared?"

"He's dead," she said dolefully. "They killed him in his office and set the whole place alight – probably after they'd ransacked it looking for the USB stick."

Charlie shook her head.

Something didn't make sense.

"But how did they know about it in the first place?"

Portia let out a heavy sigh. "D messed up. He said that, when Jonas was swearing at him and threatening him during one of their arguments, he got so angry, it slipped out."

Charlie nearly stopped in her tracks. "He told them about the recording?! The copies?! Why on earth would -?"

"No – just that he had dirt on them which would be released if anything happened to him. At the time, he thought it would give him leverage. But as soon as he'd said it, he realised he'd just signed his own death warrant. That's when he knew he had to run. I assume targeting his lawyer was just a lucky guess on their part."

Some guess! However, that still didn't explain why the information hadn't yet come out. If Murdoch was alive, surely he would have released it to change the narrative and prove his innocence? Position himself as a victim in fear of his life, rather than someone with murderous intent. Particularly given the fact that no one had yet put forward a motive for why Murdoch would want Jonathan dead. After all, there would be no reason to silence him since Murdoch's dirty washing was already on full display! So, why was Murdoch still silent? Unless he no longer had it?

"And the other copy?" Charlie asked.

"D took it with him to Joburg. Said he placed it in the safest place he could think of. Where no one would dream of looking, even if they turned everything upside down."

"And where was that?"

Portia grimaced, "He swallowed it."

If Murdoch had gone to such lengths to keep his evidence hidden, he wouldn't have simply lost it by chance. So, the fact that such information had not yet been made public seemed to confirm her initial hunch and Portia's tale. Murdoch was dead and no longer in a position to tell his side of the story. Yet, without his body, how could she prove it?

They reached the grassy clifftop and came to a stop, Charlie needing to go left to her car and Portia right towards her hotel. They were done but there was just one thing that kept nagging at her.

"You said Maharaj was one of them," Charlie said. "Who else was involved?"

Portia's face turned sour. "Jonas wasn't the only one who wanted D dead. Who do you think introduced them in the first place? The silent partner. The one always lurking in the background, pulling all the strings."

"Who?" Charlie said pressed.

"Who do you think? The man whose voice was on the tape. The top dog himself."

Hate blazed in Portia's eyes.

"Spencer."

51. Whitewash

Islington
London, UK

She hurried across Kings Cross station, heading towards the Kiss the Hippo coffee shop. She'd spent the past week working from home, partly to avoid the scorn she knew she'd get from Bulldog's boys as soon as she set foot in the office, and partly to give herself time to check out Portia's story. Whilst her claim that Murdoch's lawyer was dead had checked out, the investigation - according to Charlie's source at the Met - had concluded that the fire had been an unfortunate tragedy rather than malfeasance. It could be that Portia had got her wires crossed or, given how good Maharaj seemed to be at covering his tracks, the investigators might have missed something. Either way, for now, it was Maharaj 1, Portia 0.

In terms of the alleged puppeteer, Charlie found it difficult to imagine anyone more old-school-tie than Dovecroft. So entrenched was he in the City of London hierarchy that he was virtually finance royalty, close friends with the Chancellor of the Exchequer and rumoured to be on the brink of a knighthood. Though the photo Viper had discovered had already established a link between Maharaj and Dovecroft, that was a very long way from proving they were partners in crime. And while Dovecroft's avoidance of the camera had also pointed to a man who might be willing to go to great lengths to protect his reputation, which made Portia's version of events at least plausible, it also meant that they would need a lot more than Portia's word to go after him. Leaving the score where it stood: Maharaj/Dovecroft 1, Portia 0.

Which had sent her back to the beginning, painfully trawling through the evidence she had gathered to date for clues she might have missed, double-checking and rechecking until she felt like tearing her hair out. Then this morning, she had received a small part of the ammunition she needed. Not for everything but hopefully enough to make people stop and think. Which brought the current score to 1 all.

As was the norm at that time of day, the coffee shop was packed, excited chatter battling with shouted orders and coffee machine hisses, gurgles, and pops. Thus, when she first felt a tap on her shoulder, Charlie assumed it was a mistaken jostle. The second time, however, the tap was unmistakable. Spotting who it was out of the corner of her eye, Charlie kept staring straight ahead and stepped forward. Still studiously pretending to be oblivious to her shadow, she placed her order and quickly made her way to the pick-up point. However, when the third tap came in the form of a loud cough accompanied by a sharp-elbowed nudge in the ribs, she had no choice but to recognise the elbow's owner.

"Connie!" Charlie said brightly, "What a nice surprise!"

"Indeed," Connie's face, today packed with lightening powder and surrounded by an Aryan white bob, was the picture of smug triumph. "*I'm surprised you're out and about, pet. Thought you'd be nursing your wounds in a corner somewhere.*"

"Oh?" Charlie blinked innocently. "Why would I need to do that?"

Plastering on a smile for the benefit of those around them, Connie leant forward and hissed in her ear, "I knew you wouldn't be up to snuff. You lot never are. Tried to help you out, show you the ropes, but you were too proud for that, weren't you love? And now look at you - your knickers down and your arse hanging out!"

Charlie angled her body, her palm tingling, itching to smack the bitch right out of her. Then she looked at the faces around them and realised the angry-black-woman trap. Taking a deep breath, she clutched both hands around her backpack strap to keep them in check and settled on a haughty stare, "Well, you know what they say about chickens, don't you, *lovey*?"

"Shit coming home to roost?"

Charlie shook her head then, with a knowing look, lowered her voice to a conspiratorial whisper, "I was thinking more about not counting them before they hatch. Know what I mean?"

Connie sneered dismissively, "I don't what you're talking about. What I *do* know is that the SFO has nearly finalised their report. *And*, according to a very well-placed source, are about to give Yeats a clean bill of health, putting everything down to the work of a few rotten apples. All of whom are now safely out of the barrel!"

A barista placed an order on the table and called out Connie's name.

"But it goes deeper than that!" Charlie said, "Surely, they -"

"Oh dear – is our little lamb lost?" Connie tutted as she reached across Charlie and grabbed her cappuccino. "Did you really think that a grubby, little worm like you could take on Yeats and win? That the higher-ups would let you?" Connie snickered. "It's time you learnt your place, Ms Tate!" As she turned to leave, Connie made sure that her stiff bob smacked her across the face. Shocked, Charlie could only watch her go, spluttering to get the taste of hairspray out of her mouth, so angry she felt like crying.

"Don't mind her, darling," the barista said with a warm smile, gently pushing her vanilla latte towards her. "People like that always get what's coming to them. You mark my words."

Still out of sorts, all Charlie could do was mumble a thank you, grab her latte and rush to the Torch.

Did Connie really have an inside scoop on the SFO report?
Impossible!
Then again, Jake did say she had high connections.
Had Woodhead been right?
Had the fix been in all along?

She fumed as she barrelled forward, each stride a mark of defiance.
No way.
Not this time.
Not on her watch!

Arriving at The Torch, she sought out a hot desk away from the main newsroom floor, put down her stuff and went to look for a private pod. Once inside, she hurriedly called Jake. Not getting a response, she sent an urgent text. He called back thirty seconds later.

"Charlie - can't this wait? I'm in the middle of a shit show here!"

"Is it true that the SFO is going to give Yeats the all clear? Chalk it down to just Murdoch and his collaborators?"

He sighed, "There's a rumour to that effect, yes."

"What if I had evidence that suggested the contrary? That it wasn't just Murdoch and his crew, but it went to the very heart of Yeats? At the most senior level?"

Jake was quiet for a moment before saying, "Then it would need to be iron clad. Even then, there's no guarantee. Between you and me, following Jonathan's murder, I've been told that people – and here I'm including the Chancellor himself – now want all this Murdoch business to go away ASAP."

"But that would be a whitewash!!"

"Only if you can prove it." She heard someone swearing in the background. "Look – can we discuss this later? I've really got to go."

Charlie started to protest but Jake had already dropped the call. Rushing out of the pod, Charlie went to The Ferret. It being lunchtime, the News

Editor's door was closed with a big 'do not disturb' sign pinned at eye-level for the especially dim-witted. Ignoring it, she knocked and popped her head inside before Kathy could object. "Got a minute?"

The Ferret looked up in annoyance just as she took a huge bite of her toasted sandwich. "Can't you read?" she said with her mouth full.

"I thought you'd want to be the first to know," Charlie said sweetly. "Didn't you say you wanted another scoop?"

Her eyes narrowed suspiciously, before she gruffly said, "Come in and make it quick."

Charlie closed the door and went to stand in front of her desk. "Have you heard the latest about the SFO report?"

The Ferret shook her head as she took another chunk out of her sandwich, clearly not expecting to be enthralled by whatever Charlie had to say.

"It seems that the SFO intends to exonerate Yeats as a bank and lay all the blame on Murdoch and a few others."

"So?"

"What if Murdoch isn't the mastermind everyone is now making him out to be? What if there's someone else?"

"Oh?" even though she carried on chewing, a spark of interest flashed in The Ferret's eyes.

Without mentioning Spencer by name, Charlie brought her up to speed including the latest information she had received that morning. "So, you see," she said excitedly, "if Murdoch were alive, Portia would have heard from him by now. And given that the latest forensic report shows that the hair follicle is more than six months old – in other words, dating to before Murdoch disappeared - he couldn't have left it behind when Jonathan was murdered three weeks ago."

"Which you think confirms it was planted. Just like you said?"

"Can you think of a better explanation?"

"No," The Ferret said slowly, her focus now hundred percent locked on Charlie's face.

Buoyed by the small victory, Charlie rushed on, "The only person who would want to do that would be Jonathan's true killer, right? To divert attention from themselves and put people off the cent."

"Why? Because Maharaj, and this puppeteer Portia referred to, were beginning to worry you were getting too close?"

"Exactly! Now, if we can place Maharaj or his men close to Murdoch on the day he disappeared, then bingo! Motive, means and malva pudding!"

"Malva pudding?"

"You know – as in the proof is in the pudding?"

The Ferret rolled her eyes and then swiftly moved on. "All right, say I buy

The Meanness of Things

all this. Why kill Jonathan? Did he also have something on this…Maharaj and his secret partner?"

"Don't know yet. Maybe."

The Ferret grimaced, "Supposition. I don't like suppositions." Pushing aside the now empty sandwich wrapper, she wiped her hands with a napkin.

"Fine. Like I said, I'm still working on that. But the rest stacks up pretty well, don't you think?"

Kathy sat back, crossing her legs. "You sure Murdoch got all this on tape?"

"That's what my source says."

"Where's the recording now?"

"Somewhere secure but retrievable."

Not a whole lie. Just two quarters.

"Ok, here's my take," the Editor briefly scratched her cheek. "The forensic report does stir things up, but it doesn't necessarily mean Murdoch *isn't* alive, nor does it categorically prove that he had nothing to do with his former colleague's death. In addition, the hair alone also doesn't prove that Murdoch isn't the mastermind."

Charlie's heart sank, knowing what was coming.

"So, what we need is that recording," Kathy continued. "How soon can you get it to me?"

Charlie suddenly realised she hadn't paid attention to Kathy's carpet before. It had a different pattern from the rest.

"Charlie?"

Had a thicker pile too.

"Charlie!"

Her head shot up to find The Ferret glaring at her.

"I said, when can I get it?"

She licked her lips, "Well, that's a bit tricky."

"Didn't you just say it was retrievable?"

"It is, it is," she cleared her throat. "Just not until we find Murdoch's body."

The Ferret's eyes turned to ice. "He swallowed it, didn't he?"

"Uh-huh," Charlie took a step back.

Her face turning red as a snooker ball, Kathy stood up so violently her chair banged against the wall. "Really – this is the last straw!"

"Portia's telling the truth. I know it! We have to find a way of delaying the SFO report. Of buying time until we have the proof we need!"

"We? We? There is no *we*." The Ferret walked around her desk and advanced towards her, pointing to a stack of folders on her desk. "You see that? That pile there? Thanks to you, that's all the new fucking risk reports I now have to fill out on every goddamn major story. Our penance for Yeats not suing us. That's in addition to the bloody editorial review board reports I do every month. And you know what's really put the cherry on top? This morning I got a memo from the Editor-in-Chief classifying Yeats as Code Red. You want to know what Code Red Means?"

Charlie wanted to say 'no', but she had a feeling she was going to be told anyway.

"It means that, from bloody now on, every word we print about Yeats has to be checked, rechecked, and fucking checked again! Got that?"

"In other words, a gag order."

"No – not exactly. But it does mean that I don't have time to entertain bloody shots in the dark!" Kathy spun her around and pushed her towards the door. "Now get out. And don't come back until you've got that tape!"

The door banged behind her so loudly, Charlie jumped, her face burning as everyone in the newsroom turned and looked at her. Squaring her shoulders, she quickly went to gather her things and headed to the lifts. As the doors opened, a group of interns got in with her, huddled around a phone. From what Charlie could tell, they were giggling at a post from a mysterious politics blogger who went by the name of Wendy Wise.

Standing in the corner of the lift, Charlie shot them an irritated look, appalled by their frivolity. Even though Wendy had hundreds of thousands of followers, most of the stuff she published was mere rumour and innuendo. Not exactly the cutting edge of journalism. And whilst it was true that, once in a while, her gossip led to actual investigations and hasty resignations, it was otherwise a bunch of...

Charlie's breath caught in her throat.

That was it!

The perfect gambit.

As soon as the lift doors opened, she ran across the lobby and back to the station to take the tube home.

Thank the Lord for Wendy Wise!

52. The CEO Returns

The Strand
London, UK

Hilary grinned with satisfaction as he walked into his office, taking in the plush, deep-pile carpet, his wide, gleaming mahogany desk and the brooding strand skyline beyond. It was amazing what you took for granted until you lost it. Even if it was just for a little while.

Hanging up his coat, he stood looking out the window, going through everything once more in his head. So far, everything had gone to plan. The SFO investigation had turned out exactly as he had hoped, including clearing yours truly. An old friend in the Treasury had been kind enough to give him a copy of the draft report, on condition he kept it secret, of course. Then it had simply been a matter of mistakenly leaving it on the table during an early breakfast meeting with his now favourite town crier and poof! Half of London would know the SFO's preliminary findings by that evening. That was provided Connie did her job, but given the very amicable agreement they'd reached, he had no grounds to worry on that score. Even Spencer seemed to have thawed towards him, at least enough to let him come back to work, doubtless also having been tipped off about the draft report's conclusions. So, all-in-all, he couldn't have wished for a better outcome.

Ahhh! The beauty of life!

Hilary spun away from the window and rang his PA. Celebrations were in order. "Gertrude, please get a bottle of cold Moet from the cellars, would you? Along with two glasses – no, make that three. May as well have one yourself."

Gertrude chuckled, "What are we celebrating?"

"Life, Gertie. Life."

"Well, I'm certainly glad to have you back, boss."

"Glad to *be* back," he felt a sudden lump in his throat. He'd missed Gertrude. "And get Steven to come up, please. If he's available."

As he waited, Hilary scrolled through Trudy's handover report, searching for the little titbits between the lines that one always needed to look out for. Brooding staff conflicts, skittish clients, country risks hiding in a blind spot.

"And the CEO returns!" Steven proclaimed as he strode into the office, his arms stretched out for a hug.

"Yes, well…," Hilary pushed the report aside and stood, briefly hugging him back before disentangling himself. He had never been one for outpourings of affection, especially when they were contrived.

"Anyone for champagne?" Gertrude asked, walking in with a laden tray.

"I'll help you with that," the CFO enthused, uncorking the bottle, and quickly pouring the first glass before the froth went all over the conference table. "My son is playing his first cricket match this afternoon. Let's hope the weather holds."

"Really?" Gertrude's eyes twinkled with warmth as Steven handed her the glass, "how sweet!"

"What about you, Hilary?" Steven asked as he poured two more glasses, picking up his own and handing the other to his host. "You must have played lots of cricket in your day. Any last bit of advice for my son?"

Hilary shook his head, "Unfortunately, not. Turns out, I'm more a soccer man, myself."

"Is that so?" his guest replied, more sceptical than curious.

Ignoring the dig, however subtle, Hilary lifted his glass. "Cheers! It's great to be home!"

"Cheers!" Steven and Gertrude said in unison. After taking a sip, Gertrude retreated with her glass, leaving Steven and him alone.

Hilary went back to stand by the window. "It really is beautiful, isn't it? This city of ours."

"Yes, it is." Coming to stand by his side, Steven lightly circled the rim of his glass with his forefinger. "But is it ours yet?"

Hilary shot him a look of admonition, "It will be. If we take things step by step. The final SFO report will be released soon, and Spencer's successor will soon be announced. If it turns out to be the guy everyone thinks it's going to be, that will clear my path to the top. Then it's you and me, like we discussed. Once I'm divisional CEO, I'm going to need a man like you by my side."

Steven looked at him with surprise. "Then you haven't heard?"

Hilary's eyes narrowed. "Heard what?"

"There's a story going around on social media. Not someone I follow but plenty of others do, apparently. A friend forwarded it to me a few minutes ago."

"A story by whom?"

"A woman called Wendy Wise," Steven took out his phone and started scrolling, looking for the message. "Ah – here it is. The headline reads 'Another Whitehall Whitewash' question mark. The story goes on to claim that, according to a little tweety bird – that's her source which she doesn't name - the SFO investigators have issued a draft report which, the source alleges, is set to wrongly exonerate the bank on all fronts. Furthermore, tweety alleges that Murdoch didn't kill Jonathan and that the evidence was planted by the real murderer."

"What?" He felt the first stirrings of alarm. "Based on what evidence?"

Steven scrolled down, speed reading, "Says something about a forensic report." He looked up enquiringly. "Should be easy enough for our guys to establish if that's true, shouldn't it?"

"Yes – I'll get the Joburg office to check it with the South African police ASAP." The bubbly brew now bitter, Hilary went to his desk to dispense with his glass and grab his mobile. "Send that thing to me, will you?"

"Sure," Steven tapped his screen, "There. You should have it in your inbox any second now."

"Got it," Hilary opened the message and tapped on the link. The story already had ten thousand likes.

Who the hell was this woman?

"More importantly," Steven continued, still speed reading, "according to her source, Murdoch wasn't the money laundering ringleader at all but allegedly took instruction from a very senior member of bank management."

His heart starting to race, Hilary quickly read to the end of the story. "But she doesn't even name the man! This so-called *Puppet Master*!"

"She never does," the CFO said, pulling a face.

"And people still take her seriously? That's outrageous!"

"Foolish not to, some say," Steven put his phone away. "Looks like we're back on the back foot."

"Not if I have anything to do with it!" Hilary started pacing, wiping his now clammy hands on his trouser legs.

This couldn't be happening. Not when he was so close!

His guest drained his glass and set it aside before glancing at his watch. "I need to head out to my next meet. You'll let me know what you need me to do?"

"Yes – I'll keep you posted," he managed to get out just as the door closed.

What absolute nonsense! He'd put out a repudiation at once. Stop this stupid rumour in its tracks before it spread any further.

Connie answered on the first ring.

"I suppose you're ringing about the Wendy Wise post?"

Why did the damn woman sound so calm? Didn't she know this was a crisis?

"You need to leak the findings of the draft SFO report immediately. Now. Stop this gossip in its tracks."

"Sorry – no can do."

Hilary stopped dead. "What? Why?"

"The SFO has distanced itself from the rumours regarding its findings. Their press office just issued a statement saying the investigation is still underway and no findings have yet been made."

"But we have their draft report!"

"Well, clearly, they've changed their mind, so the report we have is useless."

Hilary swore under his breath, "Who is this Wendy Wise, anyway? Why is the SFO even listening to her?"

"An abundance of caution, my sources say. She's been right before. No one wants to issue a report only for it to emerge later that they overlooked critical facts. It's not just Wendy's credibility on the line here."

This couldn't be. His first day back in the saddle and this Wendy bitch comes from nowhere!

"It's strange, though," Connie murmured, half talking to herself. "How, all of a sudden, Wendy's so interested in Yeats. She hasn't paid any attention to the Murdoch story before."

Hilary's heart skipped a beat.

"What did you say?"

"She's also never cited documents before," Connie continued as if he hadn't spoken. "Her stories are always more of the 'he said, she said' variety. And how the hell did she get hold of a South African police forensic report, anyway?"

Hilary had a sinking feeling he knew the answer to that. "Where's Tate, Connie?" he asked quietly.

Connie scoffed, "How the hell should I know? The last time I spoke to her, she was -" He heard a sharp intake of breath. "Oh my God! Are you thinking -"

"I don't *think*, Connie, I know. Deep down in my bones."

He felt the rage rising in him, hot and fierce.

"And I also know just what I'm going to do about it!"

53. Hop In

Various Suburbs
London, UK

The bank had promised something young and fresh, and Sez didn't disappoint, the evening cocktail cum media briefing lively and stimulating, unlike those of some of their competitors. As the briefing came to an end, Jake was thankful to have something positive to write about for a change, as opposed to all the dirty dealings at Yeats.

'What did you think of that?" Connie said as she sidled up to him with a wine glass in her hand.

He gave her cool look. Connie never spoke to him unless she was after something. "Why? What did *you* think?"

"Impressive, wouldn't you say?" She scanned the room. "Though I'm surprised your girlfriend didn't pitch."

"Oh?" he said absently as he tapped his phone and scrolled through the Sez media pack, thinking about the angle of the story he was going to write. "And who might that be?"

Connie giggled dismissively, "Charlie Tate, of course!"

"She's not my girlfriend."

"Fuck buddy, then? There must be something, given how close you two have become lately."

Determined not to rise to the bait, Jake kept his voice level, "Charlie and I help each other out from time to time, that's all. Not that it's any of your business." Turning his back on her, he picked up his backpack, deciding it would be good to get a quote from the CEO before he headed out.

Connie put a restraining hand on his arm, her eyes hard as flint. "If you see her, do tell her to take care. Word is she really crossed the line this time."

He shook her hand off his arm, saying, "What line?"

"You'll find out soon enough," she replied with a smile that reminded him of curdled cream. "It was good to see you again, Jake."

As Connie sauntered away with an exaggerated sway of her hips, Jake's first thought was that he was glad to be rid of her. Spotting the Sez CEO across the room standing amongst a gaggle of journalists, he shifted his focus back to the task at hand and walked towards them.

What had that been all about? Was Connie just trying to stir things up? Or were his concerns finally coming true?

The CEO glanced in his general direction. Jake unsuccessfully tried to catch his eye to indicate he shouldn't leave before answering one last question.

Yet, if so, why would Connie tell him? That would be the equivalent of warning Charlie herself and Connie wouldn't want to do that, would she? At the same time, Connie loved having one up on people by knowing something they didn't. Perhaps she just hadn't been able to keep it in, unable to resist the temptation to crow at her enemy's impending demise?

In the corner, the CEO began to look restless, glancing at his watch. If he didn't hurry up, he'd miss his opportunity. Jake increased his pace.

After this, he'd find Charlie, tell her what Connie had said. Yet tell her what, exactly? About a threat he couldn't define, to take place at a time he didn't know? Last time he told her to be careful, it hadn't gone well. What would make her listen to him now?

He reached the group around the CEO and took out his phone, ready to ask his question.

But what if he did nothing and something actually happened to Charlie? What kind of man would that make him? So, the truth was he had no choice. He had to at least try.

After he had gotten the CEO on record, Jake turned and raced to the exit, dialling as he ran. It went straight to voicemail. Knowing Charlie never listened to her messages, he redialled, hoping she had just been temporarily caught up. Voicemail again. He paused to send her a text – "Call me. Urgent" - then tried The Torch. Perhaps Charlie was chasing a deadline, sitting at her desk in do-not-disturb mode. If he could get someone to her, they could get her to call him back. The receptionist politely told him that Charlie hadn't been in that day.

Shit.

Getting to the street, he turned towards his usual station and then pivoted, realising that the route to Charlie's flat was in the opposite direction. As he ran towards Embankment station, he tried her number again and again but each time no one answered. Then a dreadful thought occurred to him.

What if what he dreaded had already happened?

The Meanness of Things

He looked at the clock again and cursed. One hour. One hour of sitting in a black cab under a tree with his taxi light off, looking conspicuous. Being conspicuous, especially for a man in his line of work, was never good. That's why this really should have been a two-man job. Someone on the inside watching the mark and he outside, around the corner in the parking garage, waiting to go as soon as he got the signal. It wasn't as if the client couldn't afford it. He still couldn't believe the bullshit they'd given him when he'd suggested it. Keeping things low profile?! What a load of fucking codswallop! That was the problem with rich fuckers. All the money in the world and tighter than a monkey's arse.

As yet another hopeful punter tapped on the taxi window, he shook his head with what he hoped was a sad look on his face and pointed upwards, signalling that the cab was not in service. Watching the girl walk away, he wrinkled his nose in irritation. Couldn't they see that his light was off? Or were they all just bloody wankers? Next time someone tapped on his window, he'd get out the car and… No. Wouldn't do to draw attention to himself. Not yet anyway. Best to just sit and wait. Resisting the urge to check the time again, he turned on the radio, hoping some music would soothe his growing impatience.

Not that he had anything else to do. He had set aside the whole afternoon and night for this job alone. He had known it wouldn't take that long, but for jobs like this, he always needed extra prep time. Space to obtain a certain mental adjustment.

It wasn't the killing part. After all, work was work and money was money. Whether it was up close and personal or clean and cold from afar, it was all the same to him. That was why straight kills were the easiest. The problem with this type of job was the other part. The lying part. Looking into someone's eyes and smiling, knowing that they trusted you and had no clue that they were in for the chop. He hated that. He was many things, but there was one thing that he wasn't, and that was a liar.

He also wasn't much of a smiler. At least not since he'd taken up this line of work. Twenty years this past Tuesday. Not that he had stopped smiling immediately. In the first few years, he had kept grinning and laughing as he'd always done. After all, according to his mother, he'd always been a happy soul. Then people had started to look at him funny. Like they'd just tasted something foul and bitter. Something to do with his eyes, they said.

Dead eyes in a beaming face.

The journey to Charlie's flat took forever. Partly due to the fact that Jake was forced to take the bus because of the tube strike and partly because it had suddenly dawned on him, as he sat on the bus to Tooting Bec, that he didn't actually know her street address. Convincing the receptionist at The Torch that, one, he was Charlie's friend and that, two, this was an emergency, had taken all his powers of persuasion. Luckily, she had eventually put him through to the News Editor who, once sure that another potential scoop might be afoot, (what's wrong with a white lie now and then?), had been more than happy to give him the details.

Finally, Jake pushed through the small wooden gate and walked up the path of the Victorian terrace. There were three flats in all, Charlie's on the ground floor and two above. Still hopeful, he pressed the bell of the ground floor flat and waited. Nothing. Then he pressed the bells for flats two and three. Feeling someone looking at him, Jake glanced up just in time to see a curtain in the first-floor flat fall back into place. He pressed flat two's bell again. No response, not even the twitch of a curtain this time. He was just about to have another go when the intercom of flat three came to life.

"Who dis?" the occupant asked.

"Sorry to disturb you," Jake said, "I -"

"You sellin' somethin'?"

"No!" *Please don't hang up.* "Not at all. I'm a friend of Charlie's. Jake from Business Today. I really need to get hold of her but she's not answering her mobile and she doesn't seem to be home. It's an emergency."

Flat three was silent for a moment, then he heard, "Hold up."

A few seconds later, the front door opened to reveal a thick, black girl with suspicious eyes in a round face, dressed in a riot of colour. She took in his face, his clothes, his body, sizing him up.

"Yoh bro, you Jake from the press conference? The one who's been working with her on them Cayman Papers?"

"Yeah – that's me," he said eagerly, relieved at not having to repeat the whole back story. "And you are?"

"LaQuicha." The woman tossed back her braids and lifted her chin proudly. "Quicha for short but my close friends call me Q."

"Do you know where Charlie is? I've been trying to reach her for the last hour, and I'm worried something bad might have happened."

Quicha's eyes narrowed to slits, "Bad how?"

"I haven't got time to go into the details. Like I said, it's an emergency. Can you please just tell me where she is?"

She sucked her teeth, crossed her arms, and gazed over his shoulder, her face set.

Have it your own way.

"Ok, ok," he said, putting up his hands in supplication. "I bumped into another journalist who told me that Charlie had done something that crossed the line. I think someone is going to try and shut her up."

Her eyes snapped back to his face. "You mean like when she got jumped?"

"Jumped?"

"Yeah. By some asshole whilst she was jogging on the common. You mean like that?"

So that *was what had happened.*

"No," Jake said, shaking his head gravely. "I think they might be planning something much worse."

"Who's they?"

"Who knows? The bank? Maharaj? Does it really matter? We just have to warn Charlie."

She frowned, her eyes darkening with anxiety. "For real?"

"Yeah," he took a step forward. "Please – I need your help."

She glanced at her watch. "Given the day and the time, Charlie must be at Muay Thai class. That's probably why you can't get hold of her." She quickly gave him the directions. "She should be back home in about thirty minutes if you'd prefer to wait?"

Move Jake. Move before it's too late.

"No – I need to talk to her now," he looked up and down the street. "What's the quickest way to the gym?"

"Bus. But with this tube strike? Finding one that ain't already full is gonna be a problem." She pointed down the road. "On foot, it's about forty-five that way."

If he ran, he might just be there in twenty.

"Thanks, Quicha. I appreciate it."

He set off down the street, the weight of Quicha's worried eyes drilling into his back.

In preparation for this job, he had spent the last three days practicing his smile, thinking happy thoughts, and trying to get a twinkle in his eyes to match the twinkle of his teeth. While the mirror had assured him that he'd finally got a winner, his sister's youngest had opened her five-month-year-old mouth and wailed as soon as she'd seen it. Kids – the fucking worst and best critics on earth. So, in addition to the tinted glasses and cap he always wore, he'd donned a medical mask to cover the rest of his face. After all, with all the germs floating about lately, one could never be too careful.

Talking of germs, he twisted in his seat to check that there were no cracks in the glass partition demarcating the driver and passenger section of the cab. They had assured him that nothing could get through, not even an atom, but his missing pinkie finger had long been a reminder never to trust anything you hadn't checked yourself.

He'd already gone over the seal thrice and examined the plastic partition with a magnifying glass. It was airtight without a crack or a crease. Still, once in a while, he felt the faintest draft on the back of his neck, like deft strokes of poison ivy. Soon afterwards, he would feel the itch building, the skin on the back of his neck swelling until it felt like it was hot and red with puss and blisters. Soon thereafter his breath would catch in his throat, and his body would start writhing as he began to splutter and choke. Fighting for every breath, he'd grapple in vain with the door handle, desperate to escape until, with a final gasp, he departed. The place of his death, this godforsaken cab in this godforsaken spot, forlorn and alone as he waited to kill someone he didn't even know.

And each time the vision came, he'd raise a fearful hand to the back of his neck, convinced that the blistering was about to emerge, only to find the skin was as smooth and cool as refrigerated butter.

It was a strange thing, the mind. You never knew where it was going to take you.

Charlie stepped out of the shower and quickly dried herself off, humming Queen as she dressed, feeling like a champion. This evening, she had finally managed to land a blow on her trainer. A lucky shot but progress, nevertheless.

Zipping up her gym bag, she checked the messages on her phone. Twelve missed calls from Jake and two texts. She went to open the messages then thought better of it. She'd phone him as she sat on the bus on the way home. Slinging her bag over her shoulder, she left the changing rooms and headed to the exit. As she walked down the stairs, her phone buzzed, Quicha this time. That was strange. Q hardly ever rang her at this time of night. Either too busy studying or partying. Charlie waited for a text, but none came, suggesting that the reason for her call wasn't urgent. However, she made a mental note to swing by her place when she got home, just to make sure.

The temperature had dropped considerably since she'd gone into the gym, the ice-cold air slamming into Charlie's face as soon as she stepped into the street. Buttoning up her jacket, she walked to the bus stop and checked the timetable. The next one was due in about fifteen minutes, but the buses had been running late the whole day. She could take her chances and wait but that might mean freezing to death. Or she could splurge on a cab. With all the money she had received so far for the Murdoch series, she could certainly afford it. So, opting for the latter, Charlie stood on the edge of the pavement, looking up and down the road, hoping to get lucky.

After checking the glass partition for the umpteenth time, he began to wonder if the phone tracker he'd been given had a glitch. Why else would the target be MIA? Wouldn't be the first time. So much for modern technology! Something always didn't work at some point or other. He preferred the old ways, himself. Nothing wrong with a little bit of footwork and using your own fucking eyes. Not that anyone listened to him. Nah! Every client these days was too clever by half.

A dog came up to the driver's door, lifted its leg and pissed against the side of the cab. Reluctant to use the horn to warn it off in case it drew too much attention, he knocked on the window and glared at it, hoping what it read in his eyes would be enough to do the trick. The dog ignored him, boldly finishing its business before slinking off. He must be losing his touch.

Catching a movement out of the corner of his eye, he turned just as a woman further down the street stepped to the edge of the pavement and waved her arms at a passing taxi. Could that be her? Feeling the usual adrenaline rush, the tingle of anticipation, he quickly examined the picture they'd sent him. Slim, athletic build – check. About five foot six – check. Mohawk – check. Pointy, caramel face? Difficult to tell from this distance. He'd need to get closer. Switching on the taxi light, he started the engine and glided up the road.

Jake pumped his arms as he ran, his strides long, his feet pounding the pavement with each landing. As he sprinted, he sucked air through his nose, pushed it deep into his belly and out through his mouth, just like he'd been taught. He tried not to think of the seconds passing or the dozens of fellow travellers he pushed out of the way to clear a path. His mind was on one thing and one thing only.

Charlie.

Rounding the corner, he finally reached the street Quicha had directed him to, a busy arterial road that also posed as a high street, shops ranged on either side. Cars whooshed back and forth while commuters and shoppers flocked across the pavement, scurrying to their destinations. Jake elbowed his way forward, dodging in and out between fellow pedestrians, apologising as he went.

Quicha had said the club was between a spa and a clothes shop, below a huge black, white and red sign, lit up so no one could miss it. And she'd been right, a black glass door marking the club's entrance. He took the stairs two at a time, bursting into the central training area, his eyes scouring his surroundings.

Where the hell was she?

A tall, lithe guy wearing long shorts walked up to him, his six-pack gleaming with sweat. "Can I help you?"

"Charlie," Jake panted, "Charlie Tate?"

"I'm Greg her trainer. And you are?"

Oh God – not this again!

He grabbed Greg's shoulders. "Look - I'm a friend, ok? I've been trying to get hold of her the whole evening. If you know where she is, you've got to tell me – it's an emergency!"

The muscles in Greg's neck tensed, his eyes looking pointedly at the hands on his shoulders.

Jake quickly let go, pleading, "Please. I just need to find her."

Greg's face softened. "You've just missed her actually. Left about five minutes ago."

"Where did she go?"

"Probably to the bus stop down the road. If you're lucky, she may still be there."

Relief flooded through him.

He'd made it. He'd arrived in time.

Shouting his thanks over his shoulder, Jake dashed down the stairs and back out onto the pavement. About 30 metres away, a woman stood alone under the bright awning of a bus stop, her profile unmistakable. He broke into a run, calling Charlie's name as he zig-zagged through the evening throng, but she didn't hear him. An old black cab passed him and sped up when Charlie put out her hand, signalling for it to stop. As she leaned into the cab window, Jake called her name again. Her back stiffened and she stood upright, looking behind her into the crowd, frowning. Fifteen metres away, Jake jumped up and down, shouting her name, but she didn't see him. Then Charlie turned back to the taxi window.

"Where you going to, love?" he said, injecting as much warmth into his voice as he could.

"Not far," she said with a smile, her caramel, pointy face lighting up, "Cloudesdale Road." Quite a sweet smile when you thought about it.

"Then you're in luck, darling. Hop in. Was about to knock off but since

Cloudesdale's on my way…" As she got in the back, he switched off the taxi light and turned on the metre.

She nodded as she shut the door but didn't say anything else. Not much of a talker then. Just as well.

"Mind if I turn up the heating?" he asked, the perfect host. "Feeling real frosty this evening."

While he didn't wait for a response, she didn't object. Seemed glad of it, in fact. Poor thing.

The blast of the aircon masked the sharp click as the back doors locked into place. He watched in the rear-view mirror, waiting for the inevitable as the gas seeped into the passenger section. She took out her phone, intending to make a call but before they had even gone a few metres, her eyelids started to droop, and soon she was yawning.

"Been a long day, love?" he asked gently.

"Not really," she replied. "Must have overdone the workout." Putting away the phone, she yawned once more, rested her head against the back of the seat and closed her eyes.

"Well, you go ahead, darling. I'll wake you when we get there."

Soon her breathing grew deep and steady, her head lolling to one side as her body slumped into slumber. Confident that his charge was now dead to the world, he switched off the aircon, did a U-turn and accelerated up the road in the opposite direction.

"Yeah, you settle in, darling," he cooed. "Won't be long now."

54. Awake

Somewhere
London, UK

The first thing Charlie smelt was petrol, acrid and sour, pushing up her nostrils, triggering a faint alarm in the recesses of her brain, forcing her awake. She opened her eyes to pitch-black and instinctively tried to move but found she couldn't. She lay on her side, her mouth gagged, hands and feet bound, legs bent up to her chest. The last thing she remembered was sitting in the back of the taxi and suddenly being overwhelmed by fatigue. Now she seemed to be in the boot of an old sedan, rocked by the sound of whooshing wind, a throbbing car engine and the rumble of rubber grating on tar.

A boot.
A cage?
A coffin?

Her heart started pounding, the first strands of panic twisting around her, making her chest so tight she could barely breathe. Nausea crept up her throat, but she swallowed it back, sucking in deep breaths through her nose, trying to stay calm, to focus.

A memory from childhood flashed in her mind. 8-year-old Charlie in her mother's arms, hugging her tight after her mother had returned from a jail stint due to a confrontation with the police. "Weren't you scared, Mummy?" she had asked in a hushed whisper. Looking into her eyes, her mother had given her a reassuring smile. "Always," she had said. "But you have to learn to push past the fear. That's what it means to be brave, sweetie. What it means to fight for what's right." Now, hurtling towards an end she didn't dare to imagine, Charlie knew that she wasn't going to get through this if she panicked. It didn't matter who the taxi driver was or why he had taken her. The only thing that mattered now was getting out alive.

As her eyes adjusted to the darkness, she tried to search her surroundings but still couldn't see much in the gloom.

Wait…

Were those voices she was hearing?

Charlie tried to scream but the gag turned them into pathetic grunts. Turning onto her back, she slammed her feet against the boot lid, hoping to get someone's attention. She did it three times then waited, listening for a response. When she got nothing, she did it again, and again and again. All she got in return was her kidnapper pressing harder on the accelerator and soon the babble of voices was behind them, leaving only the unknowing, uncaring swoosh of passing traffic. Sighing, Charlie lowered her legs and turned back on her side.

Don't give up. As long as the car is moving, you still have time.

She moved on to the next option – calling the police. Working her tongue and jaw and pulling it with her fingers, she slowly got the gag out of her mouth and then rolled it down her chin until it hung loose around her neck. Reaching for her mobile, she found that the pocket she had placed it in was empty. Then she felt around the boot with her hands and feet, thinking it might have fallen out of her pocket but, again, it was nowhere to be found.

The bastard must have taken it.

Shit!

No one was going to save her. She would have to save herself. Which meant the sooner she untied herself the better. In that regard, at least the search hadn't been totally in vain, as she now knew she wasn't the only thing her kidnapper had thrown into the boot. Hoping it was what she thought it was, Charlie slowly shimmied the bag up her legs, the first stirrings of excitement rippling through her as her fingers clasped its straps.

She'd been right. It was her gym bag.

Finally, some progress!

Unzipping the left pocket, she felt a surge of triumph as her hand grasped soft leather. Taking out her travelling manicure kit, she opened the pouch, took out her cuticle scissors and began the painstaking process of snipping away at the black zip ties around her wrists, intermittently pulling her wrists apart to loosen the plastic. Beads of sweat broke out on her forehead, the ties rubbing and then cutting into her skin. However, she ignored the pain and the blood, snipping and pulling, snipping and pulling until she finally managed to get her hands free. Wiping her sweaty hands on her pants, she immediately moved on to the next task – freeing her legs. Bringing her knees up to her chin, she had just started on the ties around her ankles, when she noticed the car was slowing down. Soon, it drew to a complete stop. Charlie froze, holding her breath.

"Quicha! It's me - Jake. Open up!" As he waited, he bent forward, hands on his knees as he fought to get his breath back, having run all the way back from the Muay Thai studio.

He heard footsteps bounding down the stairs before the front door flew open, Quicha's eyes wide with surprise. "Didn't you find her?"

"I saw her get into a cab, but…" He thought about how the taxi's light had turned off as soon as Charlie had stepped inside, almost as if it had been waiting for her. "Something's not right. And she's still not answering her phone nor is she home. Could she have gone somewhere else?"

"Without coming home to change first? No way!"

Jake was quiet for a moment, going through all the options in his mind. Then he got it.

"You guys seem to be close," he said urgently. "Her phone wouldn't be linked to yours, would it?"

"As in find my phone? Sure," she pulled out her mobile then hesitated. "But shouldn't we just call the police?"

"And say what? I've got a bad feeling. I think my friend might be in danger, but why or how I don't actually know?"

"Yeah – guess you're right. Not like the Popo cares about black lives anyways." Her bright nailed fingers raced across the screen. "That's weird. Her signal's dead."

"What do you mean it's dead?"

She looked at him like he was thick, "As in incommunicado."

"Fuck!" Jake slumped against the wall, feeling defeated. "I guess that's it then. It's over."

Quicha put a comforting hand on his shoulder.

"No, it ain't."

The engine was still running, which provided some hope. Wherever they were, it was unlikely to be their final stop. Nevertheless, Charlie listened with bated breath, not sure what was coming. A window rolled down, something clanged on the ground, the window rolled up and the indicator clicked on. The car moved off once more, turning into what seemed like a downhill road, gravity pushing her to the right and then to the front of the boot. For the first time, she noticed that all the other urban sounds had gone apart from the remorseless growl of the engine and the roll of the wheels. They had entered a quieter, more deserted part of the city.

Not good.

Her heart thudding in her chest, Charlie wiped her brow and went back to work, frantically jabbing at the plastic tie around her ankles, pulling her legs apart inch by inch to break her bonds as quickly as possible. As she worked, her other senses remained on high alert, checking for signs of any change in the external environment or indications that they were about to reach their final destination. Whilst she had never been religious, had never felt the need to draw on the good offices of any kind of higher power, she now hoped that she might have been wrong. That something or someone somewhere would be listening to her silent pleas and grant her, just this once, the one thing she needed now more than ever.

Time.

The zip tie started to stretch. Further and further until, with a snap, her legs were free. Charlie exhaled, feeling a huge sense of relief. At least now she could fight back. However, she wasn't out of the woods yet. Now that she was unbound, the next task was to open the boot, roll out as they were in motion and get to safety before her capturer caught up with her. Immediately she shifted focus, feeling around the boot lock with her hands in the hope of locating the boot release lever. As she searched, the odour of petrol within the boot became intertwined with the stench of rotten eggs. Sulphur. They must have been passing a waste disposal site. She had read somewhere that waste disposal sites were popular dead body dumping grounds amongst the London criminal class. Yet, her kidnapper had driven past it, suggesting he had something else in mind. Something possibly far worse.

Don't focus on that. You can't control what's coming.

Focus on now and get a bloody move on!

Unable to locate a boot release lever, she tore up the carpet behind the driver's seat, hoping to at least find a boot release cable. Nothing. Then she probed above the wheel on the driver's side, working inch by inch in the gloom until her hand finally brushed over what she was looking for. Grabbing the cable, she leaned back and pulled as hard as she could, but the boot lock didn't budge. Wiping her hands on her top to get maximum grip, she tried again and again but the lock remained stubbornly closed.

What else?

Think, Charlie, think!

There had to be…

Wait – were they slowing down again?

Reducing speed, the car made a slight turn, went over a bump, and then started to jiggle as it made its descent, the smooth sound of wheels against tar replaced by the crunch and thwack of wheels on dirt-covered, uneven ground. To avoid being tossed back and forth, Charlie lay on her side, her back pinned against the back seats. In the distance, she heard a slapping sound like choppy water beating against a shore. A sound that grew closer and closer.

She was out of time.

When she sensed the car was about to stop, Charlie reached for her gym bag and took out her only weapon. With her tiny scissors in one hand and her knees drawn up to her chest, she waited, heart racing, ready to kick and stab as soon as her assailant opened the boot.

The engine cut. The driver's door swung open, and footsteps crunched over gravel.

Not accustomed to getting calls in the middle of the night, it took a while for Viper to realise that the ringing sound she was hearing wasn't a call from George Clooney desperately pinning for her after she had once more rejected his advances but from a source far more down to earth. Shoving up her pink and black eye mask, she groggily reached for the phone.

"Hello?"

"Viper, it's me," Quicha said hurriedly. "Charlie's in trouble."

She snapped awake, pushing herself upright. "What kind of trouble?" Viper had never heard Quicha sound so scared, even though she tried to hide it. This had to be serious.

"I'll explain later. Me and Jake need your help. We've tried to locate her but her signal's dead. Didn't you embed a tracker in her phone when you were doing all that other security shit?"

"Yeah, I did," she said gravely. "Give me a minute. I'll call you right back."

Springing out of bed, she donned her dressing gown and slippers and rushed to the computer room. After a few clicks, a map of London was on the screen. Another few taps and she'd zoomed in on a stationary red dot flashing at an intersection. Quicha picked up immediately.

"I've got her," Viper said. "She's near the Thames. I've just sent you the pin."

Charlie counted, anticipating it would take roughly three seconds for her kidnapper to get to the boot.

One…

The Meanness of Things

Two…
Thr…
Hold on – the footsteps seemed to be headed in the other direction.
She heard the passenger door open, what sounded like rustling plastic then the door banging shut again.
What the hell was he doing?
More footsteps, heading back to the driver's side, followed by the sound of sloshing liquid then the slam of the driver's door. More pebbles crunching underfoot interspersed with the sound of liquid splashing on metal, the grisly dyad continuing on repeat as he circled the car.
Wait – was he…?
Charlie couldn't help it. Blind panic took hold. She started screaming for help as she frantically beat her fists against the boot lid, knowing that there was no one to hear, that her attacker was beyond remorse, beyond mercy, but she did it anyway. As she shouted and punched, he carried on with his task without a moment's pause, whistling as he worked. Soon, the sound of splashing on metal morphed to liquid spattering on the ground, growing fainter as he retreated to a safe distance. A brief silence, an almost imperceptible click and…

WHOOOOOOSH!

Time stood still. In a split second, she was transported to another day, another death, a recurring nightmare. As the first whiffs of smoke snuck into the boot and heat crept up the back seats, she sat transfixed by the vision of her parents screaming as they were engulfed by flames in the front of their car whilst, behind them, her brother and his girlfriend battled to get out. Then, with the fluid transition of a dream, she was back at the beginning.

Driving on the motorway at dusk, the light of day dying under an orange sky. Bright lights streak by, white and yellow as, in front of her, red taillights stretch into the distance. They're heading out of the city for the long weekend. A family vacation that's been too long coming. As she drums her fingers on the steering wheel, humming along to the radio, Dad – riding shotgun - cracks another joke. As usual, he starts giggling before he gets to the punchline, his broad shoulders shaking with laughter. It's one of his worst but she smiles anyway whilst shaking her head in mock admonishment. Squashed in the back, Mum, Ben, and Pinkie laugh despite themselves. For the first time in a long while, she feels content. Happy almost. As if…

Thwack!

The steering wheel flies out of her hands. She tries to get hold of it, control it, but it's too late. Everyone is screaming, eyes wide with terror as the car flips up into the air, smacks down on the ground, reverberating like thunder, and then rolls down the escarpment. Grass, earth, trees, sky, the world spins and turns upside down. The car hits a tree, they jerk to a stop, and the bonnet bursts alight. Breaking glass, searing heat, angry orange flames everywhere. Her eyes start streaming, toxic black smoke scorching her lungs and throat. Dad, blood trickling down his face, slumps forward in the front seat. Mum, Ben, and Pinkie lie silent, passed out in the back.

Wake up.
Wake up!
We have to move!
Shift.
Now she's standing in the grass, frozen, helpless, watching them from afar, tears pouring down her face.
You have to get them out.
Mum and Dad in the front, coughing, burning.
My fault. I should've been...
Mum and Dad in the front, pleading, dying...
My fault. I could've...
Ben and Pinkie screaming, shrieking...
Do something!
Everyone's faces melting...
Can't...
Can't move. Can't breathe. Can't...
DOOOOO SOMETHIIIIIINNNG!!!

"Stop here," Jake said to the Uber driver, wondering if Viper had gotten something wrong. The GPS coordinates had brought them past a waste disposal plant to a deserted intersection. On their left, was a tall fence in front of an industrial-looking building. Straight ahead, the road had a construction site on one side and, on the other, a string of electricity pylons standing on its shoulder like silent sentries. Down the right turning, streetlamps stood in front of tall fences on both sides of the road, hiding the treasure within. Everything but a black cab, and more importantly, Charlie.

"Are you sure this is the right place?" He whispered to Quicha.

She flashed him a look of irritation. "Hey bro," she said to the Uber driver, "we're just going to have a quick look around. Please don't go anywhere, awright?"

"No problem, my sister," he replied with the tone of a man who had seen so many strange things in his life that he felt no need to ask questions. Quicha opened her door, switched on her torch, and started combing the street.

"What are you doing?" Jake said, following her out of the cab.

"If Viper says Charlie's phone is here, then that damn phone is here! So, stop acting like a motherfucking cracker and help me find it. Then, perhaps we'll be able to see which direction they took."

Feeling like an idiot, Jake switched on his own torch and began scanning the ground. Moving inch by inch, he continued up the road towards the pylons whilst she scoured the intersection and the right turning. It was slow work and, with each passing second, he had a sinking feeling that they were already too late.

"Over here!" Quicha yelled, bent over next to a streetlamp. "I found something!"

"Is it Charlie's phone?" he said as he came to stand by her shoulder.

She straightened up, making a face as she gazed at the object in her hand. "Part of it. They must have taken the phone apart and thrown it out the window."

"Still looks clean, though. It can't have been here long."

Quicha's eyes lit up, "Exactly!"

They ran back to the car.

"Go right!" Jake said to the driver, "And hurry!"

Without a word, the driver turned the wheel and zoomed down the road. They kept their eyes glued on both sides of the street, looking for an open gate, an abandoned cab or anything that might point to Charlie. The road made a sharp curve, and they passed a closed parking area on their right, before getting to open ground and the unmistakable sound of the river. The shore was bathed in darkness apart from the flicker of a red boat station light on the pier.

Quicha grabbed his arm. "Hold up!" she said urgently, squinting at a spot up ahead, close to the water's edge. "Is that a car on fire?"

A coughing fit shocked Charlie back to the present, thick, acrid smoke clogging her throat. In a flash, the gravity of her situation hit her, pushing aside the guilt and fear, and leaving only one thing. A dogged desire to survive. Hawking and hemming, eyes streaming, Charlie squeezed her body against the back seats, blocking out the pain as the heat singed her back and pulled up the carpet. The gloom now even darker due to the thick smoke, she used her hand to search the spare wheel storage area, hoping the sedan had a scissor jack. She was in luck. Putting the carpet back in place, she set up the jack on the floor of the boot and started turning the crank. When, the jack reached the underside of the boot lid, the crank starting to jam. Using her full body weight, she cranked with all her might, sweat running down her face, each breath searing her throat.

Wait – what was that?

Was someone calling her name?

"In here!' she yelled desperately, as she furiously worked the crank. "I'm in here!"

The boot lid started to buckle, the centre bending upwards.

Almost there.

Footsteps running towards her. Closer now. Two distinct voices, shouting, "Hold on. We're coming!!"

Thank God for Quicha!

And was that Jake?

Nonetheless, Charlie kept on cranking. She couldn't wait for them to get to her. If she didn't get out now, she could die of asphyxiation. The crank started to make a grinding noise, and - for a terrible moment - she thought it was about to break. Then, with a loud crack, the boot flew open. Coughing, surrounded by flames, she began scrambling out.

Pop.

Hiss.

BOOOOMMMMM!!

Quicha's shriek tore the night asunder.

"Chaaarlieeeee!"

She was thrown up into the air.

Then all was black.

55. May I Introduce

The Strand
London, UK

Feeling a mix of exhilaration and trepidation, the former inspired by the fact that he had finally arrived at his long-coveted goal and the latter by the possibility that his prize could still be snatched away from him, Hilary took a deep breath and tapped on the Group CEO's door. Inside, he could hear murmuring from what appeared to be a news broadcast.

"Thus, after an in-depth and wide-ranging investigation, we as the Serious Fraud Office, can find no evidence of widespread corruption or malfeasance in the African Division of Yeats Bank. Though we have identified the need to strengthen certain internal governance mechanisms, enhance its client vetting processes and increase the capabilities of the bank's internal audit team, it is our conclusion that the events associated with the so-called Cayman Papers are solely due to the efforts of the former divisional CEO, Mr Derrick Murdoch, and the small number of associates he recruited to his cause…"

Upon receiving no response to his knock, doubtless due to it being muffled by the competing TV, he decided to be bold, sticking his head into the room.

"There you are. The man of the hour!" Spencer said, beaming, waving him into his office as he turned down the volume on the TV. "Come in, come in!"

With a smile that he hoped did just enough to acknowledge the compliment without being boastful, Hilary did as he was bidden, following the two men who rose from the conference table where they had been sitting to the more congenial sofas by the fire. While Spencer's walk was sleek and stealthy like a cat, the other man moved more like a bull, meaty arms swinging by his side, his big, barrel chest leading the way. Those who didn't know him often assumed that his size meant he was all brawn and no brains. A perception that he deliberately cultivated amongst his rivals and the uninitiated. Yet, anyone who had been up against him in a negotiation or conflict soon learnt that his mind was as taut and sharp as his biceps and his cunning lethal.

"I take it you know Tom?" Spencer said, folding himself into a couch whilst his guest sat on the one opposite. "The Asia CEO?"

Hilary was momentarily confused but was careful not to show it.

Why was Tom here? Spencer had said he'd wanted to discuss the Africa CEO position, which under normal circumstances wouldn't need to involve Tom. Unless…

"Yes, of course," Hilary said as he hurried to shake the other man's hand. "How are you, Thomas?"

"Very well. Thanks to you!" With a rumbling laugh, he jerked his head in the direction of the SFO press conference, now silently playing on the TV screen. "I was worried that Spencer had given me a hospital pass with all the bad press the Africa division was getting. But I hear it was *you* who made that little problem go away?" Pulling Hilary closer, he gave him a congratulatory slap on the arm, nearly sending him sprawling.

In order not to lose his footing, Hilary quickly plopped down next to him on the couch. "Well, I wouldn't go that far," he said as he unbuttoned his jacket.

So, Thomas Huddleston, not Alex, was going to be the next Group CEO. Had the rumours been wrong or had something happened to bring about a change of heart?

Spencer's eyes twinkled with amusement. "Come now. Don't be so modest! You're amongst friends here, isn't he Tom?"

"Of course!" Tom's sharp-toothed smile glinted at Hilary.

Friends wasn't exactly how he would describe it, but he knew better than to say so. Casually leaning against the back of the sofa, he opted for, "Thank you, gentlemen. I appreciate your support."

Spencer opened a cigar box sitting on the coffee table between them, gesturing for them to help themselves. "I have to say, I didn't think you had it in you. But I'm glad you *eventually* proved me wrong." He took out a large, Cuban cigar and clipped it. "Now Tate is out of the way, I think it's time to focus on the next steps." Lighting it, he took a deep puff then rested his arms on the back of the couch like a hunting eagle in flight, his laser eyes focused on Hilary's face.

A burst of adrenalin coursed through Hilary's veins.

This was it. The confirmation he'd been waiting for!

However, under Spencer's judging gaze, he kept his body relaxed, his face cool, feigning ignorance. "Next steps?"

"As you know," Spencer replied, "I've decided to bring my retirement forward to the end of this financial year. Based on my recommendation, Tom here has just been confirmed by the Board as the next Group CEO."

"Congratulations," Hilary said, crafting his face into a picture of delight. "That's fantastic news. Well deserved!"

Tom's eyes dissected every crease and quiver on Hilary's face, assessing his sincerity. Unable to find any evidence of deception, a new warmth crept into his eyes. "Thank you," he said. "I'm humbled by the trust Spencer has placed in me."

"Tish-tosh. You earned it," Spencer took another puff of his cigar, rolling the smoke around his mouth before exhaling it in the direction of the burning fire. "The matter is still under wraps, mind you, until the formal announcement next week, so we would appreciate your discretion."

Hilary nodded in agreement, wishing Spencer would get to the point.

"In the lead-up to my exit, Tom will be working very closely with me as part of the handover process."

Hilary glanced at the Asia CEO out of the corner of his eye. He sat, straight-backed, on the edge of the sofa, his breathing steady, his muscles relaxed but his eyes darted back and forth between the two of them, watching the exchange keenly.

"Naturally," Spencer continued, "that also means being able to factor in on any divisional CEO appointments that will need to be made during that time."

Fuck! Another delay while he worked on winning Tom's approval! Worst still, what if it had all been for nothing? What if Tom already had his man, and this was all just a charade?

"Of course," Hilary replied evenly.

"Within this context, we wanted to chat to you about a few things," Spencer took an even deeper puff of his cigar, really sucking it in, before blowing the voluminous smoke in Hilary's direction.

"Things?" Hilary asked, trying not to cough or think about what the cigar smoke was doing to his lungs.

"As you know, being able to build and maintain client relationships is a critical part of the job of a CEO. It's for this reason that CEO posts have traditionally been filled by people with in-depth client management experience. Thus, as a former COO, your appointment would be the first in bank history. Given this, we wanted to be sure that building such relationships wouldn't be a problem for you."

Hilary sat forward, his face earnest. "I appreciate that. I also want to assure you that, whilst I haven't been centrally involved in deal-making processes, I have - nevertheless - been able to build strong relationships with most of our key clients. As, I'm sure, they themselves will attest."

Spencer arched a sceptical brow. "Certainly, but -"

"Not just in my role as COO," he continued, careful to keep the desperation out of his voice, "but also when I've acted as CEO of the division. Which, as you know, I've done many, *many* times. As a candidate, this makes me unique since I bring together the best of both worlds. Deep operational expertise combined with strong client engagement experience."

He paused, his eyes studying the jury of two, hoping his closing argument had been well received. The period of silence that followed must have been only a few seconds but, to Hilary, it felt like an eternity. Tom looked at the carpet whilst Spencer puffed away at his cigar, his face inscrutable. Eventually, the Group CEO turned to Tom and said, "Is he here?"

Tom glanced at a message on his phone. "Coming up the lift now."

"Is who here?" Hilary said, anxiously.

Spencer placed his cigar on an ashtray and stood. "Nothing to be concerned about. There's just someone I'd like you to meet. Not only an old friend of mine but a good friend of the firm, wouldn't you say so Tom?"

Tom scrambled to his feet. "Absolutely."

Taking his cue, Hilary also got up, looking at his companions warily.

What was going on?

Who was the guy coming up the lift?

And why was Tom suddenly jumping to attention?

The door opened and Spencer's PA ushered in a short, rotund, ordinary-looking man of Indian extraction. Hilary studied him behind veiled eyes. The man wore a cheap business suit and had apparently donned aftershave to match. In the absence of his business attire, one might have imagined him to be a street vendor or a short-order cook. Certainly not the type of man worthy of immediate admiration, let alone acquiescence.

So, what was his secret?

Spencer hugged the newcomer warmly, as did Tom, before the three of them turned to him, their faces expectant. Whatever his secret, it immediately became clear to Hilary that the man was someone he needed to impress. Thus, plastering on a charming smile, he extended his hand and stepped forward.

"Jonas," Spencer said with an affectionate hand on the short man's shoulder. "May I introduce the would-be new CEO of the Africa Division. Mr John Hilary."

56. Last Card

Alexandra Township
Johannesburg, South Africa

Boy gently shook his shoulder. "Come on, Thabo! You've been in bed for two weeks now. You need to get up." Shrugging him off, Thabo turned and faced the wall. Undeterred, Boy shook his shoulder again, harder this time.

"Leave me alone," Thabo said gruffly.

"I know you blame yourself, but Lucky was also stubborn and reckless," Boy said. "If he was here, he'd admit it himself. What good is moping around doing him? Doing you? We have to keep going. We can't just give up on life. You're the one who taught me that."

"He's right, you know," Innocent crossed the room and sat at the foot of the bed. "You also haven't eaten anything in days. Starving yourself isn't going to help Lucky, wherever he is."

Thabo's chest grew tight, his suppressed anger bursting through. "Don't pretend we don't know what happened to him! He's dead. We all know he's dead. And there's nothing we can do about it!"

Yanking the blanket over his head, Thabo closed his eyes, shutting out the world. He felt the mattress dip as Boy joined Innocent at the foot of the bed, the weight of their silence another load on his heart. He was wrong. He shouldn't have shouted at them, especially since they were not the ones he was angry at. He thought about the boy from the landfill. Those eyes, those gaping wounds. Was Lucky lying like that somewhere? Exposed. Birds, dogs, and all kinds of vermin chomping away at his flesh? Or was the body already decomposed? Skin, fat and muscle turned to jelly on the long trek to dust.

When he had gotten back, he hadn't told Innocent and Boy the details of what he'd seen at the landfill, just that the body had been someone else's. There had been no point. No words to explain the horror. Since then, Boy and Innocent had kept searching, visiting the group's old favourite spots every day, holding onto hope. He hadn't been able to. Hadn't been able to face it. Not after what he'd seen. So, instead of hope, now all he had was a bone-crushing sadness.

Innocent shook his leg. "My cousin said they've found another white man. In the heart of Sandton, stabbed to death."

Thabo didn't stir.

"Oh?" Boy said, moving from the foot of the bed to the middle. Thabo felt his body heat against his back, demanding his attention.

"He says the police still think that the first white guy killed the second white guy." Innocent replied, snickering. "How stupid is that? Like he came back to life or something?"

"Perhaps they don't know he's dead. After all, nobody's told them, have they?" Boy rested his elbows on Thabo's flank, doubling down on making his presence felt, driving his message home.

Cursing to himself, first at Boy and then at his own curiosity for getting the better of him, Thabo turned around and sat up. "Why do they think my white guy killed the second white guy?"

Innocent shrugged. "My cousin didn't say. Just that they used to work together."

That didn't make sense.

"There has to be some other link," Thabo said. "Two white guys from London, coming here to die? Can't just be a coincidence." Feeling the need to pee, he got up and crossed to the toilet bucket.

Boy watched Thabo traverse the room, a triumphant glint in his eyes, then he sat further back on the bed, crossing his legs and leaning his back against the wall, taking up real estate, preventing Thabo's return. "What about your cousin?" he said to Innocent. "What does *he* think happened?"

"Doesn't have a clue," Innocent replied. "Said it was strange, though. Normally, when there's a hit on someone, guys get to hear about it, even if they haven't been asked to bid. But this time – nothing. Either the hitman wasn't local, or whoever did it kept it in-house."

Realising he stank after not having washed for days, Thabo poured some water in the washing bowl, undressed, and began to lather himself all over. Out of the corner of his eye, he thought he saw Boy and Innocent smiling as they exchanged a look but when he turned, they were both staring at the bedspread.

"What if it was the same guys who killed my guy?" he asked as he washed. "With my white guy, your cousin only found out who might have been involved later, didn't he? Long after I'd discovered the body."

"That's true." Innocent sat forward, elbows resting on his knees.

"So, maybe it's like that this time too," Thabo began rinsing the soap off his body.

"What difference does it make?" Boy said. "Even if the people Cleaver told us about killed both of them, it still doesn't help us find Lucky."

Thabo opened his mouth and closed it again, unable to think of a counterargument. They all fell silent, Thabo finishing his ministrations as Innocent and Boy picked sullenly at the bedspread. Dry and dressed, Thabo opened the door to chuck out the used water. As he stepped into the street, Mrs Khoza poked her head out of her door.

"Oh, there you are Thabo," she said, drying a plate with a dishcloth, "I was beginning to get worried about you."

Not knowing what to say, he just smiled shyly.

"Did you hear? About that boy you found. Musa said they finally found his family and the parents came to claim him last week. I'm so glad, aren't you?"

"Yes, that's good news, Ma," Thabo turned back towards his shack.

"Would have been such a shame if they hadn't," she muttered to herself as she went back inside. "If he'd passed with no one to shepherd his way, leaving him as a wandering spirit, desolate and alone."

Hand on the door latch, Thabo stopped in his tracks.

Is that what Lucky had become?

A despondent, wandering spirit?

"Ma – wait!" Thabo ran to her door. "How long?"

Surprised, Mrs Khoza looked up from the paraffin stove she had just lit. "How long what?"

"How long before it's too late? When someone's spirit can no longer be saved?"

"Well, the burial rites should be performed as soon as possible after death." She put a pot on the stove, adding oil and chopped onions. "But, if for some reason that can't happen, they can still be performed when the body is found." She picked up a wooden spoon and stirred the pot. "Why do you ask?"

"Whenever that is?" he said urgently. "No matter how long it takes to find it?"

Comprehension dawned and her face softened. "Yes, my child," she said, her eyes full of compassion. "It's never too late. Especially, for good boys like Lucky."

Thanking her, Thabo rushed back home. Innocent and Boy looked up when he came in, watching him with interest as he put away the bowl and went to draw some money from the kitty. He now knew what he had to do.

"What happened to you?" Boy asked. "You seem…different."

"I have to go out," Thabo grabbed a photo from beneath his pillow and went to the row of clothes hanging on the wall.

Perhaps he should take a coat just in case it got cold?

Innocent got to his feet, his eyes suspicious. "Out where?"

"Just out," he tied a bomber jacket around his waist. "I'll see you guys later, ok?"

Innocent blocked the door. "Wherever you're going, we're coming with you."

Realising something was up, Boy came and stood by Innocent's side. Two against one.

Thabo looked from one to the other. "Look – I don't have time to explain. It's just something I have to do, that's all. Me and me alone."

"Why?" Innocent crossed his arms, the breadth of his chest as wide and strong as an ox. "Why do you need to go alone?"

"Because I…"

What? It's your fault? That's not the real reason though, is it? It's because you can't bear to risk losing anyone else.

"Just because, ok?"

Boy watched the exchange. Perhaps it was something Thabo said or maybe it was his body language, but all of a sudden Boy's eyes changed like a light bulb had gone off in his head. "This is it, isn't it?" he said gently. "Your last card?"

Thabo nodded solemnly.

Innocent scowled, "What the hell are you two talking about?"

"He's going to tell them," Boy said, his voice resigned. "Tell them what he knows in the hope that if they find his white guy's killers, that will also lead us to Lucky."

"Why do you guys always have to speak in riddles? Tell who?"

Boy didn't respond. Thabo looked away.

"Oh my God!" Innocent exclaimed when it finally clicked. "You're actually thinking of going to the police?!" He grabbed Thabo's arms and shook him as if trying to knock some sense into him. "Are you crazy! You know it isn't safe!"

Thabo broke free from Innocent's grip, frustration charging his voice. "You got any better ideas? We've tried everything else!"

"But you can't. You -" Innocent's voice cracked, and he put a hand over his face, trying to get a grip of his emotions. Boy looked down, discretely wiping away a tear. Thabo suddenly realised he wasn't the only one who didn't want to lose anyone else.

"I know this is hard," he said, putting a comforting hand on each of their shoulders and giving them a brief squeeze. "But this is the last chance we've got."

Boy took a shaky breath. "Cent's still got a point, though. Nothing's changed. Your white man's killers are still on the hunt and going to the police is still dangerous."

"Yes, but maybe there's a way to decrease the risk."

Innocent dropped the hand that covered his eyes, his game face back on. "How?"

"When I went to the landfill," Thabo replied, "Musa told me about a guy in town. A Constable. Said he always treats the waste pickers with respect. Never harasses anyone, never asks for a bribe. I've been thinking about that for a long time. Maybe, he might be able to help."

"Sounds like straight-up guy," Innocent said. "But are you sure you can trust him?"

Thabo sighed, "I trust Musa and that's just going to have to be enough. Now, please, please let me pass."

Innocent looked at Boy. Boy nodded at Innocent, then they begrudgingly stepped aside.

"I should be back by late evening," Thabo said as he opened the door. "Earlier if the guy's not around." He hesitated, wanting to say something else but the words got stuck in his throat.

Innocent playfully slapped him on the shoulder, trying to lighten the mood. "We'll…um…see you then, boss."

Thabo almost smiled. Innocent calling him boss was one for the history books.

"Later then," Boy echoed, grabbing Innocent's hand like an anchor.

Not trusting his voice, Thabo just nodded, stepping into the street, and turning towards the taxi rank. He knew it was stupid. Nothing bad was going to happen. Not if everything went well. And even if it didn't, nothing bad would happen right away. Yet, glancing back and waving, he couldn't help wondering if that was how he'd always remember them. Standing in the doorway, holding hands, faces sad but brave as if they were saying goodbye for the last time.

Sitting in the back of the taxi, Thabo thought of his mother. How, when the nuns at the orphanage had told him that she'd died, they'd said that God had taken her into his grace. He'd never understood the white man's God or the concept of his grace. Never seen any evidence of it in his life or anyone else's for that matter. However, what he did know was that everyone's ancestors walked with them, guiding, and supporting them through the trials and tribulations of life. So now, jiggling in his seat as the taxi stumbled across the pot-holed road, he clutched his mother's photo as tightly as he could and called upon her to watch over him at this time of need.

Greetings, Mama…

It took two taxis to get to the place he was looking for. A single-storey, face-brick building on the smart side of the city, lying next to a school, and standing opposite a petrol garage. Thabo took up his post behind a bush in the garage lot, watching people come and go from the police station across the street, waiting for the man he was looking for to appear. While Musa had given him a rough description, it could have applied to any number of people. However, he'd also said there was one particular thing that set the man apart. Something he would know when he heard it.

About an hour after he had arrived, a police van, with two policemen in front and unlucky soul in the back, turned into the street and parked in one of the parking bays outside the station. One of the policemen got out of the passenger side, fetched a handcuffed man from the back of the van so drunk he couldn't walk straight, and started to herd him inside. Meanwhile, the driver of the van sat writing in a notebook, before getting out and locking the car. When the arrested man almost tripped as they entered the station, the first policeman cracked a joke as he pushed the man inside. A joke Thabo couldn't hear but which had the second policeman in stitches as he followed in the first policeman's wake.

That laugh.

Just like Musa had described it.

Thabo's heart leapt, partly with fear and partly with hope. It was him. For now, alone. He would have to act fast before the man disappeared inside the station. Without looking left or right, Thabo sprinted across the road, shouting, "Constable Khumalo!"

The policeman stopped and turned, his eyes curious. "Yes, that's me."

"I'm Thabo. Musa sent me," Thabo said as he reached him. "Is there somewhere quiet we can go and talk? I have something important to tell you about a high-profile missing person. Highly confidential information."

The Constable studied him as if making up his mind whether or not to take him seriously. Trying his best to look like an honest man, though he wasn't quite sure what an honest man looked like, Thabo chewed his bottom lip, shooting nervous glances at the police station entrance. After a few moments, the Constable gave a satisfied nod, like he had weighed Thabo on Anubis scales and found him worthy, then turned and walked back to the van.

"Get in," he said, unlocking the doors. "There's a place just down the road."

Thabo jumped into the front, scooting down low so no one would see him.

"Musa sent you, you say?" Constable Khumalo said as he started the engine.

"Yes. He said I could trust you."

"Well, that's good to know!" Constable Khumalo briefly chuckled before growing serious again. "But what's got you so spooked that you don't want to talk at the station?"

"It's about that white guy that went missing six months ago. The one with the reward? Heard that the police weren't the only ones looking for him."

The Constable's eyes suddenly grew alert. "And you have information, you say?"

"Yes. But I also need help. It's my friend. He's missing. And I think the guys who killed that white guy might have gotten him too."

The Constable's face turned grave. "Don't worry," he said earnestly. "You've come to the right guy. And please, call me Vusi."

57. The Torch

Murdoch Found Dead

Mr Derrick Murdoch, the disgraced former Africa CEO at Yeats Bank, has been found dead in an informal settlement in Johannesburg. According to a source close to the South African police investigation who spoke on condition of anonymity, Mr Murdoch was stabbed, and his body mutilated prior to his death. A method often used by criminal syndicates.

Six months ago, Mr Murdoch, who was then considered by many as an anti-corruption champion, disappeared whilst on a business trip to South Africa. Through our investigation, we subsequently learnt that Mr Murdoch's squeaky-clean reputation had been an elaborate smokescreen to enable him to launder money from illicit sources in exchange for huge kickbacks. This trail of illicit money flows has now become known as the Cayman Papers. One of the parties Murdoch laundered monies for, through his various companies, was a businessman called Mr Jonas Maharaj. Mr Maharaj has also been caught up in several, high-profile corruption scandals in South Africa and is being investigated by international authorities for his alleged involvement in human trafficking.

As this paper has previously reported, there was reason to believe that there was a possible connection between Murdoch's money laundering activities and his suspicious disappearance. Our investigation can now confirm that this was indeed the case. Yesterday, the South African Police Services conducted a dawn raid on premises in Johannesburg and Durban, South Africa. These raids followed the discovery of four critical pieces of evidence. The first piece of evidence related to the type of murder weapon used to stab Mr Murdoch, a rare hunting knife. The second piece of evidence comprised witness testimony that Mr Jabu Mabasa, the Head of Security of Mr Jonas Maharaj, owned a similar weapon.

This witness testimony led to the search of Mr Mabasa's home. There, police found the knife and the third piece of evidence, the remnants of Mr Murdoch's blood lodged between the blade and the hilt.

The fourth critical piece of evidence discovered by the South African police was a USB stick found lodged in Mr Murdoch's stomach. The stick contained a recorded conversation that indicated that Mr Maharaj had a strong motive to silence the disgraced former CEO. A source close to Mr Murdoch who spoke to The Torch on condition of anonymity further indicated that Mr Murdoch and Mr Maharaj had quarrelled just before Mr Murdoch disappeared. However, it appears that Mr Maharaj was not the only one who had a motive. According to our sources, the information on the USB suggests that Mr Spencer Dovecroft, then Group CEO of Yeats Bank, not only had full knowledge of Mr Murdoch's activities, as well as those of Mr Maharaj, but may also have been a central participant. This, in turn, raises questions about the recent SFO report absolving Yeats as a whole from wrongdoing.

Today, in a brief statement, the bank announced that Mr Dovecroft had resigned with immediate effect, with Mr Tom Huddleston taking over as the new Group CEO. Mr Dovecroft had been due to retire at the end of the financial year. The bank gave no indication as to whether the revised timing of his exit had had anything to do with the new allegations against him, simply emphasising that the bank had had no knowledge of Mr Dovecroft's alleged activities. Both Mr Dovecroft and Mr Maharaj had not responded to our requests for comment at the time of going to print.

Yeats Fallout Continues

The impacts of the Cayman Papers and Mr Murdoch's murder continue to be felt. Based on documents found at Mr Maharaj's premises following a South African police raid, criminal charges for fraud and money laundering have been laid against Mr Maharaj, a Yeats Bank client, the former Yeats Bank Group CEO, Mr Spencer Dovecroft and the former Chief Risk Officer of the Africa division, Mr Reuben Stott. Whilst criminally liable, Mr Derrick Murdoch and Mr Jonathan Murphy were not charged given their recent untimely demise.

Following his arrest, Mr Dovecroft put out a statement dismissing the charges as being "based on erroneous conclusions derived from nebulous sources" and vowed to fight the case to the bitter end. Similarly, Mr Maharaj, through his lawyers, also denied all charges. At the time of going to press, Mr Stott could not be reached for comment.

The SFO has stated that, in the light of recent events, they would be revisiting the recent findings they had made regarding the Africa division as well as conducting a deeper probe into Yeats bank as a whole, now in conjunction with the National Crime Agency. When asked why these matters had not been picked up in the first investigation, SFO spokesperson, Ms Mary Cummins, insisted that no such evidence had existed at the time. The SFO/NCA investigation is expected to take several months.

Yeats bank has welcomed the combined SFO and NCA probe and its new CEO, Mr Huddleston, has committed that he, along with the new CEO of the Africa division, Mr John Hilary, would co-operate fully with the two agencies to ensure that all those involved were speedily brought to book. However, when asked to comment on the bank's criminal liability as a whole, Mr Huddleston referred all such queries to the Financial Conduct Authority (FCA).

The FCA has yet to comment on what actions it will take should the allegations against Mr Dovecroft prove to be true. Historically, banks have relied on the 'identification doctrine' to avoid criminal liability. This doctrine stipulates that prosecutors must prove that someone directing or in control of an organisation was directly involved in wrongdoing before the organisation itself can be held liable. Hence, in the past, banks (and other entities often involved in the money laundering value chain such as legal and accounting firms), have been able to easily distance themselves from the actions of individual actors. However, given Dovecroft's former role as Group CEO, it is difficult to imagine how it could be argued that the identification doctrine does not apply in this instance.

Lastly, following a plea deal by Mr Jabu Mabasa, further charges have been laid against Mr Jonas Maharaj for conspiracy to murder. So far, however, the police have not been able to make an arrest due to the fact that Mr Maharaj's whereabouts are currently unknown, with some speculating that he might have fled the country. When questioned, the South African Minister of Police, Mr Clement Ngema, assured the public that Mr Maharaj's disappearance was a temporary set-back, insisting that the SAPS would not rest until he was brought to justice. The SAPS have not yet confirmed whether a similar charge will be brought against Mr Dovecroft.

58. Lord Hain

Westminster
London, UK

SANCTIONS AND ANTI-MONEY LAUNDERING BILL
HOUSE OF LORDS DEBATE
Lord Peter Hain

"My Lords, it is a pleasure to follow such an expert and impressive speech from the noble Baroness, Lady Bowles, in moving Amendment 69B. The amendment is supported by my noble friend Lord Collins, and I have put my name to it. It introduces a failure to prevent an offence.

In June 2011, the then Financial Services Authority found shocking inadequacies in UK banks' anti-money laundering controls, with one-third of banks accepting, "very high levels of money-laundering risk", and three-quarters of banks failing to take adequate measures to establish the legitimacy of the wealth they were handling. The then acting head of financial crime at the FSA, Tracey McDermott, said publicly: "The banks are just not taking the rules seriously enough".

Yet, after all these strong words, what happened? Instead of the FSA—now the FCA—getting tough with the banks, since 2010 there have been only 10 convictions under the money laundering regulations, not one of them of a bank. It is therefore hardly surprising that there have been repeated money laundering scandals involving UK banks. There is *simply no adequate deterrent or serious regulatory risk to make UK banks turn away profitable business that they are offered, and there will not be until the FCA starts prosecuting people and banks for failing to apply the regulations.*

….The British Government must not permit any UK-based financial institution to be complicit in the plundering of state-owned companies in foreign lands, especially when that plunder affects the poorest of the poor. South Africa suffered enough repression over the apartheid years, and we cannot stand idly by while economic repression replaces racial oppression, serving the greed of corrupt leaders, when we have the ability to help stop it…."

59. Loose Threads

Tooting Bec
London, UK

Her eyes fluttered open to dusk, the fading sun seeping through the drawn bedroom curtains, illuminating the gloom. The flat was silent apart from the steady hum of rain beating against the windows, enveloping her in a soothing lullaby. Yawning, Charlie took a moment to take in her surroundings, glad to be home again after spending three weeks in a hospital ward. Now that her burns had healed and she could breathe more easily, they had finally relented and discharged her. And not a minute too soon. She had never been a good patient. Never been able to stand the helplessness of it all.

Reaching over to the nightstand, she checked the time on her phone. 4 pm. She'd been out for twenty hours straight. *And* with no nightmares. Could that be because of the juju they had given her, or had she finally learnt to face her fears? Whichever it was, now she could sleep peacefully through the night and, when each new day dawned, meet it with gratitude rather than sorrow.

The doctor had said she'd been lucky. If she'd still been stuck in the boot or the blast hadn't thrown her away from the car, she'd most certainly be dead. However, as far as Charlie was concerned, luck had nothing to do with it. The determination her parents had sown within her had played a part and so too had friends who never gave up. Friends who secretly embedded a tracker in your phone, even though you never asked them to, because they knew you were too stubborn to look out for yourself. Friends who had never stopped looking, arriving just in time to get you medical attention before your lungs collapsed. For so long, she'd felt alone, stranded by the death of her family, neither fully seeing nor appreciating the people she had in her life. Now she'd never make that mistake again.

Noticing she had four WhatsApp messages, Charlie tapped the app icon on her phone. The first one was from the Met telling her they still hadn't got a hit off the description of the taxi driver she'd given them. She couldn't blame them really since all she'd seen was his eyes. Perhaps the recent discovery Quicha had made would help? As she had been cleaning the flat in preparation for Charlie's return, her friend had accidentally knocked over a flowerpot, discovering a bug amongst its broken remains. Quicha was now convinced that her earlier mugging and the recent attempt on her life were linked, and Charlie was inclined to agree with her. Maybe the police would be able to find prints on the listening device that would lead to the people behind these attacks? Charlie made a mental note to call the Met in the morning with the news.

The second message was a voice note from The Ferret saying she'd like to discuss a full-time job offer once she was back on her feet. Charlie pursed her lips as she listened, not quite sure what to make of it. On one hand, while she'd been in hospital, Kathy had personally ensured that the truth about Murdoch, Maharaj and Dovecroft had gotten into print using the info Vusi had provided. And she had done this despite facing considerable resistance from up the ladder. She had even included Charlie in the by-line, which had been unusually kind - at least for Kathy. Permanent employment would also provide her with a steady income which was a definite plus. Yet, was all that enough to offset the nightmare of having The Ferret as her full-time boss? Charlie shuddered at the thought. Concluding it was probably better to delay the decision until she'd fully recovered, she opted for a positive reply without being over-comital, texting: "Sure. Let's talk".

The last two messages were from Vusi and Viper respectively, her cousin giving her another update on the Murdoch murder case, while Viper rather enigmatically just asked her to check her email. After listening to Vusi's missive, making mental notes as she went, Charlie was just about to open the email app on her phone when she heard keys rattling at her front door.

"Honey, I'm home!" Jake yelled as his footsteps sidled down the passage and into the kitchen. Another set traipsed after him, Quicha's rhythmic swagger unmistakable. Soon smooth jazz drifted down the hallway, accompanied by tinkling laughter and the whoosh-gurgle of the coffee machine, the rich aroma moving her to action. Charlie slowly got out of bed, put on her bathrobe and slippers, and shuffled to the kitchen.

"Hey girl," Quicha said warmly as she entered, pulling out a chair for her at the kitchen table. "How ya feeling?"

"Still exhausted but a lot better than yesterday." Charlie sank into the chair, the brief exertion having taken its toll. "Sleeping really helps."

Quicha affectionately squeezed her arm and sat down next to her, laying the dailies on the table as she said, "Looks like your boys are all getting busted."

Charlie glanced at the headlines plastered in bold on the papers in front of her. "Looks that way."

"Glad Dovecroft's going down." Her friend's eyes grew stormy. "That asshole needs to pay for what he did to you."

"You sure it was Spencer?" Jake said, placing two steaming cappuccinos and an expresso on the table as he joined them.

Quicha's look was scathing. "You know any other sly, scheming, banking motherfuckers?"

Jake scoffed. "We *are* talking about Yeats here, right?"

"All right you two," Charlie interjected, cradling her coffee in her hands. "Whether it was Spencer or someone else, they'll get what they deserve one way or another. Right now, I have other things to worry about."

Quicha scooped up the foam of her cappuccino with a teaspoon. "Thinking 'bout that loose thread, huh?"

"What loose thread?" Jake asked, looking from one to the other.

Charlie blew on her coffee, cooling it down. "The latest SAPS forensic report has ruled out any connection between Murdoch's murder and Jonathan's. Different murder weapons and different MOs. Murdoch was stabbed, and his chest cut up. Jonathan was shot. Two bullets in the back of the head, execution style."

'I knew it!" Quicha exclaimed excitedly. "I knew something was off."

"Is that so?" Jake said sarcastically. "How? Through your crystal ball?"

"Tell him, Charlie. Tell him my nose never lies!"

"Well, I'm not sure about never," Charlie said cautiously, "but you were right about money being linked to Murdoch's disappearance."

"See!" Quicha said triumphantly. "What did I tell you?"

Jake just smiled and took a sip of coffee.

"But if Maharaj and Dovecroft killed Murdoch," Quicha said, looking at her, "who killed the other guy?"

"Does it matter?" Jake replied. "Murdoch's been found, and his killers charged. At least, some of them. Surely, we can leave the rest to someone else?"

Quicha chuckled, "Man – you got a lot to learn about Charlie!" Then she grew serious. "But, even though I hate to say it, Jake's right. Doc said you need to get plenty of rest. No matter how you feel about it, you gotta sit this one out."

"I guess you're right," she said with a heavy sigh. "It's just bothering me, that's all."

For a moment, they sat in comfortable silence, each caught up in their own thoughts.

"You hungry?" Jake asked, having finished his expresso. "You didn't have much in, so we got some stuff for supper. Fancy some chicken coconut curry?"

Charlie nodded, "You must have read my mind."

He stood up and went to the fridge to start making supper.

When did Jake become so good at finding his way around her kitchen?

She was still trying to work out how she felt about this when Quicha got to her feet, hastily gulping down the last of her cappuccino.

"I'd give you a hand," she said to Jake, "but Mama comes first. Got a… um…thang I need to get to."

Had Jake and Quicha just exchanged a conspiratorial wink?

"What thing?" Charlie asked.

"Just a thang," Quicha said, with the worst poker face ever. "Later, awright?"

With a kiss on the cheek for her and a quick wave for him, Quicha vanished down the hall, leaving them alone in the kitchen. Jake didn't look up from his duties, apparently totally absorbed in cleaning the chicken. Charlie opened her mouth to ask him what was going on, then shut it again.

If something were to happen between them, would it really be so bad?

She coughed to get his attention. He put the now clean chicken on a chopping block and looked at her expectantly.

"Thank you," Charlie said demurely, "for…you know, making supper. And…um…everything."

That look again in his eyes. Subtle, tentative but there all the same. The one that made her feel warm inside.

"My pleasure, Charlie," he said with a loving smile before turning back to his task, humming as he went.

No. It probably wouldn't be bad at all.

As Jake got on with the meal, Charlie pretended to flip through the papers but, in reality, her thoughts turned inward. Who killed Jonathan wasn't the only loose end she was worried about. According to Vusi, the USB they had found in Murdoch's stomach had also included the number and password for Murdoch's burner phone. Like many people, Murdoch must have had a problem remembering all his passwords. After getting a warrant for the phone records, they'd found that Murdoch had used it to call three people in the last few days of his life.

The first number was Portia's. Confirmation of her claim that Murdoch had called her just before he disappeared. No surprises there.

The second number, however, she would never have guessed. It belonged to Jabu Mabasa, Jonas' muscle man. Why had Murdoch called a man he was hiding from? Even though Mabasa had confessed to kidnapping Murdoch and entered into a deal with the police (prompted not only by the blood on his knife but also new video evidence - courtesy of Viper - of him entering the hotel garage on the day Murdoch was taken), he had initially been very sketchy about the exact circumstances of Murdoch's demise. All he had said was that Murdoch had tried to escape en route and, in the struggle that followed, he had accidentally stabbed him. Mabasa had then claimed that, since the plan had gone awry, he had panicked and fled, leaving Murdoch alive in his haste. A version of events that the police, as well as Charlie, found very difficult to believe. Moreover, it still failed to explain why Murdoch had made the call.

Mabasa had also been unable to account for the significant amount of cash the police had discovered at his home when they had searched it. Whilst working with cash was not unusual in Mabasa's line of business, the huge amount involved in this instance had led the SAPS to examine Mabasa's bank accounts. This search had revealed that the transfer that had been made from Murdoch's Cayman account to a DM Trust on the day after he vanished had not been to his own trust but to Mabasa's. DM stood for David Mabasa.

Thinking about this, Charlie felt like kicking herself. She should have paid more attention to Mabasa's middle name - David. The evidence had been right there, and they had missed it!

Upon being confronted with what the SAPS had found, Mabasa finally admitted that, even though he had kidnapped Murdoch on Jonas' orders, his captor had convinced him to let him go in exchange for a million pounds. Over twenty million rands in local currency. Thus, instead of taking Murdoch to the kill site, Mabasa had hidden him until Murdoch had called him to confirm the transfer had gone through, whereafter they had staged the stabbing to make it look like Murdoch had escaped. When pressed about the marks on Murdoch's chest, Mabasa continued to insist that he didn't know where they came from. Then the police had discovered that there were other things Mabasa had been lying about. For instance, Murdoch's burner phone records had also revealed that Mabasa had called it numerous times in the months after Murdoch vanished. Again, Mabasa's version of events regarding this – that the calls had been due to a mistaken pocket dial - had been unconvincing.

Which brought her to Thabo. When Vusi had first told her about him, she hadn't been able to believe it. First, she had wanted to strangle the boy. After all, if Thabo had come forward sooner, it would have made her work so much easier. Then, she had realised she needed to thank him because, if he hadn't come forward at all, they might never have found Murdoch's body nor obtained the proof she needed to back her story and bring the perpetrators to book. Yet, sadly, Thabo's role in the story didn't end there. Not only had Thabo disputed Mabasa's claim that his subsequent calls to Murdoch's phone had been made by mistake, he claimed that Mabasa had been calling in an attempt to cover his tracks, which had also led Mabasa to kill his friend, Lucky. While, so far, the police had made no headway in finding Lucky or in linking Mabasa directly to his disappearance, this didn't necessarily mean that Thabo was wrong. Mabasa could have taken Murdoch's bribe, killed him anyway and then sought to recover the phone so there would be no trace of their interaction. When probed about this version of events, Mabasa had changed his story again, now admitting that he had called Murdoch's phone but only in the hope of getting more money out of him. According to him, he wouldn't have done that if he'd known Murdoch was already dead.

Charlie shook her head as she absently turned a page. Mabasa was proving to be more slippery than a wet snake!

Even though Charlie was inclined to back the police's decision to dismiss this latest twist in Mabasa's story, the muscle man did have one factor in his favour. The latest forensic report had indicated that a different knife had been used to carve the message on Murdoch's chest from the one used to stab him. True - Mabasa could have swapped knives but, to Charlie, that just didn't seem plausible. Why create more evidence that could be used against you? Thus, in her view, this new, inconvenient piece of evidence suggested something almost unimaginable. A second perpetrator.

This brought her to the third number on Murdoch's burner. It belonged to one of the drivers in the Yeats Joburg office. A Mr Victor Mkhize. When interviewed by the police at the beginning of the investigation, the driver had said he'd been on leave during the period Murdoch had vanished - a fact that had been confirmed by the Yeats HR department - and thus knew nothing of the incident. When the call was later discovered and he was asked why he hadn't mentioned it when he'd been first interviewed, he said he'd forgotten about it. When probed as to why Murdoch had called him, he'd said he didn't know because Murdoch hadn't left a message. When it was pointed out that, according to the call logs, Murdoch's call to him had lasted almost one minute, the driver had still insisted that they never spoke, claiming that Murdoch's voicemail message had just been white noise.

Whilst there was no reason to believe the driver wasn't telling the truth, Charlie couldn't help but wonder about the timing of the call. Calling an office driver when you arrive at the airport is one thing, but this call had occurred days *after* Murdoch had been taken. On the same day the money transfer had gotten through to Mabasa's account and moments after Mabasa claimed to have left Murdoch alive. Had Murdoch, stabbed and bleeding, tried to call the driver for help, only to die from his wounds when he failed to make contact? Why, in such a circumstance, would Murdoch have called him instead of the police or an ambulance? And if Murdoch hadn't been able to reach Mkhize, what then? Who had inflicted the final blow and carved up his chest?

"How do you like your curry – hot or mild?"

"What?" Charlie looked up, momentarily confused. "Sorry. I was lost in thought."

Jake held up four chillies in one hand and two in the other, "The curry. Hot or mild?"

"Hot please," she said before getting to her feet, feeling a sudden sense of urgency. "I'll be back in a moment. I just need to check something."

Without waiting for a response, Charlie dragged herself to the study. Viper's mail was brief, the attachment self-explanatory. The results of the facial recognition search she had asked her to do to see if there was any link between Joburg office staff, Maharaj and his associates, and the Yeats Africa Exco. After going through the findings, Charlie sat back in her chair, stunned.

How could she have been so right, and yet so wrong?

60. Andy

Kensington
London, UK

The street they lived on was surprisingly quiet, the rumble of the early evening rush hour muted by a creeping fog that had gradually gathered Kensington in its embrace, dulling the glow of the streetlamps to a golden amber which bathed the area in a deceptively warm glow. The road was banked by rows of Georgian alabaster terraced houses, fronted by neat black railings, broken only by stone staircases leading to Roman-pillared porticos covering shiny black doors with brass knockers. It was a street that spoke of status, wealth, and restrained respectability. A haven where scandals were deftly swept out of view with tongues tied and eyes averted, leaving only the merest blush to suggest that there'd been anything there in the first place. A place where people like her were never welcome.

The reason for her visit was simple. Viper's facial recognition programme had stumbled upon a South African newspaper article on the misappropriation of government school infrastructure funds and the negative impact it had had on service delivery. Many children had died as a consequence due to old and dilapidated infrastructure that should have been upgraded but wasn't, amongst them a young boy. A boy who had had an uncanny resemblance to a member of the Yeats Africa Exco.

Fortunate to find a rare parking space on the opposite side of the road, Charlie had waited until she was sure they were both at home, not wanting to give either of them prior warning. As she had waited, she had rehearsed various scenarios in her head, wondering what she would do if things got out of hand. Though she had spent the past two weeks getting her strength up, she still quickly tired and would be easily bested in any physical confrontation. As a result, Jake had gallantly offered to come with her, and she had briefly considered taking him up on the offer. However, she had finally decided to come alone. Not so much because she feared she might be wrong, but more because she feared she might be right.

Locking her car behind her, Charlie slowly crossed the street, walked up the steps and knocked on their front door. Leaning against the stair railings as she waited, she heard a door open inside the house, a woman yelling, "I'll get it, darling", followed by footsteps rushing down the hall before a blond, elegant lady in her early forties, opened the door.

"Oh!" the woman frowned and took half a step back, her face part annoyance, part curiosity like she'd been expecting somebody else. "Can I help you?"

Charlie flashed her ID card, saying in what she hoped was an authoritative but non-threatening manner, "Hi, I'm Charlie Tate from the Torch. I'd like to ask you some questions if I may. About the Murdoch case?"

While the woman responded with a polite smile, her eyes hardened, and her shoulders tensed ever so slightly. A woman steeling herself against an unwanted intrusion.

"Who is it, dear?" a man asked from deep within the recesses of the house.

As indecision marched across the woman's face, Charlie straightened her spine and held her stare, signalling her determination. Whether it was this or something else that tipped the scales, she wasn't sure, but thankfully the woman eventually nodded, rearranging her face into bored amusement as she stepped aside. "You better come in."

She led her to a modern, fashionable front parlour that smelt of jasmine, the lighting soft, the furnishings plush, the fire roaring. Sitting in an armchair close to the fire, Hilary jumped to his feet in alarm as she walked into the room.

"What is *she* doing here?"

His wife waved him down as she closed the door and motioned for Charlie to sit. "Don't fret, dear," Grace said soothingly. "She's just going to ask us some questions and then she'll be on her way." Then, after a slight pause, she added in a commanding tone. "Won't you, Ms Tate?"

"Yes, that's right," Charlie replied, though in truth she couldn't guarantee that. Couldn't guarantee anything at all. However, since the odd little lie was an essential tool of her trade, she flashed them both a reassuring smile and sank into an armchair opposite the one Hilary had just vacated. "And please," she added, "call me Charlie."

Still standing, Hilary glared at her, his frustration evident in the set of his jaw, then responded to his wife. "You think that will stop her? You don't know what she's capable of. This…this…*witch* nearly ruined my life." Crossing the room, he threw open the parlour door. "Now get out before I throw you out!"

Unimpressed by the theatrics, his wife languidly folded herself into a sofa facing the fireplace. "What would you have me do, darling? Send her away and see our name in the headlines? Honestly dear, I would have thought you would have tired of media attention by now."

"Well, actually, I'd like to speak to both of you," Charlie interjected, looking from one to the other. "That is, if you don't mind?"

"What?" Flummoxed, Hilary looked at his wife. "Why would she want to talk to you?"

Charlie saw something flicker in Grace's eyes, her mask splintering for a split second before falling back into place. She checked to see if Hilary had seen it too, but his face remained unchanged.

"I don't know, dear," Grace said with a nonchalant shrug. "But perhaps we can just get this over with?"

Still put out but deciding not to argue any further, Hilary reluctantly moved away from the door and sat down on the sofa next to his wife. Gently taking her hand in his, he defiantly lifted his chin and designed to cast a cold gaze in her direction.

"Well?" he said gruffly, "What is it you want to know?"

Charlie didn't immediately respond, absorbing the tableau. The perfect couple united against their interrogator. A pair so close and yet so far.

Where shall we start?
At the beginning or the end?
Or how about both?

"Tell me about Andy," she said gently.

Hilary's shoulders stiffened but he kept his gaze steady. "You're going to have to be a bit more specific, Ms Tate."

"Ok," Charlie leaned forward, getting into her stride. "Let me be more 'specific', as you put it. Eight years ago, you went on an extended business trip to South Africa. During that trip, you had an affair with a woman called Nomsa Dube. At the end of the trip, you broke off the affair and came back to the UK."

Grace sat still, eyes hooded, apparently entranced by a spot on the carpet.

"So? That affair was a mistake," Hilary glanced at his wife, then back at her. "One that my wife is fully aware of. Aren't you, darling?"

His wife didn't respond.

"Anyway," he continued, his tone clipped, "it's really none of your business. Or anyone else's, for that matter. Is that why you're here? Just for this drivel? Hoping to whip up a scandal!? You should be ashamed of yourself!"

"Nomsa didn't tell you she was pregnant, did she?" Charlie replied. "At least, not right away."

"No shame then?" Hilary chortled to himself. "Why am I not surprised!"

"So, when did she finally tell you? Was it before or after your son, Andy, died so tragically?"

Releasing his hand, Grace went to stand at the mantelpiece, facing the fire, her back rigid. Left alone on the sofa, Hilary glanced at this discarded hand, then quizzically at his wife's back as if wondering what he'd done to deserve such abandonment. Still, however, he kept his cool.

"I told you, you're talking to the wrong man."

"Must have been heart-wrenching," Charlie said. "Him dying like that. Drowning in a school pit latrine at only five years old. The air squeezed out of his lungs as he suffocated on other people's waste."

Grace closed her eyes and shuddered.

"That's enough!" Hilary spat. "Can't you see you're upsetting my wife?"

"Poor Andy," Charlie said, undeterred. "Such a grisly and unnecessary death. And all because of avarice. Maharaj's greed as well as that of all the politicians and merry men around him."

"Ok, that's it!" He got to his feet, eyes smouldering. "Time for you to leave. And, once and for all, this boy Andy was not my son!"

All of a sudden, Grace swung around and slapped her husband across the face. "Stop it! Just stop it! How dare you disown him? How dare you disavow that beautiful, beautiful boy!"

Hilary stood rooted to the spot, totally dumbfounded.

"Grace, I…"

"Did you think I didn't know?" she asked, her eyes bright with unshed tears. "Did you really think that, after thirty years of marriage, you could keep such a secret from me?"

"I…um…I thought -"

"How did you find out?" Charlie asked.

Taking in a shaky breath to calm herself, Grace turned back to stare at the fire. "Nomsa came to see me. Just turned up one day on my doorstep with Andy in her arms. He was still only a baby at the time but, as soon as I saw him, I knew. She'd been trying to get hold of John, but he'd refused to see her. Wouldn't even speak to her. Under normal circumstances, I would have been angry, enraged even. It's only natural when you're confronted with something like that. But somehow little Andy just melted my heart."

As she spoke, Charlie watched Hilary out of the corner of her eye. He sat on the edge of the sofa, wringing his hands as he took it all in, his eyes darting back and forth like a skittish rat and looking like his world had just come crashing down.

"Nomsa didn't want anything," Grace continued. "Just to know me and something of John's history. She said that, in her culture, it's wrong for a child to grow up without knowing their father's family." Grace picked up a log and threw it amongst the flames. "Soon, after that, we became friends. Then, after some time, Andy became my godson. I've always wanted children, you see. But we couldn't…*I* couldn't…"

"Why didn't you tell me?" Hilary mumbled, shaking his head in bafflement. "My God! If I'd known…"

Charlie's heart skipped a beat as one outstanding piece of the puzzle finally fell into place. After she'd received Viper's email, she'd begun to suspect but she hadn't been sure.

Not until now.

"Is that why you had Jonathan killed?" she asked. "Was he blackmailing you? Trying to get you to help him out of the hole he was in?"

"What…?" Frowning, Grace turned towards her husband.

"Is it?" Charlie pressed.

Refusing to look at either of them, Hilary's face shuttered, his hands so tightly clasped between his knees that his knuckles turned white.

"John, look at me." Grace glanced at Charlie, then back at her husband. "What's she talking about?"

Hilary buried his head in his hands.

Grace went to kneel in front of him, demanding his attention. "John, please…" She shook him to solicit a response but, like a lifeless dummy, his body just moved back and forth in her grip. She shook him harder, the first glimpses of alarm appearing on her face. "John! Talk to me! Is it true?"

His hands fell away to reveal a man in shock, his eyes vacant like he was lost in a distant dream.

"Is it TRUE??!!!" Grace yelled.

He blinked as he came to, but, when his gaze alighted on his wife, he looked at her like she was a stranger. He peeled her hand off his shoulder as if her touch disgusted him, and rudely brushed past her as he walked to the drinks stand in the opposite corner of the room.

"Look at us," he said wryly, pouring himself a large brandy. "Look at what you made me do."

He sounded so calm. Too calm, Charlie thought. Masking the storm within.

"Made you?" Grace stood and turned towards him, her face shell-shocked. "Are you saying…? I can't -"

"I had no fucking choice, all right?!" Hilary screamed then stopped himself, battling to get his emotions under control.

Charlie sat still, wanting to intervene, to press him to say more but knew that, if she did, he might clam up completely.

Grace started pacing, her face agitated, her hands on her head, muttering to herself, "This can't be happening. Not now. Not after everything we planned…"

Her husband glowered at her, the muscles working in his jaw as he tried to bring his rage to heal. "Like I said" he replied through gritted teeth. "I had no choice. At least, that's what I thought at the time." He took a large sip of brandy. "Isn't that what you wanted me to do? To man up?"

His wife stopped pacing. "Man up?"

"You know - if I was a striker and all that."

For a moment, Grace was speechless. "Are you crazy?" she eventually exclaimed. "I meant change your fucking job, not -"

"Don't you get it? I did it for us. For the sake of our marriage!"

She tossed her head dismissively. "Our marriage or yourself?"

Hilary went completely still, his face as hard as stone. Then, putting down his glass, he marched over to his wife and grabbed her arm, forcibly pulling her to him as he bent to sniff the nape of her neck.

"What's that perfume you're wearing, dear?" he asked scathingly. "Chanel, is it? Strange how, in all these years, as I got us this grand house and all our little luxuries, I never once heard you complain?"

"I never cared about all that," she said softly, tearing her arm from his grasp and turning her back on him. "I married *you*, not things. The problem is you just never believed me."

Hilary opened his mouth to speak then closed it again. Fuming, he turned on his heal and went back to the drinks cabinet. Downing the remainder of his brandy in one go, he poured another, even larger this time. Grace picked up a poker and stabbed at the coals, her movements stiff, looking defeated. An uncomfortable silence fell. As the wife worked the fire, the husband sullenly downed one brandy after another, the air so thick one would need a chainsaw to cut through it. From her observation post, Charlie began to wonder if they even remembered she was still there. She was just about to break the silence when Hilary slammed down his glass on top of the cabinet and swivelled towards her.

"Did you get what you came for, then?" he said, sneering as he crossed the room towards her with his fists clenched. "A confession from me. A sneak peek into our 'troubled' marriage?"

Charlie squared her shoulders, refusing to be intimidated, and stayed seated. "Almost."

Placing his hands on the arms of her chair, he blocked her in, his drunken breath fanning her face. "Well, if you print any of it, I'll deny it. Say you made the whole thing up!"

He would too. She knew that. And, without a full confession, she wouldn't be able to prove any of it. Hilary had covered his tracks too well for that. However, Jonathan's murder wasn't the only reason she had come.

"Do you hear me?" Hilary hissed, so enraged by her silence that tiny flecks of spit splattered on her cheeks as he spoke. "Print any of it, and I'll ruin you. Make sure you never work again!"

Charlie didn't move, didn't respond, just shifted her eyes towards the fireplace.

"Wait..." Following her gaze, Hilary stood upright, his eyes narrowing with suspicion. "What do you mean, 'almost'?"

Grace carried on poking the fire.

"Why did Victor call you?" Charlie asked as she got to her feet, pushing past him to stand in the middle of the room.

"Victor?" Hilary said as he let her pass, caught off guard by the change of subject. "Are you talking about the driver in the Joburg office? What's *he* got to do with all this?"

"His call logs show he rang the number of this house on the day we now know Murdoch was murdered. The day after he disappeared."

"He must have accidentally dialled the wrong number," Hilary said, confidently shoving his hands in his pockets as he swayed slightly before her, still fancying himself in a stand-off. "I was at work all day that day."

"I don't think so," Charlie said. "He rang here twice. The first call lasted almost ten minutes, the second less than ten seconds. Interestingly, the first call also came about an hour after Victor received a call from Murdoch. Murdoch called Victor shortly after Maharaj's man, Mabasa, claims to have left him injured but alive."

Grace put down the poker and rested her hands on the mantel.

"After the first call to this address," Charlie continued, "a sum of money was transferred from your joint account to Victor's. Would either one of you like to explain what that money was for?"

"To Victor's? Nonsense! That can't be correct. I never —" His voice trailed off as something else occurred to him. A thought that, by the looks of it, was none too welcome. For her part, Grace remained silent, the only indication that she was even listening being a slight tightening of her grip on the mantel.

Wife and husband. Husband and wife. Charlie now knew that at least one of them would not be surprised by the bombshell she was about to drop. However, she would need to tread carefully. If she pressed too hard, they would both shut down like a vault. Yet if she pressed too little, she might never push them past the tipping point.

Opening her mouth to speak, she searched for the perfect pitch. Not one that intimidated but rather one that conveyed a sort of inevitability. A sense of things marching inexorably to their inescapable conclusion. "Perhaps another interesting fact might jog your memory," she replied. "There was another person Victor called that day. Just before he rang here, in fact."

"Who?" Hilary asked as if he couldn't stop himself, surreptitiously giving his wife a nervous glance.

"Someone you both know very well." As she paused for dramatic effect, Grace scratched her cheek with a ruby nail, then carried on gazing at the fire. "His sister. Nomsa Dube, born Nomsa Mkhize."

Looking like he'd suddenly lost all the strength in his body, Hilary silently plopped onto an armrest. A few feet away, his wife took a deep breath and slowly released it. A woman finally letting go.

Charlie moved forward and rested her hand next to hers. "But you knew all this already didn't you, Grace? Isn't that what you meant when you said, 'after everything we'd planned'?"

She turned her head and smiled. The saddest smile Charlie had ever seen. "You know why my parents called me Grace?" she said as she focused back on the fire, orange flames dancing in her eyes. "They said that when I was born, I was so quiet compared to my brothers and sisters it was like a calming balm. And they brought me up to live up to my name. To be kind and generous. To always see the goodness in people. And, of course, to provide relief, in whatever small way, whenever I can."

Charlie leaned in closer. "Despite what Victor says, I think Murdoch did get through to him that day. He must have begged him for help. Maybe Victor was the only one around he could trust. Perhaps, over the years, he and Victor had become close. Drivers often get to know their charges in ways that few others do. Maybe Murdoch had even played with little Andy on the days he'd visited his uncle at work. Whatever the reason, Murdoch called Victor and Victor agreed. However, when he arrived, Murdoch was already delirious, not realising what he was saying. Or maybe he had a last prick of conscience. Either way, somehow Victor found out what Murdoch had done. The role he had played in his nephew's death."

To their left, Hilary groaned in despair.

"Imagine Victor's shock," Charlie continued. "For years, he and his sister had been seeking justice for Andy, trying to get those responsible to pay for their crimes. But at every step of the way, the politicians and Maharaj had slipped through the net, no matter what Victor and Nomsa did. And then Victor stumbles upon the next best thing. An unknown accomplice, a friend turned traitor, right there lying prostrate before him. Murdoch, the enabler-in-chief."

"Don't you get sick of it?" Grace whispered, as much to the flames as to Charlie. "The mendacity. The greed. The injustice. The dirty, fetid meanness of things. It's like a cancer, infecting everybody's lives. Turning everything inside out, corrupting the weak and destroying the innocent. And you know what the worst thing is? The perpetrators, the ringleaders, always get away with it. Always! Get rewarded even!"

Hilary suddenly stood, pulling his wife away from her and putting a protective arm around her waist. "Don't say anymore, my love," he murmured as he softly kissed her cheek. "This is all just conjecture. She has no proof."

Leaning into his embrace, Grace gently laid her head on her husband's shoulder and closed her eyes, giving herself up to his care. However, Charlie was not going to be stopped. Not now. Not when the tipping point was so close.

"This time, though, they weren't going to get away with it," she said, her eyes focused on Grace's face. "Victor couldn't let that happen. Something had to be done. Someone had to pay. So, he rang his sister, and they agreed to give Murdoch a taste of poetic justice. The problem was they couldn't risk doing it out themselves. That's why they rang you, told you of their plan and asked for money to get a contractor. Given how much you had loved your godson, you readily agreed. So, instead of taking Murdoch to hospital, Victor handed him over to the contractor to give him the send-off he deserved. Then he rang you back to confirm it was done. Meanwhile, the hired gun took Murdoch to a place where no one would think of looking for him. One of the most downtrodden informal settlements in Johannesburg. There he cut out his tongue, broke his arms and legs, branded his flesh, and threw him into a pit latrine, sealing it like a tomb. How Murdoch must have suffered! Spending his final hours alone, helpless and writhing in agony. Subsumed in human waste like the stinking piece of shit he was!!"

Grace opened her eyes and looked at her. A look that spoke of a treasured soul long loved and lost, of a suppurating wound that refused to heal, and a blazing fury so hot it could burn down the world.

"I -"

"Lies. Nothing but lies," Hilary quickly said, cutting off his wife. Leaving her side, he started manhandling Charlie out of the room. "Now, it really is time for you to go!"

"I'm sorry," Grace said, putting a hand to her mouth as if she was about to be sick. "It appears I suddenly feel rather unwell. If you'll excuse me, I'll be back in a moment."

As she rushed out of the room, Charlie tried her best to resist her husband's efforts, wanting to have just get a few more minutes with Grace, to check if what she'd seen in her eyes meant what she'd thought it meant. Then a cold breeze fanned the back of Charlie's neck.

Something was wrong.

From outside in the street, came a shriek of breaks followed by a dull thud. She heard running footsteps then a woman started screaming. Hilary let go of her and ran into the passage. Charlie went after him as fast as she could. As she stepped into the hall, she saw Hilary standing, frozen, in the open front doorway. Then he let out a harrowing cry and fell to his knees.

Coming up to stand behind him, Charlie saw a car stopped in the middle of the street, the driver hunched over next to the front bumper, keys in hand, looking dazed. In front of the car, a small crowd had gathered, and in the centre of the circle, a man knelt on the ground, barking orders. In response, some in the crowd started speaking frantically into their phones, calling for help, whilst others simply looked on in horror.

And at the man's feet, bathed in the amber glow of a streetlamp and the glare of the car headlights, a lone body lay crumpled and still, her dress torn, her face bloody, her golden mane splayed across the asphalt.

Grace.

61. A Kind of Justice

Islington
London, UK

King's Cross station was packed as usual, the concourse reverberating with passenger announcements as harried commuters checked train schedules, ate, shopped, and traipsed to and from platforms, chasing their destinations. Charlie walked among them, glad to feel herself again. It had been one week since that fateful night in Kensington, two days since Hilary had handed himself in, and she still had a few things to tie up. She had also decided to give The Ferret the bad news about turning down her offer face-to-face, which was why she now darted through the throng, on her way to the office.

Taking out her phone, she tapped a familiar number and waited for the person to pick up. "Hey V, how're doing?" Charlie said when Viper answered. "Just wanted to make sure my thank-you gift arrived in one piece."

Her friend chuckled. "Yes, it did. Though you know you didn't have to do that, right?"

"It's the least I could do after all you've done. And I know how much you love chocolate!"

As Charlie stepped off the escalator, she spotted Connie walking towards her, looking a little worse for wear. According to Jake, The Sentinel had moved Connie from the finance beat to obituaries, a humiliating demotion and without doubt a nail in the coffin for her career. In the mood for a slice of schadenfreude, Charlie lifted her hand, trying to get Connie's attention.

"I do, but now I've got stock for twelve weeks!" Viper said in mock disapproval. "Ok - make that ten. I already ate two bars yesterday. I just couldn't help myself!"

Spotting Charlie, Connie came to an immediate stop, her face panic-stricken. Then she changed direction and bolted into the nearest store, which just happened to be a hospice charity shop. Charlie burst into laughter.

"Ok," Viper said, sounding a bit put out. "I know it's funny but not that funny."

"Sorry,' Charlie replied. "I wasn't laughing at you. Someone just ate an overdue piece of humble pie."

"Anyone I know?"

"No – just a hack from a rival paper who tried to drag me on the Murdoch story."

"Murdoch? I thought that was all wrapped up?"

"Nearly. Finishing one last piece then I can put the whole thing to bed. Now that Hilary has formally confessed to arranging Jonathan's murder, including nicking hair from an old brush and planting it on the body to make it look like Murdoch did it, we can go to print."

"Didn't you have his confession on tape anyway?"

Viper knew her so well. She never did an interview without backup and her engagement with the Hilarys had been no different.

"Yeah," Charlie replied, "but he could have walked back his words with some cock and bull story. Now the police have an irrefutable confession and something that will also be admissible in court. My sources say Hilary told them that Jonathan contacted him a few weeks after he went AWOL. Tried to use Hilary's secret son to coerce him into backing some cockamamie story that would get him off the hook. Hilary says he knew if he said yes, that would be it. That the weasel would always have had a hold on him and would milk him for the rest of his life. So, in his view, he did the only thing he could do. He got rid of the problem."

"That's cold!"

"Yep. Hilary also dished the dirt on Spencer, by the way. Said that, when Spencer had originally asked him to investigate Murdoch, he had thought it was to protect the bank but now he realises Spencer was just trying to protect himself. He also says that when he realised something was wrong, the former Group CEO deliberately slow-walked the investigation he initiated into Murdoch's dealings. Moreover, he confirmed Portia's claim that Spencer was central to the money laundering scheme in the bank, talking about how, when Murdoch disappeared, he had openly wished him dead and later side-lined a prospective successor, Alex Sharpe, because he'd refused to kiss Maharaj's ring. He added that the Group CEO had also introduced him to Maharaj, making it clear that his promotion depended on him cultivating a good relationship with the man. However, Hilary still insists that he only realised all this in hindsight, and that he had no clue that Dovecroft was behind it all until the allegations against him surfaced."

"Do you believe him? That he really didn't know about Spencer?"

"Hard to tell. But the rest of his story seems to check out. Looks like all the rats are now jumping ship, telling on Spencer to save themselves. Which is great from our point of view."

Getting a story was one thing but, for her, the job wasn't fully done until the perpetrators were also brought to book. At least this time, it looked like she was going to see Dovecroft, Hilary and Stott all in the dock. Maharaj, unfortunately, was still in the wind, with rumours that he might have had help from some South African friends in high places. Yet, with an Interpol warrant out for his arrest, hopefully he would be joining his compatriots soon.

"It's a shame we still don't know who tried to kill you," Viper said. "Now that's a guy I'd like to see behind bars!"

"Well, actually we do," Charlie replied with some satisfaction. "Q thought it was Spencer but, after some tough questioning, Hilary admitted he did it. He arranged my mugging, the bug in my flat and my 'fiery little accident', as he put it. Said he needed to shut me up."

"You've got to be kidding me! He also did all *that*! Wait - wasn't he just a back-office bureaucrat when this all started?"

"He was. That's the irony of it all. Though he worked in a cesspit like Yeats, his hands were, until recently, clean. But, like Icarus, he reached for the sun. Chased his dreams no matter the cost. And that's what brought him down in the end. Part of me feels almost sorry for him."

"I wouldn't," Viper said sourly. "If he'd succeeded, you'd be dead by now."

"True."

Passing her favourite coffee shop, Charlie waved at the Barista who had been so kind to her that day, thankful to get a smile back.

"Why's he suddenly being so talkative, anyhow?" Viper asked.

"His wife's suicide really broke him, apparently. Said he'd always thought certain things in marriage were better left unsaid, but he now realises how wrong he's been. So, he decided to own up to everything. Come clean and do what he should have done when she was still alive."

"Even if he ends up doing time?"

She shrugged. "I guess he reckons that, with the wife gone, he's got nothing left to live for. That's what my source at the Met thinks, anyway."

"Mmmm," Viper said, sounding like she still wasn't entirely convinced.

"All right then," Charlie said, preparing to ring off. "I guess I'll talk to you later."

"Wait! What about Grace? Have you told anyone that she more or less confessed to Murdoch's murder before she died?"

Charlie let out a deep sigh. "No, and I've decided I'm not going to. Nomsa and Victor are also still playing dumb and, even though I think we have enough evidence to make a case, I've decided not to push that either. Remember when you said to me that not everyone deserves a saviour? I didn't agree with you at the time but knowing what I know now, in this case, I think you might be right. Murdoch got what he deserved, and justice was served. Not in a conventional way, but a kind of justice all the same."

"I couldn't agree more."

Viper was quiet for a moment, the mood growing sombre.

"Why do you think she killed herself?" she asked contemplatively.

"I don't know. Perhaps it was the fear of going to jail or the weight of it all became too much for her."

Charlie's mind drifted to the young girl she had found by Regent's Canal, now lying in a pauper's grave, to Thabo's friend Lucky, still unfound, and all the boys and girls who had come before them.

"It's always the children, V. It's always them who get affected the most by the ills of this world. So, perhaps it's fitting that Murdoch, Maharaj, and Spencer were all brought down by the love of a child."

As they said their goodbyes, Charlie emerged from the station and crossed the road towards The Torch's glass entrance. She hadn't been back since the day she'd rushed out its doors on her way to leak a story to Wendy Wise. Somehow the place felt different now. Maybe it was because, this time, she was returning in triumph rather than ignominy. Or, more likely, now that she had decided it would never be home, the place had lost its allure, becoming more part of her past than her future. A future full of bold new adventures to come.

Pushing through the Torch's revolving door, she felt a buzzing in her pocket. Another call, another hemisphere.

"Hey, didn't expect to hear from you, today," Charlie said cheerfully. "Shouldn't you be out celebrating acing your law exam?"

"On my way," Vusi replied. "Just thought I'd check on you before I go. How're you doing?"

That was sweet.

Too sweet.

"I'm fine. Thanks," she said, her guard immediately going up. "You?"

"I'm good."

He paused as if trying to find the right words before saying, "I really helped you out on the Murdoch story, didn't I?"

"Of course. I couldn't have done it without you."

"So, you must be pretty grateful, huh?"

"Some. Why?"

His words came gushing out all at once. "I saw an amazing car. Perfect for getting to and from class. And it's only -"

Charlie barked with laughter.

"Don't even think about it!"

62. The Beach

The Beachfront
Durban, South Africa

The blazing yellow sun beat down on the ragged shore, the waves rolling and breaking against the Durban sand as kids and adults frolicked in the shallows, screaming and giggling as they ran towards the sea and then back to safety.

It had been Boy's idea. To come to the place Lucky had loved most in the world. The perfect place to commemorate him. Mabasa continued to deny he knew anything about Lucky's whereabouts and, even though Constable Khumalo had promised to never stop looking for him, weeks later they still didn't know whether Lucky was alive or dead. So, the ceremony would be simple. Not to mourn a life but to celebrate it. And, hopefully, guide it home. Be it in this world or the next.

Thabo sat further up the beach, legs bent, his elbows resting on his knees, gazing solemnly at the beachgoers and, beyond them in the distance, the almost indiscernible horizon where the turquoise sea met the sapphire sky.

"I found this in the sand," Boy said, running up to him with a glass bottle. "Do you think it will work?"

He glanced at the blue bottle in his friend's hand, guessing it used to hold some sort of alcoholic spirit, long drunk, the bottle the only evidence of joys past. "It's perfect," he said, "provided it's got a lid."

Boy fished a cap out of his pocket and displayed it proudly on his palm. "We fill it with sand and seashells, right?"

"Yeah, that's right. Different coloured seashells if you can. And make sure you find some tigers and horns. Lucky loved those the most."

As Boy ran off to complete his task, Thabo looked to his left. Further along the beach, Innocent, his face the picture of concentration, painstakingly arranged wood and kindling in the centre of a circle of stones, building the fire. Thabo waved to get his attention and signalled to him, asking how far. Innocent waved back and gave him a thumbs-up.

Not long now.

Thabo picked up the bomber jacket lying next to him and clutched it to his chest. Lucky had loved the jacket almost as much as he did. So much so that he still caught whiffs of Lucky's scent in the jacket's lining. Therefore, it had seemed only fitting that this item should be the sacrifice. Something loved for someone loved, to warm him on his travels.

"Ready!" Innocent yelled, standing up straight.

Nodding, Thabo got to his feet and went to help light the fire. As the kindling burst into flames, Innocent added more wood until the fire was waist high.

"All done," Boy said, walking up to them and proudly holding the full bottle aloft.

"Right," Thabo said gravely. "It's time."

Moving as one, they formed a circle around the fire. The ceremony began with the Sacrifice, Thabo throwing the jacket onto the pyre as he recited Lucky's ancestral praise names. For the Blessing, Boy waved the bottle above the flames as he sang a verse from Lucky's favourite song before laying the bottle at the fire's edge. And, for the Pledge, they lifted their shirts, reached into the cooling recesses of the embers, and drew four charcoal lines over their hearts. Four brothers, bonded for life. Then they stood in silence, watching the embers burn until there was nothing left but ash whilst, around them, morning turned to afternoon, and the humid heat morphed into a cool breeze.

"Guess we should be making tracks," Thabo said when it was almost dusk. "Mrs Khoza's brother said he'll leave us behind if we don't get to the depot on time."

Picking up the bottle, he turned towards the beach road, relishing how the memento still felt warm in his embrace. Boy and Innocent reluctantly nodded and followed his lead.

"Can I carry it?" Boy said as he fell into step next to him, eyeing the bottle.

"Why?" Innocent said as Thabo handed it to the younger of the two. "I knew him longer than you did!"

Taking the prize in his grasp, Boy stuck out his tongue and wiggled his butt triumphantly. "But he liked me better!"

"What?" Innocent exclaimed as he lunged for the bottle. "No, he didn't!"

Boy jumped out of the way and ran, shouting, "Did too!"

Innocent gave chase but each time he got close enough to reach for the memento, Boy squealed and jumped out the way. Thabo trailed behind them, the warmth of the bottle still throbbing in his hand, watching them play cat and mouse and chuckling despite himself.

It felt good to laugh again.

About the Author

SJ Sibisi is an entrepreneur, global speaker, and writer with over thirty years of executive management experience spanning the financial services, management consulting, infrastructure development, ICT and public sectors. During the course of her career, she has spoken at numerous national and international conferences and provided expert input into various key initiatives including the World Economic Forum's Africa Strategic Infrastructure Initiative and the African Development Bank's Africa Economic Outlook 2016. She has also written various research reports, white papers and thought leadership articles one of which was recently published in the Harvard Business Review. She is passionate about social justice and global change and, in terms of fiction, seeks to write about issues that impact us all, traversing borders, cultures and social bubbles. This is her first novel.

Printed in Great Britain
by Amazon